# CARNAL KNOWING

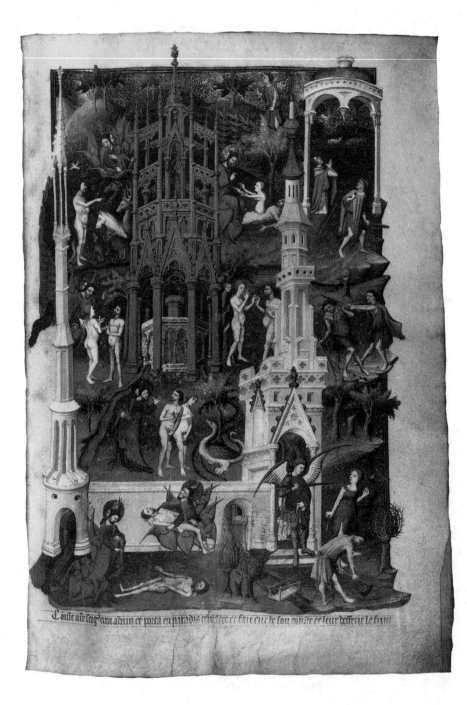

*The Creation and Fall*, Bedford Book of Hours, c.1423
British Library

# CARNAL KNOWING

———

FEMALE NAKEDNESS AND

RELIGIOUS MEANING IN THE

CHRISTIAN WEST

———

MARGARET R. MILES

BURNS & OATES

BURNS & OATES
Wellwood, North Farm Road,
Tunbridge Wells, Kent TN2 3DR

*First published 1992*

Published by arrangement with
Beacon Press, Boston, Massachusetts

ISBN 0 86012 182 8

Typeset in the United States of America
Printed and bound in Great Britain by
Biddles Ltd, Guildford and King's Lynn

FOR SIDURI, MY GRANDDAUGHTER

# CONTENTS

# LIST OF ILLUSTRATIONS

# PREFACE

*Der Schatten der Vergangenheit liegt über dem Körper.*[1]
*(The shadow of the past lies over the body.)*

This book originated in my puzzlement over the bewildering array of meanings associated with naked bodies embedded in the recorded practices, texts, and visual images of communities in the Christian West. Naked bodies gathered meanings that ranged from innocence to shame, from vulnerability to culpability, and from present worthlessness to future bliss in the resurrection of the body. Julia Kristeva has stated that "significance is inherent in the human body," but little more can be said about *what* is signified until one examines the meanings of bodies in their particular religious and social contexts.

The first theological meaning of nakedness in Christian tradition was the innocence, fragility, and vulnerability of human bodies in their initial creation. In visual images, the creation of Adam and Eve follows the Genesis account in depicting Adam's creation from the breath of God and the dust of the ground and Eve's creation from the side of the sleeping Adam. Narrations of the fall of the human race, however, focus on Eve and her initiative in sin. Paintings, mosaics, and bas reliefs, like commentaries on Genesis, reflect Ecclesiasticus 25:24: "From a woman sin had its beginning, and because of her we all die." The Fall resulted, scriptures say, in corporal punishment: Adam was condemned to hard physical labor, and Eve to laborious and painful childbearing. Nakedness in the state of sin represents the shame and pain associated with punishment.

A more positive theological meaning of nakedness was captured by Jerome's famous statement, "nudus sequi nudum Christum" ("naked to follow a naked Christ"). This became the slogan of late classical and medieval ascetics who, identifying with the spiritual commitment of the martyrs of the early church, called themselves "daily martyrs." Stripping themselves of possessions, family, and familiar environment, they entered full-time training in the Christian life. Christian tradition incorporated the motif of the naked male body, used since antiquity to represent heroic physical strength, to symbolize the spiritual exercises of the ascetic "athletes." Male nakedness represented spiritual discipline, physical control, the vigorous appropriation of a religious identity, and undistracted pursuit of an athletic crown (figure 1).

Both women and men engaged in the ascetic life; in fact, women ascetics were esteemed more highly than men because of the extra burden under which they labored, the "natural" weakness and susceptibility to temptation of their sex. Women who practiced asceticism were called "male," an interpretation of their efforts that women apparently accepted. For example, Perpetua, a nursing mother at the time of her arrest and imprisonment in early third-century Carthage, dreamed of her approaching martyrdom as an athletic contest. In her dream she was stripped of her clothing by attendants and rubbed with oil in preparation for fighting a huge Egyptian gladiator. As her garments were removed, Perpetua's body became a male body, the only body in which she could imagine herself possessing the stamina, control, and strength necessary for martyrdom.

Male nakedness symbolized religious commitment. Female nakedness, though it sometimes represented ascetic penitence, had a different role in the representational practices of the Christian West. Female nakedness received its symbolic representation in cultures that associated women with body, men with rationality, and (only) rationality with subjectivity. Eve's nakedness, described and painted in the "texts" that formed the interpretive lexicon of Christian tradition, represents religious meanings that range from innocence to sin, lust, and death. But it does not represent Eve as the subject of her experience.

Other religious meanings cluster around naked bodies: in the thirteenth century, Saint Bernard of Clairvaux popularized the idea of nudity as symbolic imitation of Christ; it took a Saint Francis to act out this metaphor. Francis announced his betrothal to Lady Poverty by publicly stripping off his clothing and flinging it at the feet of his protesting father. Similarly, in the fourteenth-century mystical tradition founded by Meister Eckhart and carried to Martin Luther by Tauler and Suso, nudity received the less literal interpretation of the soul's divestment of cares,

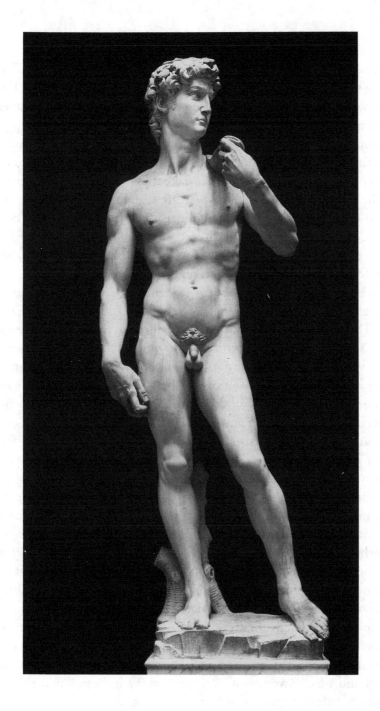

I
―――
MICHELANGELO
*David*, 1501–4
Galleria dell'Accademia, Florence (Art Resource, New York)

attachments, and ideas in order to expose the "core of the soul" where God is to be found. Ironically, the soul, departing from the body at death, was painted as a tiny, colorless naked body, carried to heaven in a napkin by angels.

Negative meanings of nakedness were formulated more slowly in Christian tradition. Nakedness and sexuality or lust were seldom associated in patristic writings. At worst, nakedness was seen as weakness. Before the sixteenth century there were few suggestions that the specific content of original sin was sexual desire, and there is even less evidence of the idea that sex brought death to the human race. In chapter 5, however, we will examine a series of sixteenth-century visual images in which female nakedness is used to represent sex, sin, and death.

Two different kinds of historical evidence will direct our exploration of social and religious meanings of female nakedness in the Christian West. The first part of the book will focus on religious practices—baptism, asceticism, and martyrdom—in which Christian women were naked, voluntarily or involuntarily, in public places; in the second part, textual and artistic representations of female nakedness will engage us. Public representations, I will contend, are closely connected to politics and social and sexual arrangements. Thus, although I will focus on texts and visual images, I will also seek to identify the most relevant features of their social contexts.

Are questions about social location, institutional affiliation, and gender politics anachronistic? Will they result in misreadings of texts and visual images? Clearly, analysis of gender constructions calls for a disobedient reading, a reading that looks for the *effect* of the artist's or author's rhetorical or pictorial strategies rather than for the author's *intended* communication. The effect we must look for, however, is not that of the image or text on either a historical or a modern reader or spectator, but the ways in which gender constructions are embedded in communications so naturalistically that the author can count on them to move an argument, to persuade, or to seduce. Moreover, the abundance of literary treatments of the relative nature, capacities, and social roles of women and men throughout Western history indicates that these were far from indifferent matters in historical societies.[2]

Historical people did not develop an analysis of gender conditioning and its social effects. In the Christian West gender difference was thought to be biologically based, scripturally attested, God ordained, and unquestionable. Yet even though gender roles were considered "natural,"

men worried enough about the potential insubordination of the "inferior" sex that they spent enormous amounts of time and energy on re-
articulating and reaffirming what women *are* and should remain. Because representations of female bodies were a vehicle for a complex
communication, we need to explore the particular expressive content
they carried.

This book seeks to clarify the religious themes by which, in the public
sphere, women's bodies were dissociated from women as subjects and
represented as figures in a male drama. By analyzing stylized depictions
and descriptions of naked bodies in the Christian West, we can identify
both an initially perplexing range of cultural and religious meanings of
"the body" and analyze different treatments of male and female bodies.
My resources for this study, then, are naked bodies as visualized and described in the art and literature of Western Christianity until about the
seventeenth century, when religious meaning no longer provided the primary interpretive framework for depictions of nakedness.

I am grateful to Robert Baldwin of Connecticut College for biblio-
graphical suggestions; to student and faculty colleagues at Harvard University, especially Constance H. Buchanan, for myriad conversations in
which the ideas presented in this book were explored and refined. I
owe—and feel—great appreciation to Deborah Haynes for research assistance and to Wendy Strothman, of Beacon Press, and Debbi Edelstein
for valuable editorial suggestions.

# INTRODUCTION

*The discourse of man is in the metaphor of woman.*[1]

*The enigma that is woman will therefore constitute the target, the object, the stake, of a masculine discourse, of a debate among men, which would not consult her, would not concern her.*[2]

*Any theory of the subject has always been appropriated by the "masculine."*[3]

*Culture, as we know it, is patriarchy's self-image. The history of representation is the history of the male gender representing itself to itself.*[4]

*Today there is a great deal of thought against representation. In a more or less articulated or rigorous way, this judgment is easily arrived at: representation is bad. . . . And yet, whatever the strength and the obscurity of this dominant current, the authority of representation constrains us, imposing itself on our thought through a whole dense, enigmatic, and heavily stratified history. It programs us and precedes us and warns us.*[5]

In about 2800 B.C. a Babylonian scribe put in writing the saga of the legendary king Gilgamesh. Gilgamesh, so the tale goes, was two-thirds god and one-third man. His appetites were voracious and his energy limitless, and he did not learn easily. At the opening of the epic, Gilgamesh's people are distressed at his lordly indifference to their feelings. He insisted, for example, on being the first to have sexual intercourse with every bride. Although we have no report from the ancient scribe as to the brides' feeling about this "honor," we are told that the practice offended husbands and fathers. They complained, but, of course, without effect. After groaning under this oppression for many years, the people found a champion, Enkidu, perhaps the strongest man alive, who might give Gilgamesh the unprecedented and edifying experience of being defeated in a fight.

Enkidu had a strange history. He had been a wild man, running with the gazelles, feeding amiably with the lions, and sleeping in the forest, until he was captured and brought to the temple. There, an unnamed sacred prostitute tamed him by teaching him the art of lovemaking and the ways of civilized people. His strength, once equal to the lions', and his speed, once equal to the gazelles', diminished rapidly, but he still possessed more strength and speed than any other man, except, possibly, Gilgamesh.

One day when Gilgamesh strode through the streets on his way to a bride, the people set Enkidu on him. They fought, and for the first time in his life Gilgamesh was prevented from accomplishing the satisfaction of his sexual desire. Rather than resenting this frustration, however, he immediately respected and loved the man who had proved his equal in strength and resolve. Enkidu and Gilgamesh became friends and shared many adventures, dangers, and triumphs, until, in the midst of one of their heroic battles, Enkidu was killed.

Gilgamesh was inconsolable at Enkidu's death, for he had lost the one person he loved. Moreover, Enkidu's death made him realize that a similar fate awaited him. Unwilling to accept his own mortality, Gilgamesh, in characteristic fashion, resolved to *do* something about it. He had heard that there was one man, Utnapishtim, who had survived the deluge that destroyed the human race and who, alone of all mankind, had been granted immortality by the gods. Gilgamesh set out to find him, intending to force him to give up the secret of immortality. To Gilgamesh's credit—he *had* learned something about fellow feeling from his experience of human limitation and love—he wanted to obtain everlasting life not only for himself, but also for his people.

As he journeyed in search of Utnapishtim, Gilgamesh came to the garden of the gods, a garden lush with bushes on which grew precious gems—carnelian, lapis lazuli, agate, and pearls. There, at the edge of the shining sea, he met a young woman who brewed in golden vats the intoxicating drink of the gods. Siduri saw Gilgamesh approaching, "wearing skins, the flesh of the gods in his body, but despair in his heart." She could hardly believe that this skinny, despairing, weather-beaten man was the legendary Gilgamesh. But he explained his anguish over Enkidu's death and his fear of his own death and then asked her to help him find Utnapishtim. Before reluctantly directing him to the next stage of his journey, however, Siduri gave him some advice:

Gilgamesh, where are you hurrying to? You will never find that life for which you are looking. When the gods created man they allotted to him death, but life they retained in their own keeping. As for you, Gilgamesh, fill your belly with good things; day and night, night and day, dance and be merry, feast and rejoice. Let your clothes be fresh, bathe yourself in water, cherish the little child that holds your hand, and make your wife happy in your embrace; for this too is the lot of man.[6]

Needless to say, Gilgamesh did not heed this advice, and hurried away to pursue immortality. The epic closes with Gilgamesh's death and the ritual lament of his people for a king who, although he was two-thirds god and one-third man, in his death was only human.

Using the metaphor of heroic struggles in the external world, *The Epic of Gilgamesh* narrates the development of male subjectivity. Three women or groups of women appear in the epic as foils for the hero's developing awareness of what is entailed in being human. First are the brides, undifferentiated and nameless women, who are raped by Gilgamesh. They present no challenge to Gilgamesh's unlimited aggression and self-assertion, and they do not stimulate in him any awareness of the real existence of another human being. Second is the temple prostitute, who, in teaching Enkidu the art of lovemaking, tames him and reduces his strength to a level acceptable and useful to society. Third is Siduri, the only human woman named in the epic,[7] who momentarily halts Gilgamesh in his frenzied quest for everlasting life and advises him to notice and enjoy the beauties and loves of this earth, the "lot of man," instead of disregarding these accessible delights and pursuing an unobtainable goal. The temple prostitute raises Gilgamesh above the beasts, and Siduri reduces him from a god, thereby defining the lower and upper limits of the human.

These women appear in the first extant text that depicts heroic struggle against the restraints of humanness. The text focuses on the development of the hero, Gilgamesh; the women's subjectivity does not develop. The women instead "stand for" twin male dilemmas: they are the endlessly replaceable objects of the hero's insatiable lust, and they represent the arbitrary limitations on an individual's potential imposed by society and mortality. Moreover, no reconstruction of these women's perspectives through *their* physical experiences is given; the interdependence of body and consciousness that has played such a prominent role in the humanization of the hero is missing from the text's representation of the women.

Where is the epic of Siduri? Why was her wisdom presented only as a foil for Gilgamesh's aspirations? What physical experiences, what struggles, shaped *her* self-understanding and the philosophy of life she articulated so poignantly? Women are not incidental to telling the hero's story; indeed, they play an essential and highly visible role in his development. Mothers, sisters, lovers, wives, daughters, and anonymous women are crucial to the definition and refinement of male subjectivity. Yet female subjectivity did not, until the nineteenth century, begin to receive the exploration accorded that of men.

Female subjectivity has occasionally appeared furtively in early Western literature, embedded in texts whose project was to describe a male journey. The story of Odysseus and Calypso in book 5 of *The Odyssey,* for example, includes a female character who reminds the hero of *her* subjectivity. Because Odysseus knows that Calypso loves him and that his preparations to leave hurt her, he suspects her of plotting to prevent his departure. Calypso assures him that, though his departure grieves her, she will do nothing to stop him; she understands his longing to sail for home, she says, but she also urges him to pause long enough to recognize *her* feelings. He has construed her as an enemy in order to rationalize hurting her, a dishonest and unnecessary ploy, a stratagem that specifically denies her subjectivity, for, she says, "The heart within me is not of iron, but yearning, like yours." Yet where can we read the epic of Calypso? Odysseus's representation of Calypso as the villain he needed her to be in order to leave her is reiterated in her literary role as nothing more than a moment in his journey.

Such an act of representing can be seen as a "laying hold and grasping," "an objectifying that goes forward and masters."[8] It is one component of the representations—mostly men's representations of women— that will occupy us throughout the book and one of several definitions that underlie the discussion. As a noun, a representation is a description or visual depiction of an object; as a verb, to represent is to characterize an object according to an (always perspectival) analysis of the essential or distinguishing features of the object. For example, Albrecht Dürer's *Artist Drawing a Reclining Nude* (figure 2) illustrates both the male artist's distance from the female model and the asymmetrical relationship of the two. The woman reclines, exposed and passive, positioned so that the artist's gaze moves from her parted legs to her upper body. The artist, clothed and upright, uses grids, a sword, and his calculating eye to reduce her body to lines on paper.

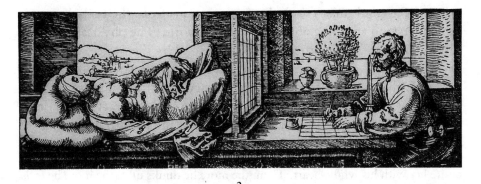

2

**ALBRECHT DÜRER**
*Artist Drawing a Reclining Nude,* c. 1527
Metropolitan Museum of Art, New York (Art Resource, New York)

The activity of representing entails two interdependent and simultaneous motions: the characterization of an object and the articulation of a subject's judgment. Further, people do not grasp something we like to call "reality" directly, but through representations of culturally construed reality. The power of representation is thus closely related to and dependent on politics and social institutions. The crucial questions about representation are: Who has the power of representation in a particular culture? Who can be represented and how? And by what "system of power" are certain representations authorized while others are blocked, prohibited, invalidated, or ignored?[9]

Theories of representation, though they have perhaps received more scholarly attention since Kant, are not exclusively a modern concern. The ancient doctrine of phantasms, described by Plato and developed by Aristotle, was rediscovered and reinterpreted in the Renaissance. The persistence of the theory demonstrates historical people's continuing interest in representation and its effects. Representation is necessary, according to Aristotle, because the soul has no sense organs with which to grasp the phenomena of the sensible world, and the body, without the soul, has no ability to codify and retain messages brought by the sense organs. "Body and soul speak two languages, which are not only different, even inconsistent, but also *inaudible* to each other."[10] Therefore, an "inner sense"[11] must coordinate and translate messages received from the body; it must, in essence, create a picture or sequence of pictures within the soul, using the "stuff" of the soul, *pneuma,* to create these phantasms.[12] The soul must create these impressions from the body before it can understand anything about the sensible world. The physical or quasi-physical nature of this process was emphasized by the Stoics, for whom *pneuma*—spirit—was a material, though highly attenuated, substance.

Ioan Culianu traces the "effective history"[13] of the theory of phantasms as it was used by later authors to explain sexual attraction; Andreas Capellanus, in his treatise *On Love,* written in the twelfth century, said:

When a man sees a woman deserving of erotic attentions, he at once begins to desire her with his whole heart. Then, the more he thinks of it, the more he feels himself imbued with love until he reconstructs her in her entirety in phantasy. Then he begins to think of her figure, he perceives her limbs, imagines them in action and explores the private parts of her body.[14]

It was this reconstruction of the dynamic of desire that prompted the thirteenth-century poet Giacomo da Lentino to ask: "How can it be that so large a woman has been able to penetrate my eyes, which are so small, and then enter my heart and my brain?"[15]

Representation theory entered the modern world with Kant's *Critique of Judgment,* which presented an aesthetic theory that jettisoned the quasiphysical nature of the theory of phantasms but retained its emphasis on the activity of inner representation. The problem Kant sought to explain is how a subject makes aesthetic judgments. Restating the ancient principle that man is the measure of all things, Kant wrote: "In order to distinguish whether anything is beautiful or not, we refer the representation, not by the understanding to the object, but by the imagination . . . to the subject and its feeling of pleasure or pain."[16] Kant's aesthetic theory might be understood as a sort of "Judgment of Paris," in which three goddesses subject their beauty to the evaluation of a man, in whose eye— "the eye of the beholder"—beauty is created (figure 3). The beauty of an "object" is thus not at all "objective," in the sense of belonging to the object, but belongs entirely to the subject of the judgment; it is "altogether referred to the subject and to its feeling of life."[17] Kant's formula rephrases Augustine's statement of more than a thousand years before, "Adam did not love Eve because she was beautiful; it was his love that made her beautiful."[18]

The subject's judgment is, in Kant's description, also universal. The subject's alleged "disinterest" makes it so. There is no "satisfaction connected to desire" attached to this judgment; it is, purely and simply, an objective judgment of taste. Emptied of any self-interest, the subject's

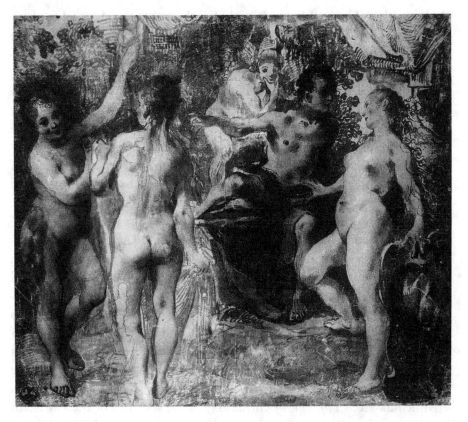

3

ANNIBALE CARRACCI (disputed)
*Judgment of Paris,* c. 1584
Fogg Art Museum, Harvard University, Cambridge, Massachusetts;
Bequest of Charles A. Loeser

judgment can be legitimately projected onto the object as a *feature* of the object: beauty. Kant also claimed that everyone who has "taste" would necessarily make a similar judgment. In fact, the test of whether a person has taste is whether s/he agrees with the judgment. The subject's judgment is universally binding.

The question that arises from Kant's analysis of aesthetic judgment is this: Who possesses the privileged judgment of "the subject"? Susanne Kappeler has noted that in Kant's theory "the position of the subject, in principle, is open to all people, but in practice the principle of universal validity has been tested among a limited number of subjects."[19] Francis

Barker adds, "The healthy male body [is] the only official vessel for lawful subjectivity."[20] In addition to gender assumptions, Kant's expectation that "the subject" will occupy a certain class, educational, and institutional niche is also apparent.[21]

Those biases have been carried forward into the twentieth century. When in 1938 Martin Heidegger claimed "that the world exists only through a *subject* who believes that he is producing the world in producing its representation,"[22] he transformed the world into a representation, with man as its subject.[23] While more recently the universal judgment of the socially and economically privileged subject has been questioned and rejected,[24] "it is [still] the man who speaks, who represents mankind. The woman is only represented; she is (as always) already spoken for."[25]

The hero's construction as subject in works like *The Epic of Gilgamesh* and *The Odyssey,* entails a journey to self-knowledge achieved through physical struggle, labor, and pain. The hero's self-knowledge is carnal knowledge, awareness recorded in the body. One who has not experienced limitation and suffering cannot recognize the suffering of others and cannot locate himself in a human community shaped by awareness of limitation and mortality. The consanguinity of human beings depends on mutual recognition of the common bond of a sentient body, whose most vivid experiences create consciousness.

Millennia after *The Epic of Gilgamesh,* in the societies of the Christian West, an understanding of oneself as body was produced by gendered religious practices and recorded in texts and visual images that represented men's and women's bodies as symbolic of different religious meanings. Carnal knowing—embodied self-understanding—needs to be distinguished, however, from historical and contemporary meanings of "carnal knowledge." "Carnal knowledge," a term from medieval canon law, means sexual intercourse. Yet a broader meaning is implicit in the several meanings for the adjective "carnal" listed by the *Oxford Dictionary of the English Language:* (1) of, or pertaining to, flesh or body; (2) related in blood, as in the phrase "according to the flesh"; (3) pertaining to the body as the seat of the passions or appetites, fleshly, sensual; (4) not spiritual, but material.[26] The first two meanings are neutral in value; the second two contrast whatever relates to body with what is spiritual, implying the greater value of the spiritual. Curiously, although the term itself seems to suggest that embodied knowledge of oneself and another human being can be attained in the intimacy of lovemaking, in usage "carnal knowledge" implied that lovemaking is defined by, if not limited to, its physical aspect. The qualifier "carnal" effectively canceled recognition that either intellectual or spiritual understanding can occur.[27]

Is "carnal knowing," then a contradiction in terms? In the Western philosophical tradition reason has often been "assumed to be disembodied and abstract," independent of physical experience.[28] In striking contrast to philosophers' esteem for "reason alone," Tertullian, a third-century North African Christian, wrote:

The soul alone is so far from conducting the affairs of life that we do not withdraw from community with the flesh even our thoughts, however isolated they may be, however unprecipitated into act by means of the flesh; since whatever is done in the heart is done by the soul in the flesh and through the flesh. . . . But if you allow that the faculty which rules the senses and which they call the *hegemonikon* has its sanctuary in the brain . . . or wheresoever the philosophers are pleased to locate it, *the flesh will still be the thinking place of the soul.*[29]

In spite of Tertullian's recognition that the soul is always dependent on the body, however, it is difficult to support my use of "carnal knowing" as embodied self-knowledge from the dominant philosophical or religious traditions of the West. Rather, the historical use of the term signals, ironically, the dualistic assumptions of Western philosophy and Christian theology. In my usage, "carnal knowing" suggests minimally (as in Tertullian's description) that the brain in which thinking occurs is a material substance. Beyond this, "carnal knowing" refers to an activity in which the intimate interdependence and irreducible cooperation of thinking, feeling, sensing, and understanding is revealed.

Carnal knowing is both embodied and social; it includes the most private and intimate experiences as well as the most public and social experiences. Carnal knowing is not a kind of "pure" subjectivity, untouched by social location and by all the particularities of experience that create one's perspective. Rather, subjectivity is itself a social construct, a cultural artifact, as Rom Harré notes: "Not only are the acts we as individuals perform and the interpretations we create of the social and physical world prefigured in collective actions and social representations, but also the very structure of our minds . . . is drawn from those social representations."[30] Men's and women's bodies are also molded by social expectations of sex/gender difference. Ruth Hubbard has written:

Sex differences are socially constructed not only in the sense that society defines sex-appropriate behaviors to which each of us learns to conform, but also in the sense that those behaviors affect our biology—bones, muscles, sense organs, nerves, brain, lungs, circulation, everything. We cannot sort out our biology from our social being because they are inextricable and transform each other.[31]

Body and subjectivity have in common, it seems, a thoroughgoing vulnerability to the transformative effects of social conditioning through gendered representations.

How do representations act in society? Representations both interpret and replace the objects they represent. Overlapping cumulative representations of "woman" select certain characteristics to "stand for" women, enabling men to "handle" the women to whom they must relate. The social function of representations, then, is to stabilize assumptions and expectations relating to the objects or persons represented.

Image-making, E. H. Gombrich has said, "is the creation of substitutes"; an image represses by producing its symbolic representation.[32] For example, literary critics like Helena Michie and Francis Barker have described a process by which the female body, transmogrified into literature, ceases to be "the immediate, the unmediated site of desire and penalty," the site of subjectivity, and becomes instead the object of writing:

The bourgeois subject substitutes for its corporal body the rarified body of the text. . . . The carnality of the body has been dissolved and dissipated until it can be reconstituted in writing at a distance from itself. . . . As the flesh is de-realized, representation, which becomes at last representational, is separated from it and puts in train a mode of signification for which, to borrow a word from Derrida, the body has become supplementary.[33]

Consistent, cumulative, and continuous representations of an object cause that object to "disappear" in its complex and perhaps contradictory "reality," subsumed in the "tidy, well-ordered totality" of the standardized representation.[34]

An established public representation, even though it may generate disagreement, resistance, and the formulation of alternatives, carries within it a behavior code. We assume that people of various races, social and economic classes, professions, and genders are as they are represented, and we treat them accordingly. Representations provide a shortcut, enabling immediate response without the laborious process of reflection that would be necessary if each person or situation were to receive an individual response. Moreover, representations often determine intimate as well as less personal relationships. Because the level of threat and the potential for pain in intimate relationships is very high, representations of the other are used to reduce her to manageability. The alternative to reliance on representations is the cultivation of a "perspectivity that confers self all around,"[35] that is, that assumes that each person possesses a unique combination of integrity, intelligence, generosity, self-interest, belief, and experience.

Finally, representations do not merely *reflect* social practices and attitudes so that analysis of representation simply reveals the prejudices or stereotypes of a society. They also re-present, reinforce, perpetuate, produce, and reproduce them.[36] There is no simple causal relationship between society and representation in either direction: social practices do not determine particular representations, nor do representations specify particular social arrangements; rather, each acts on the other—to nuance or reinforce, to correct or reiterate—at myriad tiny points. The complex nature of historical evidence makes problematic any claim more specific than that of an inevitable connection between representations and social arrangements: "Causal and principled reasoning brings the [danger of] oversimplification. The linking of cause and effect works best with few variables, demonstrable relationships, and a domain of study that lends itself to compartmentalization."[37] A reciprocal relationship between representations and social arrangements can, nevertheless, be assumed, and historians can proceed, without further assumptions, to explore in detail the nature of this connection in a particular society.

Certainly the large picture of women's place in the societies of the Christian West can be recognized without difficulty: women have lived in male-defined and dominated societies. This fact influenced the social and sexual arrangements that shaped women's everyday lives, their self-understanding and self-images, and their development of some talents and skills at the expense of others. Even though the precise nature of the interdependence of representation and society cannot be theoretically specified, however, the politics of representation are relatively easy to identify in historical societies: *who* does the public representing of women, who pays for it, where it is placed, and who looks at it? One can also analyze the content of representations of women. The sex/gender systems characteristic of the societies of the Christian West, then, can be approached in two ways: first, one can analyze the content of representations of female nakedness; second, one can study the activity of representation itself. The second approach requires the political questions I have outlined, even if the historical evidence at our disposal does not always make it possible to answer them.[38]

The study of gender can, in addition, help us map some intimate and complex relationships among laws, medicine, social arrangements, art, government, and religion. Exploration of the interdependence of religion, gender, and culture requires an interdisciplinary approach to historical evidence. Historians find that they must learn to read pictures as well as texts; art historians recognize that they need knowledge of religious and cultural history in order to interpret a painting; feminist theorists realize that to ignore religion is to risk misrepresentation of historical women; and historians of religion discover that they cannot neglect analysis of the gender constructions at the heart of the religious literature of other cultures. For scholars trained in the discrete fields of literature, art, history, and theology, learning to use effectively the tools of other disciplines is both exciting and very hard work. It is, however, remarkably engaging work because it promises to bring us closer to a past "boiling with life," in Plotinus's phrase, than reconstructions of the past that are limited to the tools of a single discipline.[39]

The art and literature of the Christian West, I have said, present the heroic saga of the development of male subjectivity. It is not, however, the development of male subjectivity through and across female bodies that interests me. Nor is it the importance, even the centrality, of female figures to the male drama that I want to examine in the chapters to follow. In this book I want instead to explore one of the most fundamental figures by which human subjectivity has been represented in the literature and visual images of the Christian West, the naked body, and to examine the themes that dominate the different representation of male and female bodies. The gender-specific associations of representations of naked, and sometimes of "nude," bodies (we will examine this distinction shortly) with subjectivity—an inner life, a construction and cultivation of a "self"—will be the book's first agenda. I will then examine the use of female nakedness in the Christian West as a cipher for sin, sex, and death.

The appropriation of the female body to represent male frustration and limitation in the societies of the Christian West has effectively precluded the formulation of a parallel representation of women's subjectivity. A historical woman who undertook to cultivate her own subjectivity necessarily incorporated the well-defined male scenario, understanding her body primarily as it appears in the male account and assimilating to her subjectivity the female figures of the male drama. One's relation to one's body—its needs and its pleasures—is not "natural" but, like subjectivity, is culturally mediated. For example, historians have long pondered why many medieval women practiced more extreme "mortification of the flesh" than did their male counterparts.[40] Medieval women, as well as many women that came before and after them, designed their religious practices around introjected images of their own bodies as figures of sin, sex, and death. They then responded to these internalized figures with severe ascetic practices that produced not only a victory over these figurations of woman—in an increase of social esteem and social leverage—but often also illness and premature death.

No one who uses representations of naked bodies as a primary resource can proceed very far without considering Kenneth Clark's famous distinction between "the naked and the nude." More than fifty years after his lecture was given at the National Gallery of Art in Washington, D.C., his analysis of the difference between nudity and nakedness continues to influence art historians and scholars. Clark described the naked body as "no more than a point of departure" for the nude:

It is widely supposed that the naked human body is in itself an object upon which the eye dwells with pleasure and which we are glad to see depicted. But anyone who has frequented art schools and seen the shapeless, pitiful model which the students are industriously drawing will know that this is an illusion. The body is not one of those subjects that can be made into art by direct transcription—like a tiger or a snowy landscape. . . . A mass of naked figures does not move us to empathy, but to disillusion and dismay. We do not wish to imitate; we wish to perfect. . . . We are immediately disturbed by wrinkles, pouches and other small imperfections.[41]

In short, "to be naked is to be deprived of our clothes and the word implies some of the embarrassment which most of us feel in that condition." The word "nude," on the other hand, connotes no such image of a "huddled, defenseless body, but of a balanced prosperous and confident body: the body re-formed."[42]

The illustrations in the 1956 publication of *The Naked and the Nude* reveal the gender assumptions in Clark's argument. All the illustrations that appear on the pages from which I have quoted are of nude females. The "shapeless, pitiful model" from which art is created, then, appears to be female. The painter-spectator, on the other hand, the "we," is the critical male who eliminates the "small imperfections" and creates a body with ideal proportions. The social practice of professional painting also insisted on the painter's maleness, as academies in which figure drawing and painting from nude models were taught did not admit women until the end of the eighteenth century. All nudes need not, of course, be female in order to substantiate the point that the role of surveillance and interpretation of the naked figure is a male role; when a male model posed for a life study, he simply assumed the female role in relation to the painter.

The naked body functions primarily as raw material for the artist: "It can be made expressive of a far wider and more civilizing experience." Furthermore, the naked body appropriated for recreation as a "nude" may contribute "associations," especially erotic associations, for the naked body, "is ourselves, and arouses memories of all the things we wish to do with ourselves; and first of all, we wish to perpetuate ourselves."[43] Questions as to whose "civilizing experience" can be inscribed on the "shapeless, pitiful" body will probably arise in the mind of a reader who has followed my argument to this point.

In Clark's distinction between "nakedness" and "nudity" the nude body is a representation of a naked body from which subjectivity, along with moles and lumps, has been elided. At the same moment when the naked body was "re-formed" to render it pleasingly balanced and proportioned and without blemishes, it lost its ability to express the personal character of the person whose body it is. "The transition from naked to nude," Annette Kuhn has written, "is also the transformation of woman into object."[44] In Clark's description, the naked body *becomes* "a nude" by having its feeling ("embarrassment") removed along with the visible symbols of its individuality and personality ("wrinkles, pouches and other small imperfections"). The nude achieves universality at the expense of particularity. The *subject* of a nude painting has been deleted, replaced by the role the nude plays in representing "a far wider and more civilizing experience."

In Clark's description of the classically proportioned nude, the religious meaning, or meanings, of naked bodies has also disappeared. Not surprisingly, this is especially evident in interpretations of the visual properties of female nudes. For Clark, "one of the few classical canons of proportion of which we can be certain is that which, in a female nude, took the same unit of measurement for the distance between the breasts, the distance from the lower breast to the navel, and again from the navel to the division of the legs."[45] Using this definition of accurate proportion, for example, he judges Hans Memling's nude *Eve* (figure 4) a failure: "The basic pattern of the female body is still an oval, surmounted by two spheres; but the oval has grown incredibly long, the spheres dis-

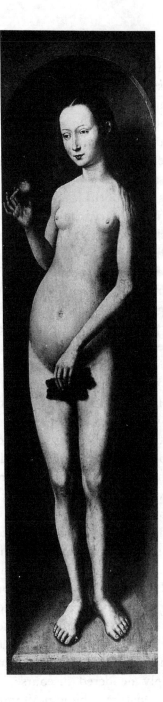

4

HANS MEMLING
*Eve*, 1467 (disputed)
Kunsthistorisches Museum, Vienna (Art Resource, New York)

tressingly small. . . . [In fact] the navel is exactly twice as far down the body as it is in the classical scheme."[46] Even if the artist's intent was to represent religious meaning through Eve's body, Clark is certain that the painter intended to produce "a figure which should conform to the ideal of his time, which should be the kind of shape which men like to see."[47]

Eve's rounded and elongated belly might, for example, have represented—to the painter as well as to his immediate audience—the womb from which all humans were born. It might in addition have evoked her association with the Virgin Mary, the second Eve, from whose womb Christ took human flesh, an association strengthened by the exposure of Eve's left ear, in which, as legend has it, Mary conceived by the Holy Spirit. The ear, painted in greater detail than other parts of Eve's anatomy, as well as her small mouth and breasts—those "spheres" which Clark finds "distressingly small"—each contribute to a subordination of sensuality and sexuality that historical painters of nude subjects found necessary to ensure the communication of a primarily religious, rather than erotic, message. Memling's Eve is not, then, "nude," but naked. Her body, through its "small imperfections," reveals her religious significance as mother of all the living. Thus, "the nude"—the reconstructed naked body—will not be as useful for my purposes as will representations in which the "naked" body is still evident, in which both subjectivity and religious meaning are expressed by the body. Even in depictions in which the author or painter intended to present a "reformed" body, then, I will seek the contours of the other body, the body formed and informed by the life of the subject.

In exploring representations of unclothed bodies in the Christian West, we must recognize religious meaning as an essential aspect of the cultivation of subjectivity. Christianity provided ideas and models for imagining a religious self, a self carefully cultivated in opposition to secular conditioning and socially prescribed roles. Moreover, Christianity has claimed to offer an alternative to secular values and conditioning without regard for race, gender, or social class. Examination of religious practices involving women and of religious representations of women reveals, however, a deeply gendered discourse, a discourse structured around assumptions of "natural" biological and social differences between men and women.

Interestingly, in Christianity religious subjectivity seems, at first glance, to be structured similarly for men and women. Men are often encouraged to adopt behavior and attitudes commonly associated with women—humility, obedience, and sensitivity to the needs of others. And for women, "becoming male," as we will see in chapter 2, meant greater assertiveness, activity in public or semipublic spheres, resistance to social expectations, and "athletic" spiritual exercise. But the religious rhetoric that encouraged women to "become male" masked a fundamental inequality. In creating and cultivating a religious self, men retained their accustomed social privileges in new institutions—church and monastery—while women, in Christian institutions as in the society at large, did not choose their own roles or help to design the new institutions in accordance with their religious needs and insights. Thus, while Christianity appears to offer both men and women support and reward for religious commitment, women were generally prevented from creating social alternatives to match their religious commitment.

Yet the limitation of women's social roles within Christianity conflicts with a religious rhetoric that explicitly acknowledged that women were capable of both rational thought and its corollary, religious subjectivity. From Augustine forward, Christian authors insisted that "inasmuch as woman was a human being, she certainly had a mind, and a rational mind, and therefore she was also made to the image of God." But Augustine qualified his affirmation, adding, "although on the physical side their sexual characteristics may suggest otherwise, namely, that man alone is said to be the image and glory of God.[48] Between men and women, "there is no difference except in relation to the body."[49] But this difference was a large one. As Augustine's statement suggests, women's "nature" was determined by their physical difference from men, that is, by their bodies. Although women possess rationality, men's "nature" was determined by it.[50] Thus, it seemed "reasonable" that human beings defined by mind should rule those defined by body. The "order of creation"—man first, woman second—was understood to reflect cosmic order and to stipulate social order; female subordination was the linchpin of social order.

In examining religious practices that pointedly engaged women's bodies and representations of female nakedness, I will bracket both theological discussions of women's rational capacities and "positive" images of good, nourishing, and socially valued women. I have done so, of course, for a reason—because, as so many Christian authors tell us, it was not women's minds that were problematic. Women's minds, they said, are "like" men's—perhaps not as fully developed, but still recognizably similar. The female body, however, was a problem for men; the control of female sexuality, reproduction, and economic labor was a perennial preoccupation and anxiety in the male-defined and -administered communities of the Christian West. Exploring social and religious practices and verbal and visual rhetoric surrounding female bodies, then, reveals not only men's concerns about women, but also features of the public environment in which women lived.

This book seeks to clarify the religious themes by which, in the public sphere, women's bodies were dissociated from women as subjects and represented as figures in a male drama. By analyzing stylized depictions and descriptions of naked bodies in the Christian West, we can identify both an initially perplexing range of cultural and religious meanings of "the body" and analyze different treatments of male and female bodies. My resources for this study, then, are naked bodies as visualized and described in the art and literature of Western Christianity until about the seventeenth century, when religious meaning no longer provided the primary interpretive framework for depictions of nakedness.

A study of practices and representations involving female nakedness will make evident an asymmetrical cultural interest in men and women as subjects in the Christian West. This is a study that must be undertaken, however, not in order to deplore the slender provision for women of symbols and images that incited, encouraged, and supported self-knowledge and the cultivation of a rich subjectivity, but in order to urge that, since the past cannot be changed, contemporary women's collaboration in creating art and literature that explores female subjectivity is all the more pressing. This project is, in fact, well underway in the last decades of the twentieth century.

# I

---

# RELIGIOUS PRACTICES OF NAKEDNESS

# INTRODUCTION TO PART ONE

The founder of Christianity, Jesus of Nazareth, carried over from Judaism the practice of baptizing converts. He himself was baptized by John the Baptist, thus setting an example for his followers. According to Gospel accounts, he instructed his disciples to preach his message throughout the world and to baptize those who believed. Jesus' specific instructions in asceticism were few: "Fast and pray" and "Sell all that you have and give to the poor." On occasion he drew criticism for allowing his disciples to relax Jewish laws regarding proper behavior on the Sabbath. The only ritual that he is reported to have urged on his followers was a eucharistic meal, to be celebrated in memory of his death.

Although his twelve disciples were men, Jesus of Nazareth sometimes demonstrated attitudes toward women that were at odds with the gender expectations of his culture. He is reported to have rescued from stoning a woman caught in adultery by calling attention to the double standard assumed by her attackers; on another occasion he was scolded by his disciples for conversing with a woman of the wrong race, class, and sexual history. Jesus regarded his society critically, questioning and rejecting practices he found incompatible with his understanding of God, himself, and other people.

After Jesus' death, his followers multiplied, attracted by his message of a loving and healing God. Communities of Christians began to meet together to remember his words and to incorporate into their lives the vivid empowerment they felt as they worshipped together. They were sporadically but persistently persecuted and executed by local governors across the Roman Empire. These communities often found it difficult to integrate the new life they experienced in Jesus the Christ with orderly communities that guaranteed unity of belief and continuity.

Jesus of Nazareth wrote nothing, and his followers recorded his words and deeds after his death. There are no contemporary paintings of this man, who nonetheless became perhaps the most frequently painted figure in the history of the world. The slenderness of historical testimony about the life, ideas, and work of Jesus has left wide arenas of belief and practice open to interpretation and development.

In the flush of missionary excitement following Jesus' death and resurrection, gender roles and expectations were temporarily transcended as women and men worked together to spread the gospel message. They felt there was little time for reenacting the social relationships in which they had grown up because they expected the imminent return of Christ and the end of the world. They experimented with new forms of relationship, like the "spiritual marriage," in which a woman and man lived and worked together without sexual contact. These relationships seem not to have worked well; they apparently strained both the willpower of the participants and the credulity of the community, and they were repeatedly forbidden by local and ecumenical councils over approximately a three-hundred-year period.

Leaders of Christian groups quickly decided that if Christianity were to survive and become plausible in Roman society, strong local centralization around authoritative leaders was needed. By the end of the first century, itinerant preachers like Saint Paul and, later, bishops, authors, and prominent laymen like Tertullian demonstrated their authority by insisting on the exclusion of women from leadership roles. By the beginning of the third century, patristic literature also reveals a preoccupation with the physical and spiritual management of women by male leaders. No aspect of women's dress, jewelry, cosmetics, or behavior was too small to engage the attention and elicit the instruction of a Clement of Alexandria or a Tertullian. Contraception and abortion were forbidden to married women, and consecrated virgins were to accept the authority of the bishop, according to Cyprian in the mid-third century, as if he were a *paterfamilias*. Clearly, control of Christian women's roles, dress, and behavior were understood as central to male authority.

By the end of the second century a fairly standardized liturgical and sacramental practice was established across the Roman Empire. Sacramental and devotional practices as well as theological treatises reveal women's subordination in Christian communities. Groups claiming orthodoxy—right belief—differentiated themselves from heterodox groups by excluding women from preaching and teaching. In orthodox groups, women were welcomed, esteemed as the spiritual equals of men, and firmly directed to subordinate roles. In a sinful world, Augustine wrote at the beginning of the fifth century, this is the best human beings can do. He saw patriarchal order simply as "peace," the only alternative to social chaos.

Nevertheless, it is not to be doubted that women found in Christian churches possibilities for self-definition not offered by secular Roman society. It is, in fact, fascinating to follow in the literature of early Christianity a familiar but still-puzzling nexus of women's simultaneous empowerment and subordination. What we must endeavor to understand in the two following chapters, then, is a complex and somewhat contradictory situating of women in the context of communal life.

# CHRISTIAN BAPTISM IN THE FOURTH CENTURY: THE CONVERSION OF THE BODY

*For each of us, sin begins at the moment when "whatever God may promise, we cannot at all apply to ourselves but, our eyes fixed on our own nakedness, we sink down dazed by fear."*[1]

*Men and women have been redeemed equally by Christ's blood, have been cleansed by the very same baptism, approach the Lord's altar to receive his body and blood together . . . with God there are no distinctions of male and female.*[2]

Historians have often assumed that people of the past acted in certain ways because they held certain ideas; they have then proceeded to identify and examine those ideas while neglecting the practices related to them. The literature of Christian devotion, however, reveals that most historical people thought it obvious that changed ideas follow, rather than precede, changed behavior. The aim of religious practices was thus not to "act out" previously held ideas or beliefs, but to realize—to make real—in a person's body the strong experience that, together with the religious community's interpretation of that experience, produced a countercultural religious self. If insight or understanding was the ultimate goal of religious experience, it was nevertheless the *method* or practices that cumulatively created the consciousness, the psychic "place" at which the insight might be achieved. Long before what we now call the "scientific method" was articulated by Francis Bacon, Christians were well aware that, by replicating the practices by which earlier candidates had achieved religious understanding, the experimental reproduction of religious experience was possible.

The earliest writings on Christian initiation describe a ritual in which an adult initiate entered the baptismal font naked in the presence of the

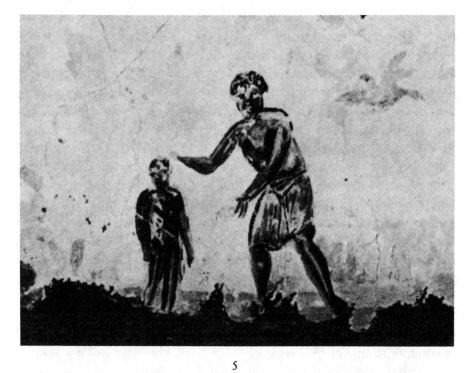

5

*Baptism of Jesus,* Catacomb of Callistus, Rome, late third century

Christian community and was baptized in the name of the Trinity (figure 5). These documents also reveal the techniques by which a strong religious experience was produced. The practices that prepared for and accompanied baptism developed a context for nakedness that removed the naked body from social meanings and identified it as the site and symbol of religious subjectivity; in Christian baptism, the naked body was no longer object, but subject. In this chapter we will explore baptism as it was practiced by Christian communities in the fourth century, turning in the last section of the chapter to its gendered aspects.

The practice of naked baptism presupposed the creation of a privileged ritual situation, a time out of time for which the initiate's associations, interpretations, even perceptions of ordinary life had been carefully deconstructed and reformed through lengthy and arduous catechetical preparation. Before examining information given by early Christian authors on the practice of naked initiation into membership in the Christian community, however, it is important to identify some aspects of secular culture that contributed to the meanings of nakedness in Christianity.

In secular Roman culture nakedness was not uncommon. In societies in which birth and death occurred in the home and bodies were prepared for burial by the family of the deceased, nakedness acquired a familiarity that is not a part of the common experience of twentieth-century Westerners. Nakedness was also a feature of public life in the later Roman Empire. Gladitorial shows in Roman colosseums regularly featured naked wrestlers as well as naked victims of unevenly matched fights with wild beasts. It has been suggested that late Roman eyes, accustomed to nudity in classical art, could have had no problem with the depictions of nakedness that soon appeared on the walls of Christian catacombs:[3] figures of Adam and Eve, Jonah, Daniel, the resurrected in Ezekiel's vision, the three Hebrew children in the fiery furnace, and naked figures in the process of being baptized, half in, half out of the water. In the Catacomb of Peter and Marcellinus (figure 6), however, the naked figures of Adam and Eve, posed on either side of an impressionistic tree, hunch forward to shield their genitals from view. They peer intently at the viewer, as if attempting to engage his eyes with theirs so that his gaze will not wander to their naked bodies. Their crossed hands, clutching leaves, both conceal and point to their genitals, in which they first experienced the most immediate and dramatic result of the Fall, the stirrings of lust. Clearly, these figures do not display a classical ease in nakedness.

But perhaps the Roman citizen's most frequent experience of nakedness took place in the public baths. Only the wealthiest of private homes included baths with running water; most Romans bathed in the sumptuous public baths that were built as part of the conspicuous benefaction of emperors, wealthy senators, or other aristocratic donors. Archaeological discoveries have provided many examples of the enormous size, sophisticated construction, and elaborate embellishment of these buildings. The Baths of Caracalla in Rome, completed in AD 217, featured mosaic floors, walls of marble, stucco reliefs, gilt bronze doors, and large-scale sculpture such as the Laocoön group.[4] Three large bath chambers—the frigidarium (cold room), the calidarium (hot room), and the tepidarium (warm room)—were supplemented by a steam room and swimming pools as well as by rooms for undressing, exercising, and massage. Hot, warm, and cold water were furnished by an intricate system involving pipes and hollow walls through which warm air could circulate.

The primary question relevant to understanding the secular setting for

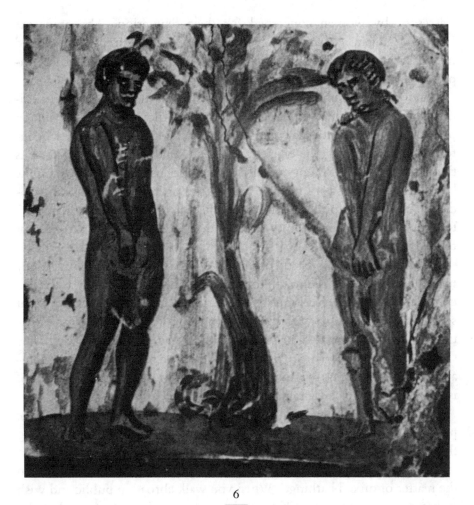

6
———

*Adam and Eve,* Catacomb of Peter and Marcellinus, Rome,
early fourth century

Christian baptism is whether Romans were accustomed to nakedness in
the context of mixed bathing. Apparently, the use of public baths
changed dramatically during the early centuries of the Christian era. In
Republican Rome men and women bathed separately, either at different
times in the smaller baths or, if the baths were large enough to contain
full facilities for both, in different rooms.[5] The first record of mixed
bathing comes from Pliny the Elder in the first century AD, but even
then, mixed bathing seems not to have been practiced by the upper

classes or by women concerned for their reputation. The emperors Hadrian, Trajan, Alexander Severus, and Marcus Aurelius prohibited mixed bathing, but Domitian, Gallienus, Heliogabalus, and other emperors permitted it.

Conduct in the public baths was apparently an indicator of the condition of public morality, though it is difficult to know whether legislation prohibiting immorality, gambling, obscenity, and vulgarity must be interpreted as implying the existence of such conditions. What is clear is that mixed naked bathing gradually came to be customary in most public baths by the fourth century. Constantine's effort to legislate morality included closing the public baths, but whether this rather unrealistic attempt to limit the opportunity for immorality was enforced throughout the empire is unknown.[6]

Although Christians participated in the secular culture in which they lived and were socialized to the tolerances of their society, they were also committed to systemic critique and rejection of aspects of the culture that seemed to be in conflict with their notions of morality. A major and continuing conflict among Christians involved the extent to which they should and could participate in the secular public realm.[7] Strong and unambiguous statements were made by Christian leaders on both sides of issues concerning acculturation as opposed to separation.[8]

Christians' use of the public baths was one such debated issue. If the public baths were frequently problematic for secular Romans, drawing the attention of emperors to their regulation, they were more so for Christians. The fourth-century *Apostolic Constitutions* addresses men on the matter of mixed bathing: "When you walk abroad in public and wish to bathe, make use of that bath which is appropriated to men, lest, by showing your body in an unseemly manner to women, or by seeing a sight not seemly for men, either you are ensnared, or you ensnare and entice to yourself those women who easily yield to such temptations."[9] Women were similarly instructed: "Avoid also that disorderly practice of bathing in the same place with men. . . . But if the bath be appropriated to women, let her bathe orderly, modestly, and moderately."[10] In the mid-third century, the North African bishop Cyprian argued that consecrated virgins should avoid public baths, while these Christian women protested that since they did not feel shame, nor did they look immodestly at anyone, they saw no problem with bathing at the mixed baths.[11] Some Christians perceived the danger of public baths as greater in the case of consecrated virgins. Jerome proposed one solution:

As regards the use of the baths, I know that some are content with saying that a Christian virgin should not bathe along with eunuchs or with married women, with the former because they are still men at all events in mind, and with the latter because women with child offer a revolting spectacle. For myself, however, I wholly disapprove of baths for a virgin of full age. Such an one should blush and feel overcome at the idea of seeing herself undressed. By vigils and fasts she mortifies her body and brings it under subjection. By cold chastity she seeks to put out the flame of lust and to quench the hot desires of youth. And by a deliberate squalor she makes haste to spoil her natural good looks. Why, then, should she add fuel to a sleeping fire by taking baths?[12]

"A clean body and a clean dress mean an unclean soul," Jerome declared.[13] His contemporary Augustine of Hippo was somewhat more lenient; he prescribed baths for consecrated virgins once a month.[14] Though ambiguous, the evidence seems to prohibit mixed bathing for Christians. Clearly, mixed bathing was a part of the larger issue of sexual morality, and nakedness was seen as potentially—though not inevitably, as we will see—a dangerous incitement to sexual lust.[15]

Similarly, gladitorial displays involving nakedness were repeatedly forbidden by and for Christians, though nakedness was probably not the central issue. The association of the colosseum with "the devil's pomp," most sharply characterized by the torture and execution of Christian martyrs, provided ample reasons for the rejection of that arena. Nevertheless, if Christians did as they were instructed and avoided the colosseum, they did not become accustomed to this late Roman travesty of classical athletic nakedness. Both the activities of the colosseum and public nakedness were associated strongly with the secularity that Christians forswore at baptism—"renuntiare saeculo"[16]—and that the Christian moralists urged Christians to avoid. As Augustine preached to his North African congregation at the celebration of the New Year:

The customs of the pagans delight their gods. However, he who said, "I would not have you become associates of devils" wished his hearers to be separated in their way of life and in morals from those who served demons. For such demons are pleased with misleading songs and with worthless shows, with the varied foulness of the theatre, with the frenzy of the games, with the cruelty of the amphitheatre . . . By acting in this way they, as it were, offer incense to the demons within their hearts.[17]

Christian naked baptism, then, cannot be understood as a continuation of secular culture made feasible by Christians' familiarity with and acceptance of secular nakedness.[18] Ironically, the appropriate context for

Christian baptism must rather be Christian aversion to secular naked-ness, an aversion informed by the sense that a human body, because of its intimate connection with the soul, should not be casually or carelessly exposed. For Christians, following an incarnated Christ meant that naked bodies have religious meaning; bodies are the site and naked bodies the symbol of religious subjectivity. Even Christian authors who differed from each other in their philosophical ideas of the relationship of bodies and souls nevertheless claimed the mutual and reciprocal influence of body and soul. Tertullian, with his Stoic conception of the cor-poreality of the soul, described the human body's full partnership in the soul's process:

There is not a soul that can at all procure salvation except it believe while it is in the flesh, so true is it that the flesh is the very condition on which the soul hinges. And since the soul is, in consequence of its salvation, chosen to the ser-vice of God, it is the flesh which actually renders it capable of such service. The flesh, indeed, is washed, in order that the soul may be cleansed; the flesh is anointed, that the soul may be consecrated; the flesh is signed with the cross that the soul too may be fortified; the flesh is shadowed with the imposition of hands, that the soul also may be illuminated by the spirit; the flesh feeds on the body and blood of Christ, that the soul may be fattened on God.[19]

Augustine, informed by a Platonic metaphysics, also insisted on the in-tegrity and mutual affect of body and soul.[20]

Despite this new sense of the human body as both the recipient and the perfect symbol of Christian subjectivity, early Christian literature, espe-cially but not exclusively in North Africa, repeatedly reveals the diffi-culty male ecclesiastical leaders had in conceptualizing women's bodies and roles in Christian communities. Attitudes toward secular gender as-sumptions reveal a fundamental contradiction between Christians' secu-lar gender conditioning and their countercultural claim to have "no dis-tinctions of male or female."[21] Secular gender conditioning is evident in the repeated fulminations of male ecclesiastical leaders who claimed that Christian women spent lavish care on their dress and make-up in order to entice men. And Christian women themselves often revealed the extent to which they had accepted the assumptions—while rejecting the acting out—of their secular role as seducers of men.[22]

To understand Christian baptism, then, we need to posit a tension or contradiction between Christians' secular socialization and what Fou-cault has called the "techniques of the self"—actually communal tech-niques—by which a chosen self-in-community was created and established.[23] In Christian initiation, a person's identity, loyalty, gratification, and responsibility were systematically and incrementally transferred from the secular society to the Christian community. The inherent fragility and instability of this complex process was minimized by the skillful arrangement of cumulative psychological, intellectual, and physical experiences. On the one hand, there were "new truth obligations: learning what is truth, discovering the truth, being enlightened by truth, telling the truth."[24] There was also a new history to be learned and the insertion of the initiate into a new human saga, a biblical rather than nationalistic scenario; there was a new scripture to be absorbed, new authorities to consult, and new activities to make habitual. On the other hand, there was a secular conditioning to dismantle and reinterpret, a past that had to be methodically remembered and confessed. As Foucault explains: "Everyone in Christianity has the duty to explore who he is, what is happening within himself, the faults he may have committed, the temptations to which he is exposed. Moreover, everyone is obliged to tell these things to other people, and hence to bear witness against himself."[25]

Christian initiation was a combination of instruction, confession,[26] and physical experience designed to produce a thoroughgoing conversion of the initiate. The word and concept of "conversion" are so familiar within Christian tradition that historians usually fail to explore their specific meanings in particular historical situations. In fact, historical Christians have meant very different things by "conversion." The best way to understand "conversion" is to examine the practices, the "techniques," brought to bear on a person in order to effect fundamental change.[27] The role of baptism in the process of conversion was pivotal. Stated most starkly, baptism, along with the lengthy and arduous catechetical preparation that preceded it, created a conversion so dramatic that Christians called it simply "new life."[28]

Augustine's conversion, one of the most famous in the history of Christianity, is misleading if it is taken as a model of fourth-century conversion. As recounted in book 8 of his *Confessions,* it was essentially a solitary struggle to resolve certain intellectual and emotional issues, a passionate inner turmoil in which Augustine felt himself the passive recipient of God's activity.[29] His baptism followed this conversion, confirming and reinforcing a *fait accompli.* Most fourth-century converts, however, came to the catechumenate with nothing more than a willingness to acknowledge belief in Christ; catechetical instructions, exorcisms, examinations, fastings, prayers, and baptism then undertook to create the process of birth into a Christian community. The ritual of baptism itself was necessary but was not sufficient to confer salvation without change of life.[30]

Moreover, many fourth-century people were willing to place their names with the bishop—the first step in affiliating with a Christian church—but were not willing to proceed with the process of initiation. The strenuousness and seriousness of the life change involved in baptism may account for some of this reluctance. In a time when a very wide range of interpretations were being given to what was entailed in becoming a Christian, it was, no doubt, frightening to enter a process that might end with a change of professions (as in Augustine's case),[31] a life of sexual abstinence[32] (like *all* the converts described in such Christian popular literature as the apocryphal Acts),[33] or the sale of all one's goods for distribution to the impoverished (like Melania the Younger). Not everyone could envision with equanimity the deconstruction of secular socialization.

Frederic van der Meer speculates that there were hundreds of converts each year in Augustine's North African diocese of Hippo at the turn of the fifth century. Not all of these were baptized immediately or in the next several years, however; even so, baptisms each Easter must have included sizeable numbers of people.[34] Although infants were baptized if they seemed in danger of dying, adult baptism was the rule in the fourth century. By then, a majority of the candidates for baptism were from Christian families.[35] Many people, like Augustine's father, postponed baptism indefinitely or until they were close to death. A century before Augustine, Tertullian had argued that baptism ought not to be "rashly granted": "all who understand what a burden baptism is will have more fear of obtaining it than of its postponement."[36] Augustine, on the other hand, vehemently urged Christians to "hurry to enter the bath."[37] Baptism was, after all, a matter of life or death; Augustine was "quite unable to conceive of a pious catechumen's being saved if he died a sudden death and was not baptized at the time."[38] But emergency baptism was always possible. And, since in the fourth century only one penance was permitted after baptism, catechumens—like Constantine—often waited until death was imminent to be baptized.[39]

Part of the reason for people's reluctance to undergo baptism may have been the rigor, humiliation, and physical discomfort of the intensive period of training, probation, and instruction that preceded baptism. Augustine was not reluctant to use fear to motivate people to enroll for baptism:

I must warn you in the words of Holy Scripture: "Defer it not from day to day, for his wrath shall come on a sudden." God knows that I tremble in my *cathedra* myself when I hear those words. I must not, I cannot, be silent. I am compelled to preach to you on this matter and to make you fearful, being myself full of fear.[40]

Naked baptism was observed as one of the two essential elements in Christian initiation, along with the invocation of the Trinity. Hippolytus, presbyter in Rome after AD 212, specified removal of clothing for baptism,[41] and in the fourth century instructions for baptism throughout the Roman Empire stipulated naked baptism without any suggestion of innovation or change from earlier practices. A sampling of these instructions will demonstrate the central importance of naked baptism to Christians.

In the Eastern empire, Cyril of Jerusalem or John, Cyril's successor, bishop of Jerusalem from AD 387 to 417 (there is some question of authorship) explained to the recently baptized what they had experienced. He wrote:

Immediately, then, upon entering, you removed your tunics. . . . Having stripped, you were naked. . . . Marvelous! You were naked in the sight of all and were not ashamed! Truly you bore the image of the first-formed Adam, who was naked in the garden and "was not ashamed."[42]

The Syrian bishop, Theodore of Mopsuestia (before 428), wrote:

You draw therefore near to the holy baptism and before all you take off your garments. As in the beginning when Adam was naked and was in nothing ashamed of himself, but after having broken the commandment and become mortal, he found himself in need of an outer covering.[43]

About a century later, the Greek author Pseudo-Dionysius gave a similar detailed account:

The deacons divest him [the initiate] completely and the priests bring the holy oil for unction. The hierarch begins the process of unction with a threefold sign of the cross, leaving it to the priest to cover the body of the man completely with oil. . . . Then the priests guide the man to the water [and the hierarch] immerses three times the initiate whose name is called out across the water by the priests to the hierarch with each immersion. Each time the initiate is plunged into the water and emerges, the hierarch invokes the three persons of the divine blessedness.[44]

Similarly, John the Deacon, writing in about AD 500, said:

They are commanded to go in naked, even down to their feet, so that [they may show that] they have put off the earthly garments of mortality. The church has ordained these things for many years with watchful care, even though the old books may not reveal traces of them.[45]

Narsai, founder of the Nestorian School at Nisibis in the middle of the fifth century, described the candidate for baptism: "Naked he stands and stripped before the Judge that by his wretched plight he may win pity to cover him."[46] Several paintings in the Christian catacombs in the first centuries of the common era also depicted naked baptism (see figure 5).[47]

We have seen that secular practices of public nakedness which habituated people to the sight of naked bodies do not supply the reason for naked Christian baptism. Why, then, did Christian leaders insist on its centrality in Christian initiation? We will need to look in two further directions for an answer to this question. First, what suggestions did they receive from other religions in the Roman Empire? Second, what theological understandings warranted and prescribed naked baptism?

Several historians have suggested that cultic nudity in the mystery religions of the later Roman Empire informed Christian baptismal practice.[48] Jonathan Z. Smith has argued, however, that proselyte baptism in postbiblical Judaism was the most immediate and direct influence on Christian baptism. Postbiblical Judaism not only practiced naked baptism, but also evidenced a similar ambivalence over nakedness. Judaism, Smith writes, "did not share with its Hellenistic neighbors the notion of sacral nudity; indeed, it was prudish to the highest degree."[49] Moreover, the Hebrew Bible reveals a "horror of nakedness," and rabbinic literature reiterates this attitude in a "series of proscriptions against praying, reading the Torah," and conducting other religious exercises while naked. Within such a context, Smith writes, "it appears all the more striking that the texts which describe Jewish proselyte 'baptism' consistently suggest that the proselyte was nude."[50]

Christian apostolic and patristic writings support Smith's claim that early Christianity shared both Judaism's horror of nakedness and its insistence on naked baptism.[51] Smith interprets naked baptism in the light of catacomb depictions of naked figures in which they symbolize new life and represent a present sign of the promised resurrection of the body. In short, Smith argues convincingly that the practice of nakedness associated with Christian baptism seems most likely to have been influenced by Jewish practice, though naked initiation in the mystery religions of the Roman Empire cannot be ruled out as another influence.

Theological meanings of nakedness in baptism are puzzlingly unfocused for a feature of the Christian rite that seems to have had such great importance. Let us briefly survey some of the interpretations of naked baptism given by Christian authors, including not only some that were, by the fourth century, considered orthodox, but also some from gnostic Christianity that were, in their own time, valid alternatives.

1. Stripping off the "old man with his deeds."[52]

2. Imitation of Christ: "Having stripped, you were naked, in this also imitating Christ, who was naked on the cross, by his nakedness 'throwing off the cosmic powers and authorities like a garment.'"[53]

3. Leaving the world; Jonathan Z. Smith suggests a pun between *kosmos* (the world) and *kosmos* (ornament): "to take off one's ornaments, one's dress, is to take off the world."[54]

4. Death and rebirth: "In the same moment you were dying and being born, and that saving water was at once your grave and your mother. . . . One time brought both, and your death coincided with your birth."[55]

5. New life: "[The newly baptized] are called *infantes* because they, who were first born to the world, are now born to Christ."[56]

6. "Naked and unashamed" (Genesis 2:25): Theodore of Mopsuestia speaks of two different "moments" of nakedness in baptism: before baptism, the nakedness of shame, like that of Adam and Eve after the Fall, and a nakedness without shame, after baptism, "a nakedness," Jonathan Z. Smith remarks, "which will be fully realized by the believer only at the resurrection, . . . a nakedness of transcendence."[57]

7. Quasi-martyrdom: martyrdom was frequently called "baptism by blood," and it could replace baptism for martyrs who had not yet received the rite at the time of their death. Tertullian urges confessors—those condemned and awaiting execution for their adherence to Christianity—to fast in preparation for martyrdom, just as *competens* fasted in preparation for baptism.

Three further meanings appear in heterodox baptism:

8. Sexual neutrality;[58] and, in Naassene material preserved by Hippolytus: "This is the gate of heaven and the house of God where the good

God dwells alone; where no one impure enters, no psychic, no one fleshly. It is reserved for the *pneumatikoi* alone. When they come they cast away their garments and all will become bridegrooms having been made male (anēroseōmenos) by the virginal spirit."[59]

9. Stripping off the body.[60]

10. Bridal chamber: "The baptism which we previously mentioned is called 'garment of those who do not strip themselves of it,' for those who will put it on and those who have received redemption wear it. . . . It is also called 'bridal chamber' because of the agreement and individual state of those who know that they have known him."[61]

In this brief survey of theological meanings of nakedness in Christian baptism, the symbolism of death to former commitments and socialization and birth to a new existence predominate. The stripping of clothing followed by nakedness and, after baptism, the donning of a white linen garment was a paradigm of the deconstruction of secular socialization; it was a symbolic regression to an infantile state, a conscious choice of allegiance to the Trinity, and a reinvestment of loyalty in the Christian community witnessing the baptism—a new "public" in which the body of the initiate had been incorporated into the Body of Christ and the naked body, along with the soul, redeemed from secular meaning and assimilated to religious meaning.

Religious ritual would not, however, require the literal reenactment of nakedness to image and reinforce its symbolic meaning. In later centuries authors who also interpreted baptism as death and rebirth—rather than as enlightenment or cleansing, for example—did not find this meaning impaired by the baptisee's clothing. Why, then, in the first centuries of the Christian era, was naked baptism such a central feature of Christian initiation throughout the Roman world? Neither Jewish precedents nor theological rationalizations provide a fully convincing reason for the unanimity in historical writings. The answer is most likely to be found in the interweaving of intellectual, psychological, and physical experience in the extended preparation for baptism. Only after that experience, Augustine said, were initiates in a position to understand the two mysteries of Christian faith that were never divulged to the uninitiated—baptism and the eucharist.

We have sufficient historical evidence to reconstruct not only the practices and architectural setting, but also the emotional tone of baptism in the North African town of Hippo Regius—Augustine's diocese—at the end of the fourth century. By that time preparation for baptism in Augustine's basilica in Hippo had acquired a settled pattern.[62] First, it was a secret process,[63] unlike regular worship services. Anyone could come to the church and attend the first part of the regular service, the "service of the Word." The unbaptized were then dismissed to stand behind a curtain or screen; they could still hear, but could not see, the "liturgy of the faithful."

A person desirous of becoming Christian would go to the bishop's palace, usually accompanied by a Christian friend who would certify his or her intention to become a Christian to one of the priests. A catechist would then instruct the applicant for an hour or so in the primary aspects of the faith and the duties of a Christian. If the applicant agreed to continue the process of becoming Christian, this initial instruction was concluded by the administration of four rites: the tracing of the sign of the cross on the forehead; the catechist's laying on of hands; an exorcism in which evil was "breathed out" of the applicant; and the giving of the sacrament of salt,[64] probably along with some of the blessed bread that was given to the unbaptized, signifying "a shadow of the Eucharist" in which the applicant would eventually share as a baptized Christian.

The next stage of preparation might take place years after the preliminary enrollment; in North Africa in Augustine's time, the initial stage of the catechumenate lasted for at least two years. It began when the catechumen enrolled as a *competens,* a "seeker along with others." A time of strict probation for *competentes* took place in the seven weeks before Easter. During this time, they were required to practice strict abstinence from sexual activity, were forbidden to bathe, and were required to fast[65] every day until evening as penitential acts. In worship services during Lent, the *competentes,* "unbathed and with their clothing neglected, stood apart in a special portion of the church where the whole congregation could see them."[66] In addition to these ascetic exercises, *competentes* were also rigorously instructed in not only the essentials of the faith, but also the evils of pagan amusements, moral responsibility, and sexual morality.[67] On several occasions, *competentes* were questioned, "in front of the whole congregation about their conduct and their resolutions, and . . . quite possibly on at least the first of these occasions, they underwent some kind of bodily examination to check whether they suffered from possession, leprosy, or ritual uncleanliness."[68] This examination, the

*scrutinium,* was followed by a "blowing out" or exorcism of the Evil
One: "Contemptuously and almost hissing, the exorcist blew at the un-
seen enemy. . . . Then using [an] ancient prayer . . . he would cry,
'Come out of him, Accursed One!'" While this was done, the *competens*
stood on a cloth of harsh sackcloth or on rough animal skin, as described
in a sermon by Theodore of Mopseustia:

You stand also on garments of sackcloth so that from the fact that your feet are
pricked and stung by the roughness of the cloth you may remember your old
sins and show penitence and repentance of the sins of your fathers. . . . You
stand barefooted on the cloth while your outer garment is taken off from you,
and your hands are stretched towards God in the posture of one who prays.[69]

Toward the end of the period of fasting, introspection, and repentance,
the *symbolum* of the Passion—almost identical to the Apostles' Creed—
was recited to the *competentes.* They had never heard it before but were
now expected to commit it to memory, word for word.[70] Truths of the
faith that were often heard in sermons and scripture were only now
"handed over" to the catechumen, "gathered together, arranged in a
fixed order, and condensed" into the *symbolum.*[71] Each candidate for baptism recited the *symbolum* alone before the whole congregation during
the Easter Vigil.

On Maundy Thursday catechumens were allowed to break their fast
and to take a bath. On Good Friday, however, they fasted again, and a
ceremony occurred in which the bishop washed their feet. They also at-
tended a service in which the Passion story was read from the Gospel of
Matthew, along with a sermon on the Passion. The Easter Vigil represented the climax of the seven weeks of strenuous physical and mental
preparation for baptism. On Easter Eve the most joyous celebration of
the liturgical year began. In Hippo, the great basilica blazed with the
light of many lamps and of the huge Pascal candelabra as crowds of
people streamed into the church and readers read the scripture lessons
that recount the saga of the human race from creation to redemption.
After the lessons, Augustine preached; in his *extempore* Easter sermons,[72]
recorded by stenographers as he spoke, the subject was often light:
"When the devil had power over you, 'you were once in darkness, but
now you are light in the Lord. Walk, then, as children of the light.'
Keep vigil against the darkness and its rulers in your mother, the light;
and from the bosom of your mother, the light, pray to the Father of
Lights."[73]

At the end of the vigil—probably at the first cockcrow—the baptism service commenced with the whole congregation choosing to leave the darkness and turn to the light. At the ritual question, "Doest thou forswear the devil? And his angels? And his pomp?" the congregation, along with the *competentes,* loudly denounced them and turned toward the west, the direction in which the sun set and from which the demons came. They then turned to the east, the direction of the rising sun, to dedicate themselves to the God of light, after which they processed to the baptismal chapel beside the basilica, singing Psalm 42, "As the hart pants for the fountains of water, so my soul pants for thee, O God."

"The baptistry too," according to Van der Meer, "is blazing with lamps, and the curtains are withdrawn between the pillars that carry the roof of the holy pool." The pool, which is octagonal, has three rows of steps leading down to it. "These steps are in part decorated with mosaics, as is also the floor of the pool. . . . The basin is filled by 'living,' that is to say, by streaming, water."[74] After being anointed with oil "from the topmost hairs of [the] head to the soles of [the] feet"[75] and removing the one robe in which the initiate was clothed, the candidate entered the baptismal pool.

The water in the pool is not deep. It reaches up to the breast of a boy, while an adult is immersed scarcely up to the navel. When the candidate has entered the pool, the ancient questions are put: Do you believe in the Father? Do you believe in the Son? Do you believe in the Holy Ghost? Do you believe in the Holy Church, the remission of sins, and the resurrection of the body? . . . Three times the candidate is baptized in the water.[76]

The shallowness of the baptismal pool makes it difficult to visualize how the immersion actually took place. Baptisees may have been placed by the deacon under the stream of water pouring into the pool; or they may have knelt down so that their heads and shoulders could be pushed under the surface of the pool after each of the first three questions was answered, or water may have been poured over their heads and shoulders while they stood or sat in the pool.

Augustine addressed the "seekers of baptism" as fetuses *in utero:*

The beginnings of . . . . your conception, when by heavenly grace you are beginning to be generated in the womb, ought to be sustained by prayer . . . you who are now being born whom the Lord has made, strive to be born in a sound and healthful fashion, lest you be prematurely and disastrously delivered. Behold the womb of your mother, the Church; behold how she labors in pain to bear you and bring you forth into the light of faith. Do not, by your impatience, disturb your mother's body and make narrow the passage of your delivery.[77]

After baptism, *competentes* became *infantes*. The neonate, still naked, appeared before the bishop to receive confirmation and another anointing. He or she also received a laying on of hands, prayer, and a sealing or *consignatio* by which the cross, Christ's "owner's mark or *titulus*" was signed on the forehead. The *infante* was then clothed in a white linen robe symbolizing purity[78] and donned slippers because the sole of the foot must not touch the earth for eight days. Finally, the *infante* was given a small portion of milk and honey, "the ancient ritual food of the newly born."[79]

The physical focus of baptism, so clear in these accounts, received a great deal of attention in North Africa, not only in Augustine's time, but also in earlier African Christian authors. The body, like the soul, was seen as changing ownership in the process of baptism: "As you presented your bodies to sin as the instrument of iniquity," Augustine told the *competentes,* "so now you may present your members to God as instruments of justice."[80] Similarly, descriptions of the weeks of preparation for baptism focus less on verbal instruction and learning than on physical activities: "Behold where the stadium is; behold where the wrestling grounds are; behold where the racecourse is; behold where the boxing ring is! . . . If you wish so to fight that you do not beat the air in vain but so as to strike your opponent manfully, then chastise your body and bring it into subjection."[81] The body is the stadium, the wrestling grounds, the racecourse, the boxing ring in Augustine's vivid imagery of the *competentes* struggling to break free from indenture to evil. It is important to note that Augustine did not use this energetic ascetic imagery in general advice about the Christian life, but only in specialized instruction for "seekers after baptism." The key to a victory of Christianity in the life of the person is the physical practices—fasting, sexual abstinence, vigils, prayers, and exorcisms—that effectively deconstruct the person's physical and social habits and make possible the reconstruction of a new orientation. Just as the unbaptized were seen as the property of the devil, bearing evil in their bodies, so the baptized became, body and soul, flesh of Christ's flesh and bone of his bone.

Augustine emphasized the need for secrecy about two, and only two, aspects of the faith: baptism and the eucharist. In sermons to *infantes,* the newly baptized were told for the first time the meaning of the eucharistic celebration:[82]

In the night that is passed you saw what stands here upon the altar, but what manner of thing it is, what it signifies, and the great mystery that it shows forth, you do not yet know. Well then, what you see is bread and a chalice. Your own eyes tell you that, but what you have yet to learn is this: that the bread is Christ's body and the chalice is his blood.[83]

Moreover, baptized Christians, Augustine continued, become themselves the eucharistic bread they see on the altar, the "body of Christ": "You are what you have received."[84] This strong interpretation of the result of the sacrament of baptism was part of the secret of the faith not divulged to the uninitiated. "If, then, you are Christ's body and members, it is your own mystery that lies here upon the table of the Lord, and it is your own mystery that you receive. . . . It is *what you are yourselves*."[85] The secrecy of this information, the physical condition of the initiate at the end of seven weeks of physical, psychological, and intellectual dehabituation and deconstruction, and the vivid experience through which the *infante* had recently passed all contributed to the recognition that the eucharist also represented a self-offering, a being eaten as well as an eating.[86] The initiate was at once food and eater, eating the body of Christ and, by eating, becoming that body.

This imagery gives us an important suggestion about the role of the body in baptism, a suggestion that may help to clarify the importance of nakedness in baptism. Let us consider in more detail the preparation of the *body* for baptism, the ascetic practices by which the body became the locus of the conscious choice to become Christian. In the first treatise on baptism, written at the end of the third century, Tertullian said that the candidate for baptism must "pray with repeated prayers, fasts, and bending of the knee, and vigils all the night through, and with the confession of all by-gone sins."[87] Fourth-century descriptions of the seven-week preparation for baptism explicitly stipulate that two exercises relate directly to the body: fasting and exorcism. Although the long daily instructions and prayers, culminating in the Easter Vigil,[88] also required physical endurance, they were not, like fasting and exorcism, understood as exercises directed to the cleansing of the body.

Modern people, usually unfamiliar with the physical effects of fasting, often interpret the requirement of fasting in ancient texts as representing rejection of the material world for the spiritual world. Interpreting fasting in this way, however, loses sight of the effect on the body and consciousness of short fasts. We need to consider the possibility that Christian authors were at least as interested in the effect of fasting as in fasting as a symbolic statement.[89]

Historians are able to reconstruct the effects of food deprivation through experiments and by observing contemporary fasting.[90] Although social meanings and the specific symbolic content of fasting practices differ enormously across time and in the different religions in which fasting has been found effective, many of the effects of fasting on the human body appear to be cross-cultural. In his exploration of ancient ascetical fasting, Herbert Musurillo cites a study conducted in 1950 at the University of Minnesota[91] which lists among the psychological effects noted in modern patients apathy and irritability, reduction of sexual interest, emotional volatility, a tendency to introversion, and lack of independence and social initiative.[92] These effects, however, were the result of prolonged fasting, while fasting in preparation for baptism was much gentler, consisting, for most of the seven weeks, only of food abstinence until sundown, or one meal a day. Compare a fourth-century author's description of the effects of fasting with the 1950 study: "Consider the effects of fasting: it cures disease, dries up the bodily humors, puts demons to flight, gets rid of impure thoughts, makes the mind clearer and the heart purer, the body sanctified, and raises man to the throne of God."[93] Despite the differences in interpretation, Athanasius's description of the effects of fasting focuses on one of the effects described by the 1950 study as reduction of sexual interest. Augustine also testifies to the effectiveness of fasting in relieving not only sexual but also social and psychological pressure: "The temptations of the world, the snares of the devil, the suffering of the world, the enticement of the flesh, the surging waves of troubled times, and all corporal and spiritual adversities are to be overcome by almsgiving, fasting, and prayer."[94]

What were the practices of fasting surrounding baptism and the Easter celebration? The *Apostolic Constitutions,* collected in the fourth century but containing much older material, prescribes the following periods of fasting:

Fast on the days of the passover [holy week], beginning from the second day of the week until the preparation and the Sabbath, six days, making use only of bread, and salt, and herbs, and water for your drink; but do you abstain on these days from wine and flesh. . . . You who are able, fast the day of the preparation and the Sabbath day entirely, tasting nothing until the cock-crowing of the night.[95]

A more strenuous fast is prescribed for the time immediately preceding the Easter Vigil:

From the even of the fifth day till cock-crowing break your fast when it is daybreak of the first day of the week, which is the Lord's day. [On Saturday] from evening till cock-crowing keep awake, and assemble together in the church, watch and pray and entreat God; reading, when you sit up all night, the Law, the Prophets, and the Psalms, until cock-crowing, and baptizing your catechumens, and reading the Gospel with fear and trembling.[96]

Fasting was so crucial to the Easter celebration that, at least in some geographical areas, failure to fast was grounds for deposing members of the clergy.[97]

The connection between food and temptation was constantly reiterated, though differently interpreted, by many Christian authors.[98] Although patristic authors seldom associated eating with the assimilation of demons into the body, popular apocryphal Acts frequently made this connection. Evil spirits, they said, can enter the body through the mouth along with food—particular demons with particular foods. Conversely, demons can be eliminated by the strictest control of the amounts and kinds of food one eats. Compulsive eating, with its lack of self-control, was understood as both evidence and cause of moral laxity. Moreover, eating rich and abundant food was thought to have a direct physiological effect in stimulating sexual desire. According to Basil of Ancyra:

As the body grows fat it is inordinately stimulated by the sexual humors seething deep down, and it is goaded and driven on to sexual intercourse. . . . As the stomach swells with food, the organs beneath it are necessarily stimulated towards their proper function by the deeply seething humors. For the overhanging stomach supplies these organs with the things which act on these faculties like a spur.[99]

Fasting as antidemonic strategy and fasting as penitence were integrated—or conflated—in fasting as catechetical exercise and annual religious practice for all baptized Christians. Perhaps the most ingenious theological rationale for fasting is the suggestion that since Adam and Eve's sin was caused by desire for food and the pleasure of taste, restraining the pleasure of food is the most direct method for dissociating oneself from the fall of the human race: "We fast now because Adam did not fast."[100]

The second catechetical practice that directly addressed the body of the candidate for baptism was not unrelated to fasting. Exorcism, like fasting, was thought to purify the body. Daily exorcisms accompanied the instruction of catechumens throughout Lent. Cyril of Jerusalem wrote:

Let your feet take you swiftly to the catechetical instructions. Submit to the exorcisms devoutly. Whether you are breathed upon or exorcised, the act spells salvation. Imagine virgin gold alloyed with various foreign substances: copper, tin, iron, lead. What we are after is the gold alone, and gold cannot be purified of its dross without fire.[101]

All early descriptions of Christian baptism include exorcisms in the preparation for baptism. It was considered fully as important for Christians to identify what they turned away from in becoming Christians as it was to name what they turned toward. Evil had to be "breathed out" of the body in order to free the person from the devil's possession, "for it was believed that the devil literally possessed the unbaptized, as though they were his property, just as the Holy Spirit took possession of the baptized."[102] The daily exorcisms during the period of catechesis reached their goal and climax in the candidate's renunciation of the devil just before baptism. However, demons would also need to be expelled on many occasions after baptism by the sign of the cross, which Cyril of Jerusalem called "a terror to devils."[103] Tertullian wrote that demons were especially vulnerable to expulsion by Christians:

Fearing Christ in God and God in Christ, they become subjects to the servants of God and Christ. So at our touch and breathing, overwhelmed by the thought and realization of those judgment fires, they leave at our command the bodies they have entered, unwilling and distressed, and before your very eyes put to an open shame.[104]

Practices of fasting and exorcism reveal the extent to which Christians understood the process of instruction and baptism to be incomplete without a rigorous engagement of the body. The continuous attention to the conversion of the body in the seven weeks of intensive catechetical exercises reached its climax in naked baptism, the moment in which the stripping of secular socialization was most complete. Clothing, which represented the candidate's lifelong accumulation of secular interests, values, and loyalties, was laid aside, and the candidate entered the baptismal waters in the same condition of naked vulnerability in which he or she originally entered the world. The power of such a religious experience can only be imagined; stories of the quasi-magical effect of the ceremony are frequent in the literature of the fourth century. But analysis of the physical, intellectual, and emotional practices by which the ceremony of naked baptism was prepared indicate that more skill than "magic" was involved. A change of beliefs and values was certainly a desired effect of catechesis and baptism, but it was not the only effect. A new integration of the body in religious commitment was produced by the practices surrounding and including naked baptism. The naked body, the exposed body of birth, baptism, and death, came to represent religious subjectivity, aspiration, and commitment.

"The body," especially the naked body, is, however, a gendered body. The process that created a new relationship of body to individual subjectivity also constructed a social relation. Everyone who was baptized did not receive exactly the same experience and meaning from the baptismal rite.[105] Certainly, no one in the early centuries of the common era was critically aware of the social *construction* of gender roles and expectations. Quite the contrary: Christians, like their secular neighbors, assumed that there are "natural" intellectual and psychological as well as biological differences between men and women. Belief in natural differences between the sexes was explained by the Genesis account of Eve's creation after Adam and from his side. Since women were considered derivative from and inferior to men, social arrangements both reflected this assumption and guaranteed that differences were readily *observable* in society. We now turn to an exploration of baptism as a gendered ritual.

Saint Paul invoked the baptismal rite in his statement to the Galatians that in Christ "there is neither Jew nor Greek, slave nor free, male nor female."[106] But men and women were differently treated in baptismal practices. In describing these differences, we must acknowledge that women evidently both shared in the empowerment witnessed to by Christians and were firmly confined to supportive roles in Christian churches and communities. We must refuse to resolve this apparent contradiction by concluding either that women were freed to new experiences of self-definition or that they ultimately received nothing more in Christian communities than a reinforcement of secular gender conditioning. According to existing evidence, both appear to be accurate, so we must explore their puzzling coexistence.

How was baptism a gendered experience? In my earlier description of baptism, I glided rather too hastily over the statement that during the baptismal rite, naked people were anointed with oil by clergy "from the topmost hairs of your head to the soles of your feet."[107] Let us examine more closely that part of the ceremony. The third-century Syrian *Didascalia Apostolorum* stipulated:

When women go down to the water, those who go down into the water ought to be anointed by a deaconess with the oil of anointing; and where there is no woman at hand, especially a deaconess, he who baptizes must of necessity anoint her who is being baptized. But where there is a woman, and especially a deaconess, it is not fitting that women should be seen by men: but with the imposition of the hands do thou anoint the head only.[108]

Evidence of the existence of deaconesses, however, is found only in the Syrian and Greek churches; there were apparently none in Egypt or Palestine, and the office was "generally unknown in the West."[109] Clearly, women assistants were used in the baptism of women in some places, but in many others, they were not.[110]

In the sixth century the Palestinian monk John Moschus recounted the story of the monk Conan, who was in charge of all baptizing in the monastery of Pethucla.[111] Conan was disturbed, John wrote, when he had to baptize women. One day a particularly beautiful Persian woman came to be baptized, but Conan did not have the courage to anoint her, so he fled from the monastery. He was stopped, however, by a vision of John the Baptist, who made the sign of the cross three times over Conan's genitals, thus symbolically castrating him. Conan returned to the monastery, baptized the Persian woman "without even perceiving that she was a woman." He continued to perform this office for twelve years without "experiencing any movement of the flesh, and without noticing the sex of those whom he baptized." Jonathan Z. Smith, who quotes this story, comments, "Significantly, in this narrative, when the leader of the monastery thought to send for a deaconess to perform the rite on women, 'he could not as it was not the custom.'"[112] It appears that male clergy customarily baptized women in most parts of the Roman Empire. It is difficult to determine how long this practice continued, but it was certainly going on in the numerous baptisms of the fourth century when Christianity became, under Constantine, a licensed cult and, in the 380s, under Theodosius, the official religion of the empire.

Since Christian initiation was the entry into Christian communities, the administration of baptism was a key issue for church order. The bishop was the final authority on how baptism should be administered, how preparation was conducted, and who was eligible for baptism; all other church officers had to confer with him and ask him for approval of their practices and methods of instruction. Women were excluded from the administration of baptism and were severely warned to relinquish any aspirations to teaching or clerical roles: it was "illegal and impious" for women to baptize:

And about a woman's baptizing, we are informing you that there is no small danger to the women who attempt it. Therefore we do not advise it. For if "the man is the head of the woman" (1 Cor. 11:3), he was chosen for priesthood; it is not right to set aside the order of creation and *leave what is chief to descend to the lowest part of the body.* For woman is the body of the man, being from his side and subjected to him, from whom she also was separated for the production of children. . . . For the man is the ruler of the woman, since he is also her head.[113]

It is worth noting, however, that John Chrysostom permits women to "baptize" themselves and other women through martyrdom. After telling the story of a woman who led her two daughters to martyrdom by drowning in the midst of a persecution, he commented: "It was the mother who baptized them. 'What are you saying? That a woman baptizes?' Yes, such baptism women also administer; just so this woman also then baptized and became a priest."[114]

Chrysostom was willing to include women in suffering, but they were not included in leadership roles in churches. Since the woman he described was dead, he was willing to acknowledge that she had acted as a priest. Yet the male prerogative of priestly roles was, as late as the third century, a debated issue across Christian groups. Tertullian refers to Christian groups (perhaps Marcionites) in which women baptized as well as performed other priestly functions, such as *docere, contendere, exorcismos agere,* and *curationes repromittere.*[115] Orthodox Christians contrasted their communities with those of "heretics" on the basis of women's participation in leadership; interestingly, they also contrasted Christianity with paganism on the issue of women in administrative and liturgical roles:

For this is an error of Gentile atheism to ordain women as priests to the goddesses; it is not in the dispensation of Christ. And also, had it been necessary for women to baptize, certainly the Lord would have also been baptized by his own mother, not by John, or when he sent us to baptize, he would have sent women with us as well for this purpose. But now, nowhere, neither by command nor in writing did he transmit this, since *he knew the order of nature and the fittingness of things,* being the Creator of nature and the Legislator of the arrangement.[116]

In heterodox Christian groups women were both teaching and baptizing. Tertullian connected the prohibition against women as baptizers directly to their descent from Eve:

But the impudence of that woman [of the Cainite sect] who assumed the right to teach is evidently not going to arrogate to her the right to baptize as well [because she taught, according to Tertullian, that baptism was unnecessary or ineffectual]—unless, perhaps, some new serpent appears, like that original one, so that as that woman abolished baptism, some other should of her own authority confer it.[117]

In orthodox churches a rite that could not be conferred by a woman but in which naked women were anointed by male clergy made explicit in practice what was repeatedly asserted in the literature of early Christianity, namely that the subordination of women to men was reinforced in Christian baptism.

A second aspect of the genderization of baptismal practices can be seen in the order in which *competentes* were baptized. The *Apostolic Constitutions*, as do other descriptions of baptism, states that women were baptized last. Children were baptized first, followed by men and then women. I have not been able to find any rationale for this procedure, but the order is puzzling. Were children baptized first because they were assumed to be nearest the state of innocence to which preparation for baptism aspired? If so, were women baptized last because they were thought of as farthest from this state, due to their association with Eve, who introduced sin into the world? In the absence of patristic statements that directly connect the practice of baptizing women last with Eve's transgression, we can only speculate as to why this was done. Yet it was not only the more misogynist patristic authors who stated their view that women are "all Eves."

A further stipulation for women appears in Christian baptismal manuals. Hippolytus's instructions read: "and last the women, who shall all have loosened their hair."[118] The order that women's hair be unbound at baptism is ancient, though it is not mentioned in the New Testament writings.[119] What did it signify, in the context of naked baptism? We can identify a cluster of meanings without selecting one as decisive or central. The simplest and most general meaning was probably the symbolic nakedness of undressed hair, a reiteration of the literal nakedness of the female candidate for baptism. But the treatment of hair is also linked, in early Christian writings as in many other cultures, with social order; in secular Roman society, hair was arranged in accordance with a woman's sexual status—long and flowing if the woman was a virgin, or bound on the head in a chignon if the woman was married. By adopting the pre-scribed style, a woman announced her willingness to be defined by her sexual status in the social order. In Roman culture the loosened hair of women who would normally have had bound or veiled hair had quite specific meanings. In Roman funerals it was customary for female mourners to loosen their hair and remove all signs of wealth and dignity, a rejection of the marks of social placement and prestige. Baptism, understood in part as a funerary rite, may have rendered appropriate this "neglect of the appearance" as a sign of mourning. On the other hand, during the ordeals that resulted in her martyrdom, Perpetua pinned up her loosened hair, "for it was not right that a martyr should die with her hair in disorder," her *acta* reports, "lest she might seem to be mourning in her hour of triumph."[120]

The significance of hair arrangement was an issue in Christian com-munities as well as in secular culture. Wayne Meeks has argued per-suasively that in Christian communities an "intensified sense of role op-positions" ironically resulted from a new flexibility in social roles. When people perceived this flexibility as a lack of order, anxiety and a reaction of misogyny often resulted, motivating renewed attention to defining opposite and complementary roles and dress for women and men. Tradi-tional social roles were not "taken for granted, but debated, consciously violated by some and vigorously defended by others."[121] Women's hair, a heavily loaded symbol of social order, was a focus of this debate, as the Apostle Paul's instructions to the church at Corinth (1 Corinthians 11:2–16) reveals. Paul instructs men to pray in public worship with un-covered head; women are always to pray with covered head. Apparently some women were praying without a head covering "as an overt sign of their sexual liberation and equality, since in Christ there is 'no male or female.'"[122]

But stable social roles were not all that was at stake. J. Duncan Derrett describes a further issue involved in women's hairdos: "The real reason why Eastern women's hair is covered is, as Paul himself indicates, its uni-versal acceptance as a sign of sexual attractiveness. It is not merely that the hair needed to be covered out of respect: it was because of the long tresses that it needed to be covered." Uncovered hair was a signal of sexual availability, an insult, Derrett writes, to a woman's husband. He paraphrases Paul's concern: "The husband is entitled to his wife's modesty in public. . . . For the husband's rights are not forfeited simply because their spiritual status has been changed by their conversion. . . . They had a right to their wives behaving as married women do."[123] Similarly, the second-century *Shepherd of Hermas* described the deplorable situation of Christian men who were seduced by women.[124] The author contrasts the virtues with vices—both personified as women. The vices, clothed in black garments and wearing their hair loose, are the image of the diabolical seductress.

The management of hair was also debated hotly in North African churches. As in other parts of the Roman world, veiling the hair signified modesty, loss of virginity, or subordination to a father, husband, or, in the case of consecrated virgins, to a bishop. Tertullian's preoccupation with hair appears repeatedly in his instructions on women's dress and, fifty years later, Cyprian, bishop of Carthage and martyr in the Decian persecution, required consecrated virgins to cover their hair. Tertullian placed the responsibility for seduction of men directly on Christian women who did not use the veil: "I pray you, be you mother or sister or virgin-daughter . . . veil your head: if a mother for your sons' sakes; if a sister for your brethern's sakes; if a daughter for your fathers' sakes. All ages are imperilled in your person."[125] Was the requirement that women's hair be let down during Christian baptism a reminder, at the very moment of their initiation into the Christian, community that all women participate in Eve's perennial guilt for the seduction of Adam and the human race?

It is clear that secular, social, and religious meanings converged in an area of enormous sensitivity—women's sexuality, spirituality, and social status within Christian communities. Women's loosened hair in naked baptism becomes more, rather than less, puzzling when we begin to unravel the complex issues surrounding women's hair, but it is important to understand this complexity and the intensity of the debate if we are to arrive at a recognition of what was attempted and, apparently, achieved in baptismal rites.

W. C. Van Unnik suggests another source for the practice and meaning of loosened hair for female baptisees. In the Palestinian Jewish rites of purification after menstruation, according to rabbis, it was believed necessary for the water to touch all parts of the body in order to cleanse the woman. In the Hebrew Bible rites of lustration were also stipulated for funerals, for prayers for successful warfare, and for women suspected of adultery.[126] In Judaism loose hair, Van Unnik states, indicated that a woman was ritually impure in some way, the most frequent of which was menstruation. Furthermore, in Jewish proselyte baptism pagans were considered impure—like menstruating women—and therefore required to undergo the ritual cleansing of baptism.[127] The stipulation of women's loosened hair may have been one of the several Christian baptismal practices that were directly derived from the baptismal rite for Jewish proselytes.[128]

Since Christian initiation represented the creation of a religious subjectivity, Christian leaders seem to have found it crucially important to establish the role of women in this new social order within the initiation rite itself. This was done in two ways: by baptizing women after children and men, and by stipulating that women's hair must be loosened. Moreover, flowing hair can act as a veil, as Saint Paul suggests when he calls hair a "natural garment" in 1 Corinthians 11:15. Dennis MacDonald writes: "Among the curses on Eve, the rabbis included the wearing of a veil . . . as a sign of mourning for Eve's sin."[129]

A closely woven set of religious meanings of loosened hair—as associated with penitence and impurity—was held in tension with secular meanings of loosened hair—as wantonness, insubordination, subversiveness, and sexual availability. In addition, the loosened hair of woman at baptism also signified the loosened hair of a virgin or unmarried woman, a woman not engaged in sexual activity. At baptism every woman, whether married or virgin, became virgin temporarily, both by literally abstaining from sexual activity during the extended period of catechism and by her initiation into a new life and community. Penitence for the sin of Eve, a sin which, according to Jewish interpretations of the Genesis account, caused menstruation and ritual impurity, may also have been among the associations of loosened hair. This cluster of conflicting meanings recapitulated male leaders' ambivalence about women in Christian communities, a tension amply documented by the enormous amount of writing devoted to issues related to women. Definition of the place of women in church organizations was a major issue, requiring both rhetoric and legislation.[130] Since baptism and the preparation that led to it were for all Christians the central training in Christianity, and for most Christians the only systematic training they would receive, it

# 2

# "BECOMING MALE": WOMEN MARTYRS
# AND ASCETICS

*I am a woman in sex, but not in spirit.*[1]

*For what thing might there be more glorious than these women, whom men may wonder at sooner than they may imitate? But this chiefly the glory of Him in whom they that do believe and they that with holy zeal in his name contend with one another are indeed, according to the inward man neither male nor female; so that even in them that are women in body the manliness of their souls hides the sex of their flesh and we may scarce think of that in their bodily condition which they suffered not to appear in their deeds.*[2]

*She had a life without vanity, an appearance without pretense, character without affectation, a face without adornment: she kept watch without sleeping, she had an immaterial body, a mind without vainglory, intelligence without conceit, an untroubled heart, an artless spirit, charity without limits, unbounded generosity, contemptible clothing, immeasurable self-control, rectitude of thought, undying hope in God, [and] ineffable almsgiving.*[3]

*What a woman she is, if it is permissible to call such a manly Christian a woman!*[4]

The construction of female subjectivity in patriarchal cultures is always highly complex. Every society directs individuals to the performance of approved social roles, a socialization in which a sense of self, identity, and integrity is also developed. The processes of socialization and subjectification are thus interdependent and complementary: subjectification accompanies "the process by which individuals work themselves into social structures they themselves do not consciously determine, but to which they subordinate themselves."[5] In both processes, "the body becomes the decisive pivot around which the true self is defined,"[6] the medium through which individuals are "inserted into the prevailing social order."[7]

According to the German feminist Frigga Haug, subjectification focused on the body is peculiarly a form of female development. Women's subjectification revolves around two tasks, managing sexuality and acquiring the skills necessary to fulfill a "constant requirement to arouse desire,"[8] as constitutive of female self-worth and value to society. Male development, she writes, follows a somewhat different course in being less focused on the body: "Neither bodily strength and agility, in sport or in work, nor their concomitant pleasures are reduced to their sexual meaning alone—on the contrary, they offer multiple potentials for men's development."[9] Thus, the female body as *seen*—dress, hair posture, and ways of walking, standing, and sitting—plays a central role in defining women, both in the eyes of others and in their own subjective esteem. Haug's theory, however, is based on contemporary European women; this chapter will explore whether it can help us to understand the presentation of women, their dress, their behavior, and their roles in early Christian literature.

I will first examine descriptions of involuntary nakedness in accounts of women's martyrdoms and then discuss attitudes toward the female body in the literature of asceticism. I will try to demonstrate that within these texts the reader can glimpse the forging of a countercultural connection between the female body and women's subjectivity: these women used their nakedness as a symbolic rejection, not only of sexuality, but also of secular society's identification of the female body with male desire, its relegation of the naked female body to spectacle and object. According to the hagiographical literature, ascetic women and martyrs insisted on assimilating their bodies to the religious identity they had chosen and developed. Their bodies became, for ascetic women, both the location and the symbol of a religious self.

Most of our information about what historical women did and thought comes from male authors and is often explicitly prescriptive, so I will not attempt to identify forms of religious thought and practice that may have been unique to women.[10] Writings *about* women often provide glimpses of conflicts between male ecclesiastical leaders and laywomen in Christian churches, but they are too filled with the authors' own agenda to serve as a basis for speculation about whether women understood or practiced Christianity differently from men. Nevertheless, literary reports of women and men ascetics reveal some significant differences that can help us to reconstruct assumptions about women and attitudes toward them in Roman culture and in Christian communities in the fourth century.

The metaphor most frequently used for women who undertook to live an uncompromising Christian faith was that they had "become male." Women apparently referred to themselves in this way; male authors also repeatedly referred to women whose courage and commitment they admired as "more like men than nature would seem to allow."[11] In his *Life of St. Macrina* Gregory of Nyssa wrote, "It was a woman who was the subject of our discourse, if indeed you can say 'a woman,' for I do not know if it is appropriate to call her by a name taken from nature when she surpassed that nature."[12] Women's aspirations to union with Christ, in martyrdom or by an ascetic life, were also described as attempts to "become male."[13] Perpetua, an early third-century Carthaginian Christian, saw herself as fully invested with Christ's power and therefore invincible when, in a dream shortly before her martyrdom, she acquired a male body. "Becoming male" could also be very practical for a Christian woman: Thecla cut her hair and put on men's clothing in order to be able to travel with more freedom and to avoid rape. Pelagia "dressed as a man and secretly went off" to join a monastery, where she "passed" as a male eunuch for the rest of her life, to be discovered only at her death.[14]

For men as for women, the development of a religious self required choice. Moreover, that initial choice had to be followed by active, vigorous pursuit of the new identity and membership in the new community. The models for such choice, in the social, intellectual, and religious world of the Roman Empire, were male. For women, then, courage, conscious choice, and self-possession constituted gender transgression. Non-Christian Romans who witnessed Christian women's behavior sometimes characterized it as "madness." Some Roman parents felt so thoroughly betrayed by their daughters' rejection of the social roles for which they had been trained that they became violent. In *The Martyrdom of Ss. Perpetua and Felicitas,* Perpetua's father, failing to convince her to renounce Christianity, "bore down on [her] as if he would pluck out [her] eyes"[15]; and in the late-second-century Christian novel the *Acts of Paul and Thecla,* Thecla's mother, on hearing Thecla publicly reject marriage, cried out, "Burn the lawless woman, burn her who is not a bride in the middle of this theater, so that all women who have been instructed by [Paul] may be afraid."[16]

Christians were not alone in insisting that women who undertook to live as Christian "overachievers"[17] had "become male." Hellenistic Jews, Valentinians, and members of the Hellenistic philosophical schools agreed that for women to cultivate a religious identity was to become male.[18] But the metaphor did not carry with it the disapproval of male authors, who saw becoming male as progress, as the highest spiritual achievement, and as healing the rift of gender created by the Fall.[19] For example, Philo, the first-century Hellenistic Jewish philosopher, urged the gender transformation by outlining the qualities and behavioral traits he associated with maleness and femaleness: "Progress is nothing else than the giving up of the female gender by changing into the male, since the female gender is material, passive, corporeal, and sense-perceptible, while the male is active, rational, incorporeal and more akin to mind and thought."[20]

"Becoming male" was applauded by gnostic as well as orthodox Christians. In the Gospel of Mary, Mary says to the disciples, "Praise his [Jesus'] greatness, for he has prepared us and made us into men."[21] And in the Gospel of Thomas, Simon Peter says to the disciples: "'Let Mary leave us, for women are not worthy of life.' [But] Jesus said, 'I myself shall lead her, in order to make her male, so that she too may become a living spirit, resembling you males. For every woman who will make herself male will enter the Kingdom of Heaven.'"[22]

The motif of "becoming male" was also a recurring theme in the baptismal formulae of the gnostic Christian groups. The Gospel of Philip describes the original human being as male and sexual differentiation as the painful result of the Fall: "If the woman had not separated from the man, she would not die with the man."[23] Baptism restored the integrated wholeness of Adam before Eve's creation, before the woman was split off from Adam's side. In the Gospel of Thomas, baptism is viewed as beginning the process of "making the female male," a process that will ultimately lead to eschatological fulfillment.[24] In this image of the "two becoming one," however, the female is incorporated into the male, completing his lost integrity.

Martyrdom—public execution as the result of confessing, "Christiana sum"[25]—was an occasion on which women were often stripped of their clothing before crowds in late Roman colosseums. The regularity with which the female body and female nakedness were featured in *acta* and popular novels indicates that their readers expected such details, though

they seldom note male martyrs' nakedness. Women's bodies seem, however, to have had different and often contradictory meanings for Christian women themselves and for the crowds who witnessed their martyrdom. *Acta* report women's insistence on their bodies' assimilation to their
faith so that they were undaunted by their public display. The body was
the site and symbol of resistance to a society they saw as wicked and lawless. *Acta* also regularly comment on the reactions of governors, gladiators, and crowds to naked women martyrs. These reactions range from
grief at the imminent destruction of their beauty, to horror at the sight of
a young woman who had recently given birth, to voyeuristic glee. Martyrdom literature, though it reveals women's attitudes to their bodies,
also indicates that Christian authors and audiences shared the interest of
late-classical crowds in female nakedness. In many martyrdom accounts,
respect and esteem for women martyrs vies with textual interest in their
bodies or concern to establish the inferiority of their sex, disclosing male
confusion and conflict over heroic Christian women.

In the late second-century *Letter from the Churches of Vienna and Lugdunum,* the story of the martyrdom of the slavewoman Blandina features
her body as a powerful symbol of her faith. After torture, in which "her
whole body was torn and opened up," Blandina was

hung up, fastened to a stake, and exposed, as food to the wild beasts that were
let loose against her; and through her presenting the spectacle of one suspended
on something like a cross, and through her earnest prayers, she inspired the
combatants with great eagerness: for in the combat they saw, by means of their
sister, with their bodily eyes, him who was crucified for them, that he might
persuade those who trust in him that everyone that has suffered for the glory of
Christ has eternal communion with the living God.

To this poignant description of the identity of Blandina's body with
Christ's in the eyes of those who suffered with her, the author added the
following interpretation: "For though she was an insignificant, weak,
and despised woman, yet she was clothed with the great and invincible
athlete Christ."[26]

According to legend, the twenty-year-old Syrian woman Febronia was
"so beautiful that the eye could never be sated by gazing upon her," but
she had been so carefully sheltered in a female monastery that she "did
not know what a man's face looked like."[27] Arrested in a persecution during Diocletian's reign, Febronia resolved, "In a woman's body I will
manifest a man's valiant conviction."[28] During her trial, the judge
"ordered the soldiers to tear off her clothes, tie her up with rags, and let

her stand there undressed, an object of shame in front of everyone. 'Let her see herself naked like this and lament her own folly, now that she has fallen from honor and respect to shame and ignominy.'"[29] Febronia, however, had an alternative interpretation of her naked body; she responded:

What athlete entering the contest to fight at Olympia engages in battle wrapped up in all his clothes? Doesn't he enter the arena naked, until he has conquered his adversary? I am waiting in expectancy for tortures and burning by fire; how could I do battle with these while I have my clothes on? Should I not meet torture with a naked body, until I have vanquished your father Satan, throwing scorn upon all your threats of tortures?[30]

Another Syrian woman, the maidservant Mahya, "who was always very masculine in her manner of acting," was similarly treated at her trial: "The king ordered her to be stripped naked. When they had done this, she said to the king, 'It is to your shame . . . that you have done this; I am not ashamed myself . . . I have been naked in the presence of men and women [referring to baptism] without feeling ashamed, for I am a woman—such as was created by God.'"[31]

The romantic early Christian novel *The Acts of Paul and Thecla* describes the trials of its heroine, Thecla. Clothing and nakedness are leitmotifs of this story, for Thecla's nakedness caused even the governor to weep, during unsuccessful attempts to burn her or have her killed by wild beasts, over the imminent destruction of her beauty.[32] Thecla is stripped in front of the crowd but is miraculously clothed with a cloud of fire, "so that neither did the animals touch her, nor was she perceived as naked."[33] Public nakedness is clearly conceived by the anonymous author as part of Thecla's punishment and torture; when she was momentarily reprieved by the governor, "he ordered clothes to be brought and said, 'Put on the clothes.'" Thecla dressed, but, like Febronia, reinterpreted her nakedness, removing it from the governor's power and aligning it with her strength as a confessor of Christ: "The one who clothed me while I was naked among the beasts shall clothe me with salvation on the day of judgment."[34] Thecla insists that her body is not ultimately at the disposal of the governor to cover or strip, but is an aspect of her religious integrity, incorporated and included in her salvation. In this novel the integrity of body and will is dramatized by Thecla's escape from all attempts to execute her. After her ordeals in the arena, she undertakes a preaching mission to Seleucia and, after converting many, "she slept with a good sleep."[35]

Perhaps the most complex and detailed account of a woman's martyrdom is that of the early third-century *Martyrdom of Ss. Perpetua and Felicitas*. This description of the trial, imprisonment, and martyrdom of a
small group of Carthaginian Christians on March 7, 203, is a compilation
of several documents. The account is introduced and concluded by an
anonymous editor, thought to be Tertullian. Among those martyred
were two young women, Perpetua, a twenty-two-year-old wife and
mother with a nursing infant, and Felicitas, a slave woman who gave
birth to a child in prison shortly before her martyrdom. The central section of the *acta* is composed of Perpetua's prison journal,[36] a description
of her experiences, dream visions, and the physical and emotional feelings of her last days. *The Martyrdom of Ss. Perpetua and Felicitas,* because
of its dual authorship, gives two perspectives on a female body within its
few pages: female body as spectacle and female body as the site and symbol of religious subjectivity. Both the editor's and Perpetua's texts use her
body as a leitmotif around which to focus the narrative of her martyrdom. Perpetua's body was the locus of the progressive deconstruction of
her secular socialization as it was increasingly aligned with her Christian
identity.

In a brief introduction the Montanist editor introduces two themes
characteristic of North African Christianity: the high value of spirit-
inspired prophecy and martyrdom as the ultimate Christian witness. The
editor then introduces Perpetua's journal, presented, he says, "according
to her own ideas and in the way she herself wrote it down."[37] As might
be expected in a society in which women's socialization and subjectification revolved around their relationships with men, Perpetua mentions
her mother only once and never alludes to a bond with Felicitas, the
woman with whom she will die. Her journal is filled, however, with real
and visionary males—her father, brother, and son, fellow prisoners,
gladiators, guards, and God.[38]

Perpetua begins her story with an encounter with her father in which
she tries to explain her resolve to confess Christian faith. She points to a
vase, asking him if any name other than "vase" can be used for it. He
agrees that it cannot be called by any other name, and Perpetua replies
that, like the vase, she cannot be called "by anything other than what I
am, a Christian."[39] In Perpetua's theory of language, the vase—or her
body—participates in the essence of the word that names it. Shortly after
this, Perpetua reiterates the identity of her body and religious subjectivity as she describes her prison baptism. Her only request, in the privi-

leged prayer of the newly baptized, was to ask for the "perseverance of the flesh" (*sufferentiam carnis*); that is, that her body would continue to act out her name, "Christian." In the *Acta minore,* a shortened and somewhat later version of Perpetua's martyrdom, the relation between Perpetua's name and her Christian identity is emphasized by wordplays that assimilate her given name to her chosen name: "I am a Christian, and I follow the authority of my name, that I may be perpetual (*ut sim perpetua*)." [40] Throughout her account Perpetua focuses her vivid description of conditions in the prison, her anxiety and physical discomfort over the absence of her child, and her dreams around her body. She narrates her incremental weaning from her socialization and her family—from the parents who gave her birth and the child to whom she gave birth—until her only connection is with her Christian confession and with the other confessors who share her experience. When after her condemnation, her father refuses to send her child to her, the incorporation of her body into her Christian subjectivity is finalized and revealed by the fact that her breasts neither become inflamed nor cause her any discomfort though nursing has been abruptly terminated.

Perpetua formulates her withdrawal from parents and child—curiously, she does not mention her husband—in dream images. In her first dream, she climbs a perilous ladder to a garden in which a shepherd gives her some of the coagulated milk or cheese he is milking from a sheep. Awaking from the dream, Perpetua notices that she still tastes "something sweet" and realizes that she has, by eating in paradise, become not merely a temporary visitor but an imminent resident of that other world. She therefore concludes that she "would no longer have any hope in this life." [41]

The last stage of Perpetua's dissociation from her "earthly" connections occurs the day before her martyrdom. In a remarkable vision she images "becoming male" as a physical gender reversal. She is led into an arena to fight a vicious gladiator. As "handsome young men," her seconds and assistants, strip Perpetua, her body becomes a male body (*facta sum masculus*). [42] After defeating her opponent, Perpetua is given a branch in token of her victory, and "I began to walk in triumph towards the Gate of Life." She concludes her account, "I realized that it was not with wild animals that I would fight but with the Devil, but I knew that I would win the victory." [43] She has been granted the male body she needs to emerge victorious from the unimaginable suffering she will encounter.

After Perpetua's account of this vision her diary ends and narration of the *acta* shifts from first to third person as the editor relays the stories and visions of several of Perpetua's companions. He then describes the day of their martyrdom. Perpetua approached her martyrdom "with shining face and calm step as the wife of Christ and the beloved of God."[44] Because she and Felicitas refused to put on the dress of a priestess of Ceres for their entrance into the arena, they were instead stripped naked and brought into the arena in nets: "Even the crowd was horrified when they saw that one was a delicate young girl and the other was a woman fresh from childbirth with milk still dripping from her breasts. And so they were brought back again and dressed in unbelted tunics."[45] No similar details regarding the dress or nakedness of their male companions are given in the *acta*. Rather, the men's words and actions provide the content of the account of their heroic deaths. To be sure, Perpetua's words and actions during her martyrdom are also narrated; her heroism has warranted that attention. But the editor cannot ignore her dress, demeanor, and the arrangement of her hair.

Although, in the bonding of her body to religious subjectivity, Perpetua has "become male," her body remains spectacle to the observer, even though he is a fellow Christian. The editor remarks that, after being tossed by a mad heifer, she rearranges her tunic to cover her thighs, "thinking more of her modesty than of her pain."[46] He also supplies a conventional motivation for Perpetua's act of fastening her disheveled hair: "for it was not right that a martyr should die with her hair in disorder, lest she might seem to be mourning in her hour of triumph." In the editor's portrayal of Perpetua's martyrdom, her body is a textual device, a useful figure on which to advocate modesty for future female readers of the *Martyrdom*.

Is this the same Perpetua who described her own body as so integrated to her religious self that lactation immediately ceased after her infant was taken away from her? Is this the Perpetua whose body in her final dream vision became male, the perfect reflection of her religious resolve? The susceptibility of the female body to alternative and even conflicting interpretations is clearly illustrated in *The Martyrdom of Ss. Perpetua and Felicitas*. Perpetua's body could represent "male" heroism, commitment, and courage even while it remained an object for the male gaze.

Perpetua's diary reveals her socialization even as it narrates her resistance. Her exclusive attention to men and male dream figures discloses her assumption that her spirituality, like her social identity, will take form in relation to a male-defined reality. We must also consider whether, in these circumstances, women's acceptance of the naming of their spirituality as "becoming male" was not, perhaps, a more-or-less conscious strategy for claiming the esteem of communities in which women's religious empowerment was problematic. Tertullian's invectives against female leadership in Christian churches, like Cyprian's insistence, fifty years later, on his authority over consecrated virgins, are only two examples of conflict over women's roles within Christian communities. The anxieties of male ecclesiastical leaders over their ability to control women are repeatedly signaled by the amount of time and energy they spent in attempting to resolve these issues in print, if not in actuality.

Perpetua's journal was preserved and transmitted because the editor found it a useful vehicle for furthering his theological and social agenda. Concerned to record contemporary martyrdoms for the edification of posterity, the editor included the journal to support his Montanist claim that the Holy Spirit continued to act and speak through contemporary Christians, especially through confessors condemned to execution for their faith. In fact, he argued in the prologue, "the more recent events should be considered the greater." In the midst of a conflict over the status of prophecy in relation to ecclesiastical authority, the editor directs his readers to interpret Perpetua's story in light of his theological interest. Similarly, it is through the editor's eyes that the reader visualizes Perpetua's death. The conclusion emphasizes her "shining face and calm step" as she entered the amphitheater, her modesty in torture, and her active role in her own death as she guided the gladiator's trembling hand. *The Martyrdom of Ss. Perpetua and Felicitas* is an unusually vivid example of the appropriation of a woman's writing as support for theological and ecclesiastical concerns that her text does not acknowledge as her own.

Christian women accepted "becoming male" as a characterization of their behavior that was consonant with their resolute choices, their courageous and triumphant behavior. "Becoming male" removed the female body from the realm of secular social and sexual arrangements and made it the ally of the religious self, no longer to be defined by, or associated with, the biological or social functions of women's bodies. Two centuries after Perpetua's martyrdom, Augustine would tell readers of the *City of God* that women will not have male bodies in the resurrection since to have a female body is not a defect or imperfection. Even in

Augustine's time, however, lacking language and symbols for a specifically female bravery, overcoming the socially constructed limitations of their gender was an intimate and apparently exhilarating part of ascetic women's religious commitment.


Asceticism, the "daily martyrdom," came, in the course of the fourth century, to carry many of the religious meanings and metaphors associated with martyrdom. Although women's bodies—as temptation—figure prominently in the literature of male asceticism, my focus here is not the figure of "woman" in male asceticism and monasticism but ascetic women's attitudes toward their bodies. We can reconstruct the ascetic styles approved for women from the prescriptive historical texts, though we cannot claim that women ascetics actually behaved in the ways depicted. Nevertheless, the popularity and survival of these texts indicates that they played a role in shaping the ideas, self-images, and behavior of women ascetics.

The literature of asceticism from the fourth century through the medieval period is a rich source of evidence relating to attitudes toward the female body. Both women and men ascetics fetishized the female body, though in different ways. In ascetic practice, nakedness became a metaphor for divestment from the cares and entanglements of secular life. Jerome instructed consecrated virgins, "Let the words be ever on your lips: 'Naked came I out of my mother's womb and naked shall I return thither.'"[47] His famous adage "Nudus nudum Jesum sequi" ("Naked to follow a naked Christ")[48] became the slogan of monasticism for over a thousand years. The Sayings of the Fathers relates an incident in which a monk was asked, "What must I do to be saved?" To answer, the monk "took off his clothes and put a girdle about his loins, and stretched out his hands and said 'Thus ought the monk to be naked of everything worldly and crucify himself against temptation and the world's struggles.'"[49]

Actual ascetic nakedness is more difficult to document. John Cassian and others list nakedness among effective ascetic practices, and it was an essential component of medieval ascetic legends, but I have looked in vain for historical accounts of practices of nakedness and for descriptions of what nakedness was thought to achieve. Instead, sexuality became a preoccupation for male ascetics, both as temptation and as an energy to control and direct to spiritual pursuits. A different theme dominates women ascetics' understanding of the body and sexuality. Though some of them acknowledged sexual temptation, it was primarily involuntary sex—rape—that they feared increasingly as their societies became vulnerable to attack and plunder in the late classical and medieval world.

Despite the lack of evidence for nakedness as an ascetic practice, hagiographical literature and artistic depictions continued to circulate legends in which naked female ascetics are featured. The legend of Saint Mary of Egypt is an example. In the absence of historical evidence for the existence of Saint Mary of Egypt, the legend must illustrate for us medieval readers' fascination with a saint they could visualize with a combination of spiritual and prurient interest. First circulated in the second half of the fifth century in the writings of a Palestinian monk, Zosimus, the legend was repeated and embellished in a popular medieval collection of saints' lives, Jacobus da Voragine's *Golden Legend*.

One day while crossing the desert, the story goes, Zosimus chanced upon a hirsute figure he at first took to be a wild beast. Discovering, however, that the "beast" was actually a naked woman who was deeply tanned by the desert sun and covered with curly hair, he asked how she came to be there. She was born in Egypt, she said, and had lived a dissolute life in Alexandria from the age of twelve. At the age of seventeen she joined a group of pilgrims en route to Jerusalem. On the day of the Adoration of the Cross, she attempted to enter the Church of the Resurrection five or six times, but an invisible force restrained her. After vowing repentance she was able to enter the church. The next day she went to the desert to begin her repentance, taking nothing but three loaves of bread. When Zosimus happened upon her, she had been in the desert for forty-eight years. On the next Holy Thursday, according to her instructions, Zosimus brought her communion. He returned the following year on Holy Thursday to find the holy woman dead. Zosimus buried her, with the help of a friendly lion, and departed to tell the tale of such uncompromising and admirable penance.

The legend of Saint Mary of Egypt was often conflated, in medieval religious painting, with gospel accounts of Mary Magdalene, the female figure *par excellence* of passion and penitence (figure 7). An altarpiece by the thirteenth-century Italian "Master of the Magdalene" combined their stories. Mary Magdalene receives Saint Mary of Egypt's body-concealing hair, and around the central figure scenes from the legend of Mary of Egypt, such as Zosimus bringing communion to her (bottom left) and an angel carrying bread to her (third from top on the right), are

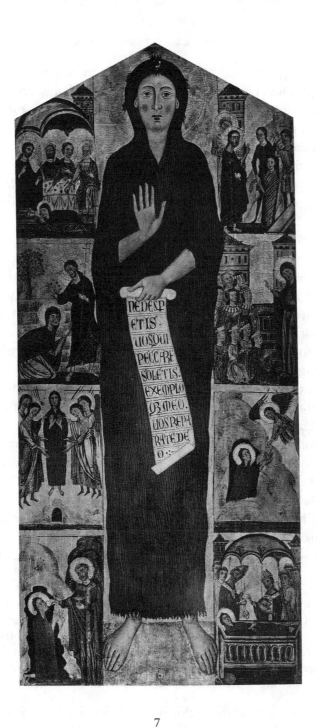

7

MASTER OF THE MAGDALENA
*Mary Magdalene and Stories of Her Life*, 1250–70
Galleria dell'Accademia, Florence (Art Resource, New York)

mingled with gospel and apocryphal stories of scenes from the life of Mary Magdalene. The result is a complicated and ahistorical figure but one that appears to have appealed strongly to medieval piety. Though Mary is completely clothed by her hair, viewers of the altarpiece were tacitly invited to visualize her nakedness. Here, religious associations of loosened and flowing hair discussed in chapter 1 in connection with women's baptism seem to be amalgamated in an image which might equally suggest Mary's association with Eve, the originator of sin, or penitence.

Nakedness also specifically symbolized virginity. Jerome regarded marriage as a skin or covering, a protection from the solitary condition of human life; he admonished Christians "enveloped in the skin of matrimony" that it is too late to "seek the nakedness of virginity and of that eternal chastity which [you] have lost once and for all."[50] But virginity was not first a metaphor; it was the *sine qua non* ascetic practice. By the end of the fourth century, the persecution and martyrdom of Christians was no longer living memory in the West. Moreover, the asceticism practiced in the West did not feature the more dramatic harsh practices of Egypt, Syria, and Palestine. Virginity took the place of both in Western ascetic practice.

By renouncing sexual and reproductive activity, a woman could become the equal of a man, since it was precisely her sexual organs and reproductive functions that differentiated her from a man.[51] For ascetic women as for women martyrs, transcending gender effectively meant that both sexuality and socialization were simultaneously rejected. Clement of Alexandria saw in ascetic renunciation of sex not only a way to modify secular socialization, but also the prefiguration of an eschatalogical asexuality:

[To the true gnostic] his wife . . . is as a sister . . . as being destined to become a sister in reality after putting off the flesh, which separates and limits the knowledge of those who are spiritual by the peculiar characteristics of the sexes. *For souls themselves by themselves are equal.* Souls are neither male nor female when they no longer marry or are given in marriage. And is not the woman translated into a man when she is becomes equally unfeminine, and manly and perfect?[52]

Virginity was prized among orthodox Christians, but gnostic Christians considered it mandatory. Their uneasiness about sexual activity had a common source: both rejected secular socialization, in which sexuality played such a prominent role.[53] Orthodox Christians managed to accept

sexuality by reinterpreting its meaning; for example, Jerome said that reproduction was good in that it created more virgins, and childbearing
was considered one of the routes women might take to salvation. Many
gnostics, on the other hand, apparently held the view that secular conditioning so thoroughly informed all sexual activity that Christian commitment and sexual activity were incompatible. What was clear to both
orthodox and heterodox groups was that sexuality was uniquely problematic because of its connection to secular culture.

In orthodox Christianity two roles were acceptable for women—virginity or motherhood. Women could "become male by living in ascetic
virginity, or they could, according to 1 Timothy 2:15, be "saved in
childbearing." The two roles were not equally valued, however. Patristic
authors consistently denied any aversion to marriage, but their writings
praise virginity with passionate excitement. Ambrose wrote:

Virginity has brought from heaven that which it may imitate on earth. And not
unfittingly has she sought her manner of life from heaven, who has found for
herself a spouse in heaven. She, passing beyond the clouds, air, angels, and stars,
has found the Word of God in the very bosom of the Father and has drawn him
into herself with her whole heart.[54]

No reader of patristic literature could miss the difference in interest,
tone, and length in discussions of virginity and marriage. In his treatise
*Against Jovinianus,* for example, Jerome gave an unprecedentedly narrow
interpretation to the passage in 1 Timothy: "The woman will then be
saved if she bear children who will remain virgins: if what she has herself
lost, she attains in her children, and makes up for the loss and decay of
the root by the excellence of the flower and fruit."[55]

In short, virginity was by far the more praiseworthy option. Gregory
of Nyssa extolled virginity at the expense of marriage: "The more exactly we understand the riches of virginity, the more we must bewail the
other life, . . . how poor it is."[56] He added: "Marriage, then, is the last
stage of our separation from the life that was led in Paradise; marriage,
therefore, . . . is the first thing to be left; it is the first station, as it were,
for our departure to Christ.[57] As we might expect, Jerome was even more
luridly graphic about the sexual bonds of marriage for a woman, refer-
ring to the "vomit of marriage"[58] and arguing that virgins should not
bathe along with married women since "women with child offer a revolting spectacle."[59]

Patristic authors frequently had to defend themselves against charges that they harbored a gnostic disdain for marriage. Responding to such accusations, Jerome wrote defensively: "I do not detract from wedlock when I set virginity before it. No one compares a bad thing with a good. Wedded women may congratulate themselves that they come next to virgins."[60]

Authors who urged ascetic virginity also described marriage and child-bearing as difficult and dangerous for women. Jerome reminds himself that he has promised not to dwell on the "woes of marriage," but he refers the reader to a list of patristic accounts of these "vexations, from which a virgin is free and to which a wife is fettered."[61] Denying that he thought of marriage as evil, Ambrose wrote:

The marriage bond is not to be shunned as though it were sinful, but rather declined as being a galling burden. For the law binds the wife to bear children in labor and in sorrow, and is in subjection to her husband, for he is lord over her. So, then, the married woman is subject to labor and pain in bringing forth children, and she only that is married, not she that is a virgin, is under the power of her husband. The virgin is free from all these things who has vowed her affection to the Word of God. . . . And so she is moved by counsels, not bound by chains.[62]

John Chrysostom takes up the same theme in order to argue for virginity:

If in apparently happy marriages so many disagreeable events and misfortunes occur, what can be said about those who agree about their distress? . . . Many women are born of illustrious parents, raised in great luxury, are given in marriage to some man who has great power; then suddenly, before the woman could be deemed happy on account of these things, some danger arises, just like a tempest or a hurricane, and they too have sunk, they too partake in the horrors of shipwreck, and they who before marriage enjoyed thousands of good things, through marriage fall to ultimate misfortune.[63]

Even children are not unambiguous blessings for a woman. According to the apocryphal *Acts of Thomas:*

For the majority of children become unprofitable, possessed by demons, some openly and some in secret; for they become either lunatic or half-withered [consumptive] or crippled or deaf or dumb or paralytic or stupid. Even if they are healthy, again will they be unserviceable, performing useless and abominable deeds; for they are caught either in adultery or in murder or in theft or in unchastity, and by all these you will be afflicted.[64]

In a similar vein, the Syrian woman Ruhn of Najran is reported to have said to her friends:

You, my fellow women, know very well that a woman has no days of joy like those of her wedding feast; after the wedding feast there are only griefs or pains. When children are born, it is accompanied by pains and groans; or when a woman loses her children, there is anguish and sorrow, while when she buries her children, there is weeping and mourning.[65]

Indeed, these descriptions of marriage as grim for women are supported by demographic evidence from the later Roman Empire. Inscriptions testify to "heavy mortality among younger women." A. R. Burn, analyzing these statistics, observes that although the "dangerous age" for women "coincides more or less with the reproductive period," childbirth alone was not responsible for the heavy mortality rates for women. Among reasons for the greater threat of death to women are "better feeding and nurture of boys than girls during childhood," and "physical exhaustion, nervous breakdown, and other ailments which are the aftermath of premature childbearing."[66]

Vowed virginity represented both a life-style by which women could gather self-esteem and the esteem of their communities and the rejection of a life determined by sexual activity, with all its entailments. "Becoming male" was not, however, originally a female construction of an ideal life, but was accepted by women as an approved alternative to marriage. Fetishization of physical *integritas* was defined and stimulated by vivid textual accounts of the rewards of virginity, together with lurid descriptions of the fallen virgin.

The consecrated virgin who "fell" into any form of sexual activity became, in the eyes of Christian leaders, a public whore. There was apparently no female figure between chaste virgin and whore with which to describe a virgin who decided that she had mistaken her religious vocation and could better serve God as a virtuous wife. Jerome painted the contrast between a virtuous virgin and a fallen virgin with his characteristic vivid rhetoric. Quoting prophets of the Hebrew Bible who used the image of the prostitute to characterize Israel's desertion of its God, Jerome wrote:

Uncover thy locks, make bare the legs . . . thy nakedness shall be uncovered, yea, thy shame shall be seen. . . . Yes, she of whom the prophetic utterance once sang . . . shall be made naked, and her skirts shall be discovered upon her face. She shall sit by the waters of loneliness, and shall open her feet to everyone that passes by and shall be polluted to the crown of her head. Better had it been for her to have submitted to the yoke of marriage, to have walked in level places, than thus, aspiring to loftier heights, to fall into the deep of hell.[67]

The nakedness extolled earlier by Jerome as the symbol of virginity, religious commitment, and detachment from the cares of life in society, has become the shameful nakedness of sex.

In the literature of asceticism from the fourth century forward, both male and female ascetics were preoccupied with women's appearance. Christian, and especially ascetic, women must, according to prescriptive texts by male authors, give the same amount of attention to studied neglect of their physical appearance as secular women were thought to lavish on their dress, cosmetics, and hair. Advice given to consecrated virgins counseled constant attention to the body, while, ironically, denying care for the body and dress. An unattractive appearance was, moreover, crucial to maintaining the virgin's most prized possession, her intact, "closed" body, which must be anxiously protected. "I would have you draw from your monastic vow not pride but fear," Jerome wrote, in his letter to Eustochium on the preservation of virginity, "You walk laden with gold: you must keep out of the robber's way." [68] The dress and comportment of consecrated virgins must avoid any suggestion of seductiveness, as Augustine's *Epistle* 211 clearly states:

You should not let your clothing be conspicuous, nor should you strive to please by your clothes but by your behavior. Do not have such delicate headcoverings that your hairnets show underneath. Do not let any part of your hair remain uncovered nor should you be outside with hair either carelessly strewn or painstakingly arranged. [69]

The standard of minimal maintenance, combined with disinterest, was Augustine's idea of the ideal appearance of a vowed virgin.

Female beauty created temptation for male Christians; it therefore became a heavily worked topic in the writings of early Christianity. Tertullian urged that all Christian women neglect their appearance: "Even natural grace must be obliterated by concealment and negligence, as being equally dangerous to the glances of eyes. For although beauty is not to be censured, as being a bodily happiness . . . yet it is to be feared." [70] Concealed in Tertullian's rhetoric is the crucial factor of the assumed maleness of "the beholder." Women were to obscure their beauty to protect men's salvation. Apocryphal novels of the second and third centuries, as well as many *acta,* carried the same message. Even in this literature, the physical beauty of the heroine was not an unambiguous sign of spiritual beauty; it was also a temptation for celibate men. As Stevan Davies suggests, the apocryphal Acts may have gained their popularity by formulating the contradictory experience of devoted women in Christianity.[71] Thecla's experience may have been typical: lustful men, backed by civil authority, try to use her sexually, and "Christian men, even Paul, do not take her seriously, but regard her as a beautiful woman prone to temptation despite her status as a confessor."[72]

Almost all Christian virgins are described as beautiful, though beauty, as we often learn from more detailed accounts of a woman's appearance, is firmly located in the eye of the beholder. Jerome is drawn to Paula, "the only lady in Rome who had power to subdue me," because "she mourned and fasted, she was squalid with dirt, her eyes were dim from weeping," and he notes that "the only woman who took my fancy was one whom I had not so much as seen at table."[73] He also praises her for never entering "a bath except when dangerously ill."[74] Jerome advised her not to ruin her eyes by weeping copiously for her sins, but she responded, in Jerome's words: "I must disfigure that face which, contrary to God's commandment I have painted with rouge, white lead, and antimony. I must mortify that body which has been given up to many pleasures. I must make up for my long laughter by constant weeping."[75]

Although young virgins were consistently beautiful, women who, like Paula, converted to Christian faith after "sinful" lives regularly showed their zeal, according to the texts that describe them, by penitential exercises that destroyed their beauty. Pelagia, before her conversion a fabulously beautiful prostitute in Antioch, proved the seriousness of her repentance by the remarkable change in her appearance after her conversion. "I failed to recognize her," the narrator of her *Life* wrote approvingly:

because she had lost those good looks I used to know; her astounding beauty had all faded away, her laughing and bright face that I had known had become ugly, her pretty eyes had become hollow and cavernous as the result of much fasting and the keeping of vigils. The joints of her holy bones, all fleshless, were visible beneath her skin through emaciation brought about by ascetic practices. Indeed the whole complexion of her skin was coarse and dark like sackcloth, as the result of her strenuous penance.[76]

Images of Mary Magdalene by medieval artists and authors also contrast spiritual beauty and physical beauty in the same figure. In Donatello's famous 1455 wood sculpture of the praying Magdalene, her smooth and shapely hands, arms, and feet contrast sharply with her haggard, tear-funneled face, twisted hair, and veined neck. A similar *Praying Magdalene* by a disciple of Neri di Bicci combines and contrasts beauty and the ravages of penitence in a figure with flowing, gently waving hair, smooth hands, and a face permanently marked by mourning (figure 8).

Unlike ascetic women whose beauty vanished as a result of their austerities, Saint Antony, after twenty years of penitential practice in the solitary desert, retained his youthfulness, "so that all remarked on it" when he returned to town.[77] Apparently the loss of male beauty was not considered necessary for effective penance; on the contrary, the spiritual exercises of the male "athlete" enhanced the appearance of his body. Female beauty was, however, problematic for male authors. Associated with spiritual beauty, it was noted and honored. Beauty of body for its own sake, however, was suspect and dangerous to men who might enjoy it and lose their control, and hence their salvation.

Christian authors imply, by their repeated warnings to women on the topic of their dress and comportment, that it is largely a woman's responsibility to avoid producing desire in men. The *Lausiac History* reports that the maidservant Alexandra, having taken this message to heart, shut herself in a tomb, leaving an opening only large enough to receive the necessities of life. Asked why she had done this, Alexandra replied, "A man was distressed in mind because of me and, lest I seem to afflict or disparage him, I chose to betake myself alive into the tomb rather than cause a soul, made in the image of God, to stumble."[78]

Women were, if not always considered responsible, at least strongly suspect in the case of sexual assault; they may either have invited attention by their dress or comportment, or, as Augustine suggested in the *City of God,* once assaulted, they may have enjoyed it. In the pain and chaos following the Sack of Rome in AD 410, Augustine found himself in the unenviable position of counseling Christian women, both consecrated virgins and married women, who had been raped. Though admitting that the human body is neither accidental nor ancillary to human being—"A man's body is no mere adornment, or external convenience, it belongs to his very nature as a man"—Augustine nevertheless attempted to relieve Christian women's anguish by assuring them that purity—of body as well as of soul—is "a virtue of the mind" that remains undiminished by what happens to the body:

Virtue . . . holds command over the parts of the body from her throne in the mind. . . . The consecrated body is the instrument of the consecrated will; and if that will continues unshaken and steadfast, whatever anyone else does with the body or to the body . . . involves no blame to the sufferer.[79]

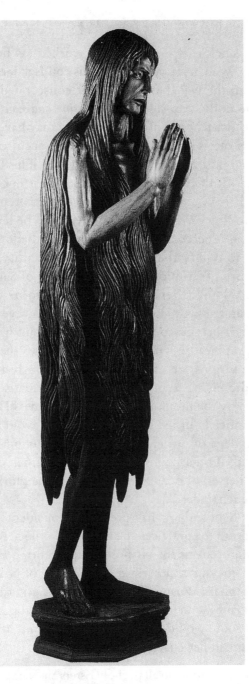

8

DON ROMUALDO DE CANDELI (?)
*Praying Magdalene*, 1455
Museo della Collegiata di Sant' Andrea, Empoli

Whether Augustine's rhetorical strategy worked, as he intended, to re-assure Christian women is not recorded; his counsel does not seem to take seriously enough the fact that, at least for consecrated virgins, physical integrity of the body was valued as the *sine qua non* of their religious identity.[80] His consistent use of male language may have also undermined the effectiveness of his advice, even for readers accustomed to it: "What sane man will suppose that he has lost his purity if his body is seized and forced and used for the satisfaction of a lust that is not his own?"[81]

In most Christian literature, however, rape was represented as a fate worse than death for Christian virgins.[82] More to be feared than martyr-dom, which was, if necessary, to be welcomed, the loss of bodily integ-rity threatened to nullify the virgin's primary identity. For example, in the fourth-century description of the martyrdom of Saints Agapê, Irenê, and Choinê at Saloniki, Irenê was condemned to be placed naked in a brothel. She miraculously escaped violation, however, since "no man dared to approach her, or so much as tried to insult her in speech."[83] In popular hagiographical literature from the third to the tenth century or later, Christian virgins are often saved miraculously from rape. At the beginning of the eighth century, the didactic treatise *De laudibus vir-ginitatis,* written by the monk Aldhelm to the Abbess Hildelitha of Bark-ing Abbey, specifically urged suicide in order to avoid rape: "Therefore, great is the privilege of purity, which someone who by force was com-pelled to give up, if on account of this hateful human coupling she will-ingly deprived herself of ordinary life, she will be gloriously honored in the heavenly bedchamber."[84]

Jane Tibbitts Schulenberg has presented considerable evidence from the medieval period for practices she has called "the heroics of virginity," that is, self-disfigurement for purposes of preventing rape. One account of such drastic measures describes the actions of Saint Ebba and the nuns of Coddingham during the Danish invasions of the 870s. When rumors of the Danes' cruelty and lust reached the abbess, along with the news that their route would inevitably bring them to the monastery, she gathered the nuns in her charge together, and,

with a heroic spirit, affording to all the holy sisters an example of chastity profit-able only to themselves, but to be embraced by all succeeding virgins for ever, took a razor, and with it cut off her nose, together with her upper lip unto the teeth, presenting herself a horrible spectacle to those who stood by. Filled with admiration at this admirable deed, the whole assembly followed her maternal example.[85]

When the invaders arrived the next morning, they were so repulsed by the hideous sight that they "retired in haste from the place," only taking time to burn to the ground the monastery and its inmates. The virgins' desperate ploy was successful; never expecting to save their lives, they were nevertheless determined to preserve the integrity of their genitals.

Although the evidence for "heroic virginity" in the Middle Ages comes from prescriptive tracts and hagiography, making it impossible for the historian to estimate how frequently such heroics actually occurred, the model of heroic virginity defined precisely what was valued most in a virgin—her physical *integritas*. The inseparability of women's bodies from their religious commitment was clearly one of the primary messages circulated by accounts of heroic virginity. The actions of the nuns at Coddingham were simply the literal extension of a religious choice that began when a woman rejected the social roles and sexual arrangements of her society in favor of a cultivated religious life.

It was not, however, only as a model for women that women's bodies played such a central role in ascetic literature. Woman as temptation is a constant feature of monastic literature. As Geoffrey Galt Harpham has shown, this female figure was central to the male monk's inner dynamic of temptation and resistance.[86] Temptation, Harpham writes, provided an essential energy in asceticism:

One could not be held accountable for having an image of dancing girls if girls were dancing before one. In the desert, however, every thought other than the thoughtless thoughts of perfect prayer appeared as a residue of the world. Such thoughts gave evidence of a still-unpurged and desiring will, and were subject to critical scrutiny and judgment. The temptations of the desert had, in short, a number of distinct advantages. They illuminated the secrecies of the self like a flare shooting over enemy territory, and thus promoted self definition and self-externalization. . . . Temptation, [then,] may be "courted" as a way of burning off impurities, enabling the ascetic to "take cognizance" of desire without approving it.[87]

As temptation, women's bodies played an indispensable role in the fantasy lives of male ascetics, a concentrated and localized form of the world-as-temptation, grist for the mill of the monk's resistance. When the harsh ascetic practices of fasting, penitence, watchfulness, and exposure to the burning sun had brought Jerome to a condition in which emaciation and disfigurement had wasted him almost to death, he still experienced temptation. He remembered:

Now, although in my fear of hell I had consigned myself to this prison where I had no companions but scorpions and wild beasts, I often found myself amid bevies of girls. My face was pale and my frame chilled with fasting; yet my mind was burning with desire, and the fires of lust kept bubbling up before me when my flesh was as good as dead.[88]

Examples such as Jerome's could be multiplied; fantasies of women's bodies focused and energized the ascetic endeavors of countless ascetic men. The fetishization of the female body in ascetic practice, both for men and for women themselves, clearly carried enormous motivational power.

Even the real women encountered by male ascetics, according to ascetic literature, were to be treated as if they existed only as male fantasy. *The Sayings of the Fathers* and John Cassian's *Conferences,* like other ascetic treatises, are replete with tales of encounters with women—mothers, sisters, fellow ascetics, young and old, harlots and married women—in which monks react to the woman from the perspective of the monastic maxim "A woman's body is fire." Male ascetics were repeatedly advised to consider all women without exception as threat, danger, and potential object of male lust, as the following anecdote indicates:

On a journey, one brother had with him his mother, who had now grown old. They came to a river and the old woman could not get across. Her son took off his cloak and wrapt it round his hands, so as not to touch his mother's body, and carried her across the river. His mother said to him: "Why did you wrap your hands like that, my son?" He said: "Because a woman's body is fire. Simply because I was touching you, the memory of other women came into my soul."[89]

Monastic talk about the real and fantasized women who provided the temptation they needed in order to exercise resistance is harshest in stories that describe the monk's attempts to handle physical passion. One monk, troubled by fantasies of a beautiful woman, subsequently learned of her death, and devised a way to rid himself of fascination with her:

When he heard the news, he put on his cloak in the night and went to the place where he had heard she was buried. And he dug the place, and wiped the blood of her corpse on his cloak, and kept it in his cell when he returned. And when it smelt too much, he put it in front of him and hurriedly said to his temptation: "Look, this is what you desire. You have it now, fill yourself." And so he chastised himself with the smell until his passions died down.[90]

Nor should we too hastily name as "repression" the mechanism by which women's bodies came to figure so centrally in the ascetic endeavors that excited all Christians and attracted so many in the late Roman and medieval worlds. Unless a more complex notion of "repression" is adopted, the term will be inadequate for the phenomenon. Harpham writes:

When the pleasures of satisfaction conflict with certain consciously held values, so that the gratifications, as Freud says, "cause pleasure in one part of the mind and 'pain' in another," then repression even becomes strategically desirable as a way of concealing gratification. Repression is not, then, sustained only by cultural and ethical imperatives, but by covert forms of pleasure of which the consciousness is kept blissfully ignorant.[91]

Clearly, room must be made in any theory of ascetic practice for what Gregory of Nazianzus called "the pleasure of no pleasure."[92] Far from a progressive and cumulative exercise in renunciation of pleasure, ascetic practices were, as Harpham puts it, "a means of securing a complex species of pleasure."[93]

Just as, in the case of male ascetics, recognition of the dynamic of temptation and resistance must replace the notion of simple suppression of desire, so our interpretation of ascetic women must become more complex. Clearly, in Christianity as in secular society, women did not define their own roles. Rather, they worked both to embody and to reinterpret existing expectations. The absence of the conditions essential for effective self-definition—access to the public sphere and the construction of a collective voice—suggests that their alternatives were more circumscribed than those of male Christians. While women were not consciously "victimized" by men, textual preoccupation with women's bodies indicates that women were perceived as a potentially destabilizing factor in Christian communities and Roman society. Women, their bodies, and their roles were often the focus of legislation, teaching, and preaching; men also attempted to ease their anxiety about actual women by creating the figure of "woman" and thereby defining women and prescribing responses to them. That Christian women accepted these figures and learned the skills involved in avoiding identification with negative figures and embodying images of positive figures is suggested by the unquestioned use, by both men and women, of "becoming male" as the image of women's religious subjectivity.

# II

---

# REPRESENTATIONS OF FEMALE NAKEDNESS

# INTRODUCTION TO PART TWO

While religious practices of nakedness often masked their gender specificity under the rhetoric of a religious faith common to women and men, visual representations and textual descriptions usually reveal more pointedly the different symbolic meanings associated with male and female nakedness. Artistic and textual representations of nakedness reiterate and interpret one another, helping us to reconstruct the sometimes subtle, sometimes flagrant encoding of gender. Throughout most of the history of the Christian West, idiosyncratic or "creative" interpretations were not sought or valued. Rather, nakedness is treated similarly, with different nuances and emphases, in different societies of the Christian West.

Religious representations of nakedness were generally statements of committed resistance to secular or "fallen" society. Thus, many were unambiguously positive: to be stripped of clothing was to be stripped of secular socialization, to be divested of acculturation, to repudiate investment in the social world.[1] Nakedness in martyrdom, in asceticism, and in medieval practices of evangelical poverty was voluntary and active, the result of an adamantly confessed faith.

Social meanings of nakedness in the Christian West were, on the other hand, generally negative. The mark of powerlessness and passivity, nakedness was associated with captives, slaves, prostitutes, the insane, and the dead. Also, as we have seen in martyrdom accounts, the prerogative of imposing nakedness on others to humiliate, torture, or punish was an important social power. In social meanings, the humiliation of nakedness was emphasized.

Only when gender is engaged as a category of analysis do we begin to see that our impression of the positivity of religious nakedness must be revised to account for female nakedness presented as symbol of sin, sexual lust, and dangerous evil. In depictions of the naked female body, interest in active religious engagement, exercise, and struggle is often subordinated to, or in tension with, the female body as spectacle. Insofar as women and their bodies were assimilated to religious meanings, they "became male." But the female body ultimately and visibly resisted becoming male, and thus represented the fall of the human race into sin, sexual lust, acquisitiveness, and hunger for power. In short, although religious nakedness generally contradicted social meanings of nakedness, in the case of the naked female body, social meanings were reinforced.

In the following chapters we will examine some artistic and literary devices by which "woman" was represented in the Christian West. Standardized female figures preclude the effort—for men—of relationship, of dealing with women as subjects. For the male subject, the existence of a similar but different subject, unpredictable, mysterious, and seeming to require constant management, was apparently threatening. Figuration works to displace threat in that women seem to be understood in advance of any relationship with a real woman. The appropriate male response is also prefigured. Geoffrey Harpham describes figuration as "money," a kind of coinage that permits an abstract and distanced appropriation of the world.[2] Ultimately, however, the male subject knows or suspects that female figures do not capture the complexity of women. Thus fear of "woman" is both kept at bay and stimulated by female figures.

Let us imagine that a fourth-century monk meets a woman as he gathers reeds with which to weave a basket. The woman, he notices, is beautiful. The monk immediately recognizes her beauty as a danger to him. The image of the woman has already entered his mind as a phantasm that will undoubtedly reappear later to disturb him as he tries to pray. The demons, he thinks, will bring her image to him as distraction and temptation. This disturbance could dismantle years of patient and sometimes painful ascetic labor. The monk also notices that the woman is distressed about something. He is not fooled by this, however; he recognizes the woman's apparent distress as a trick of the demons to lure him to his downfall.

If he were to attend to the woman's distress instead of to her beauty, he would need to treat her as a person, like himself, with an interior life, her own integrity, her own perspective, and her own universe. To respond to her in such a way, however, would seriously jeopardize his carefully cultivated tranquility and his spiritual progress. If he lingers to speak to her, temptation might overwhelm him. So he overcomes the momentary temptation to respond to her need. He responds, instead, to a readily available Christian figure of "woman." She is, he concludes, a mirage conjured by a demon in order to test his progress in asceticism. She is temptation, Eve, the "devil's gateway." He can resist, dismiss, and flee her, congratulating himself on his perspicacity and his narrow escape. Or he can rape her.

*Either response will bring him pleasure,* the "pleasure of no pleasure," or physical pleasure. He cannot lose. And it is his saga, after all. The text exists because *he* is interesting, because he—and his ascetic deeds—have an audience, a public. He is interesting because he has internalized a totalizing figure that enables him to manage not only this woman, but the whole world: he sees the "world" as temptation. She is nothing but an instance of his remarkable ability to force his governing metaphor onto someone who might falsify his construction of the world, not by her beauty, which contributes to his reading of "woman," but by her different subjective world. The possibility that she might succeed in appearing to him as a suffering, struggling human being, resistant to his figuration, constitutes his temptation.

He is admired; people are fascinated by his intransigent determination, his power *over* the personal, the idiosyncratic, the individual, the subjective. Yet the text must ultimately replace him because only the text is absolutely invulnerable to the possibility that the figured entity—the woman—will resist, will overcome his interpretation of her with her own. The living monk was only a stage on the way to the text; the *text*, not the monk, represents the world as temptation.

Although the monk and the text successfully consigned the woman and her perspective to figuration, the real woman is not peripheral to the monk or to the text. She is needed, indeed, essential. Nothing else in the world-as-temptation is as tempting as she is. She is both desirable body and fascinating subjectivity. She is difference and *différance,* mysterious, unknown. She localizes, focuses, "reduces"[3] all temptation to the time and space occupied by her body. She is the litmus test of his ascetic practice, the "trial by seduction"[4] that proves his accomplishment.

The reconstruction of the dialectic of temptation and resistance suggests why there is so much writing about women in the literature of early Christianity, not only in the literature of male asceticism, but also in descriptions of Christian churches and communities. In Christianity women were understood to be capable of religious subjectivity. Women, like men, were seen as ultimately "before God," engaged in their own struggles, their own pilgrimage, sometimes their own martyrdom. Simultaneously, however, the vision of women as subjects of religious commitment escalated male anxiety because it threatened to nullify the figure "woman" by which men could understand and manage women. In the early Christian movement and in its medieval and early modern successors, then, two conflicting images of woman must be taken into account: a vision of equality (Galatians 3:28) *and* the reaction to that vision: "You are all Eves." Neither of these contradictory views can be collapsed into the other so as to make one of them central, decisive, normative. The second figure exists because of the first; it was the tension between these two views of women that held them in suspension, unresolved, highly volatile, and carrying great affective energy.

Did historical women resist these constructions and formulate alternatives? To expect, or even to suggest the possibility of a body of writing untouched by patriarchal culture is unrealistic. Women's access to the public sphere was limited; Christian communities, despite their greater flexibility and volatility, in practice reinforced rather than challenged existing gender expectations, even while recognizing in theory the possibility of a countercultural equality of men and women. The early curtailment of leadership roles for women meant that in addition to isolation from the public sphere (except in martyrdom), women had no opportunity to construct the collective voice that could have enabled them to speak and write about themselves. For example, Perpetua's voice, in all its poignancy, urgency, and vividness, is, in the document in which it was circulated in her century and transmitted to ours, bracketed by her editor's theological and social agenda.

The two conditions necessary for adequate self-representation—public space and collective voice—did not exist together for third-century Christian women or for their later counterparts. In martyrdom women spoke and acted in public, but at terrible cost. In medieval female monasteries, on the other hand, it was possible for a collective voice to emerge; women may have been able to define themselves in relation not to patriarchal societies, but to each other and to God. Yet this collective voice was achieved by retirement from the public sphere. Moreover, collective voice was undermined by women's dependence on male priests who fed them the primary nourishment of their religious life, the body of Christ. In the following chapters we will explore some historical representations of women and will conclude, in chapter 6, by asking if it is possible for women in the last decades of the twentieth century to represent women publicly as subjects of their own epics.

# 3

## ADAM AND EVE: BEFORE AND AFTER

*And the eyes of them both were opened and they realized that they were naked.*[1]

*Adam did not love Eve because she was beautiful; it was his love which made her beautiful.*[2]

*Your own nature does not make you beautiful; it is due to the weak eyesight of the people who see you.*[3]

*She would carry herself around like Eve, mourning and penitent, that she might more fully expiate by each garment of penitence that which she acquired from Eve—the degradation of the first sin and the hatefulness of human perdition. . . . You know not that you are also an Eve?*[4]

The story of Adam and Eve provided the Christian West with a palimpsest on which attitudes toward bodies, sexuality, and women were inscribed.[5] However, interpretations of the Genesis account represent not so much a "unified set of shared notions," but a "series of arguments among people"[6] about the significance of sex difference and the social construction of gender. This mythical story, far from people's direct experience, served to explain the daily experience of the difference between and asymmetrical social value of men and women, their different roles in social and sexual arrangements, and women's exclusion from social, political, and ecclesiastical leadership. Because relationships between men and women are perennially one of the most volatile and intimate aspects of communal life, strong social conditioning in the management of these relationships is crucial for maintaining workable societies. The story of Adam and Eve—their creation, fall, and punishment—played a pivotal role in training individuals to accept and support social arrangements. In the societies of the Christian West, in which public life was organized and

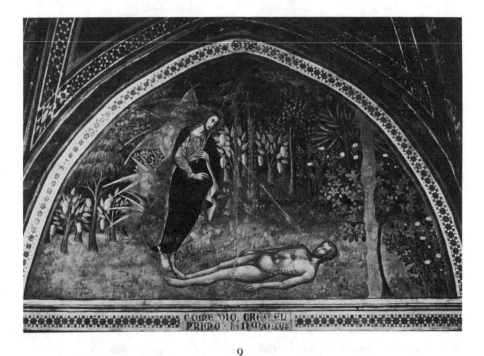

9
―

*Creation of Adam,* San Gimignano, Italy, fourteenth century
(Photograph: Katherine J. Gill)

administered by men, the story of the creation of human beings and their fall into a permanent state of disorientation, distorted values, and sinful behavior highlighted the role of "woman" in bringing evil into the created world.[7] The Genesis story also "explained" why it was the continuing duty and responsibility of men to control women. Historical women lived in societies in which the rhetorical and pictorial figure "woman" was an essential component of public male discourse, and it is, therefore, only by reconstructing historical compositions of the figure "woman" that we can understand an important aspect of the public environment.[8]

Eve, more than any other scriptural woman, was represented as the prototypical woman; her personality traits and behavior were understood to be characteristic of all women and to be instructive about how men should regard and treat women. The exact nature of her guilt and responsibility was repeatedly debated. As "figure" she collected generalizations about "woman" that were not open to falsification by men's experience of actual women. Eve provided an important rationale for the

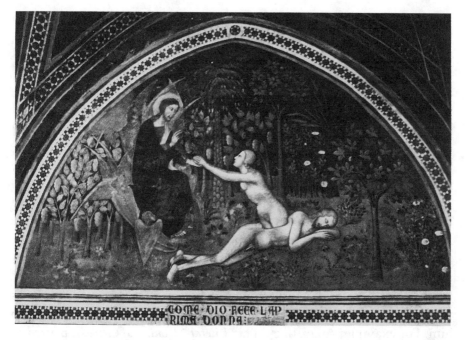

10

*Creation of Eve,* San Gimignano, Italy, fourteenth century
(Photograph: Katherine J. Gill)

treatment of women in patriarchal societies. Although there have been many interpretations of the Genesis account of the creation and Fall, the orthodox interpretation that became normative for centuries of Western Christianity featured Eve's derivation from Adam's body—"a sort of second human being"[9]—her leadership in disobedience, and her condemnation to subordination and painful childbearing.

In paintings and mosaics throughout the medieval period, God's breath animates the newly created Adam; then God pulls Eve by the hand from Adam's side (figures 9, 10). Nevertheless, Christian authors agreed with one another that despite her derivation from Adam, Eve was "built" by God and was not created by angels at God's bidding. Augustine wrote:

I would say without hesitation that the flesh formed in place of the rib, the body and soul of the woman, the shaping of the bodily members, all the inner organs, all the senses, and whatever there was by which she was a creature, a human being, a woman—all this was done by the work of God, which God did not do by the angels but by himself.[10]


In this chapter I will explore some of the most influential literary representations of Eve in orthodox Christianity. I will not attempt a survey of literary treatments of the creation and Fall across the centuries but will explore in some detail versions of the story by several notable authors—Saint Ambrose, Augustine, Saint Hildegard of Bingen, Martin Luther, and Søren Kierkegaard.

Christian leaders who undertook to reinterpret or reform Christianity frequently began by reestablishing the Genesis story as the authoritative account of sex and gender difference. Sometimes they understood the distinction between sex difference—male and female bodies—and gender hierarchy—the social privileging of maleness—as the evidence and result of a fallen world. Most frequently, however, they argued that Eve's physical difference from Adam decisively defined her role in relation to him. For example, Augustine, in his *Literal Meaning of Genesis,* paused as he described the creation of Eve from Adam's side to warn: "[Woman was made] for the man from the man. . . . Whoever calls these facts into question undermines all that we believe, and his opinions should be resolutely cast out of the minds of the faithful."[11] Augustine's use of the language of anathema shows that he considered belief in the secondary creation of woman both in sequence and rank to lie close to the heart of Christianity.[12]

If we understand Christian authors' discussions of the Genesis account of creation and the first entrance of sin into the world not only as religious statements, but also as social proscriptions and prescriptions, we can regard them not as normative statements and even less as consensuses, but rather as a series of arguments among people about a matter that intimately concerned their daily lives. Then we can begin to reconstruct, from a text that presents one of the sides of the debate, the different positions that were taken and argued. The question to which the text provides an answer seems frequently to have concerned "woman's" place in family and society.

Language practices and social practices reflect and nourish each other: the social fact of women's subordination to men seems to have justified literary treatment of women as a collective. For example, when Au-

gustine explained why the patriarchs of the Hebrew Bible were allowed
to marry more than one wife, he wrote:

It was permitted for one husband to have several wives, [but] it was not permitted for one woman to have several husbands, even for the sake of offspring. . . .
For, by a hidden law of nature, things that rule love singularity; things that are
ruled, indeed, are subjected not only each one to an individual master, but also,
if natural or social conditions allow, many of them are not unfittingly subjects to
one master . . . just as many souls are properly subjected to the one God.[13]

Over a thousand years later John Calvin defended the primacy of the individual male subject in similar terms, extrapolating from Paul's injunction to women to obey their husbands[14] a general rule that all women
must be subordinate to all men. Calvin wrote:

Paul is not here speaking of individual persons, nor of an individual household.
Rather, he divides the human race into two parts. . . . Thus there is the male
and the female. I say this for the benefit of any unmarried man, lest he at any
time abandon his privilege by nature, namely that he is the head. Of whom? Of
women, for we must not pay attention to this only within a household, but
within the whole order that God has established in this world.[15]

Religious explanations of male dominance and female subordination
played an important role in reproducing societies that continued to be
organized and governed by men. Let us examine several expositions of
Adam and Eve, looking especially at discussions of the moment—a historical moment, Christian authors insisted—in which, in the self-
conscious nakedness of Adam and Eve, gender hierarchy was established
as normative and inevitable for human beings.

Saint Ambrose, bishop of the imperial city of Milan during the last decades of the fourth century, when Christianity became the official religion
of the Roman Empire, commented extensively on the first chapters of
Genesis. A thoroughly political Christian leader, Ambrose consistently
worked to establish the authority of the Christian church over that of the
imperial power in matters of faith and morality, at one time excluding
the Emperor Theodosius himself from communion until he had re-
pented publicly for ordering the massacre of seven thousand people at
Thessalonica. Ambrose also successfully resisted an imperial edict that

made the cathedral in Milan an Arian church by barricading himself with his congregation in the church and singing hymns until the emperor relented. The time in which he lived as well as his own role in the establishment of Christianity in the empire made him aware that religious beliefs inevitably carried political significance.

Ambrose's *Paradise* tells the story of Adam and Eve's existence in the paradise of the Garden of Eden. Traces of the arguments of dissidents appear throughout his discussion as Ambrose responds to one disputed point after another. His account begins after the six days of creation, when Adam and Eve enjoyed perfect happiness in the delightful garden provided by God. After discussing the much-debated question of whether the devil existed in paradise and deciding that he did, Ambrose comes to the fall of the human race. The issue of gender difference rises immediately; observing that Eve was created in paradise while Adam was not, Ambrose says that this is intended to demonstrate that the "grace" belonging to each person is independent of locality of origin or race since, "although created outside paradise, that is, in an inferior place, man is found to be superior, whereas woman, created in a better place, that is to say, in Paradise, is found to be inferior." His proof is that "she was the first to be deceived and was responsible for deceiving the man."[16] Ambrose next discusses Adam's responsibility for sin; if Adam did not know good and evil, how could he be held responsible for his choice? Ambrose argues that "it was not a question of technical knowledge, but of fidelity,"[17] and that, in this sense, Adam and Eve recognized both the good of obedience and the evil of disobedience. Quoting Genesis 3, "When they both ate, their eyes were opened and they realized that they were naked," Ambrose comments on Eve's role:

The eyes of their mind [singular] were opened and they realized the shame of being naked. For that reason, when the woman ate of the tree of the knowledge of good and evil she certainly sinned and realized that she had sinned. On realizing this, she should not have invited her husband to share in her sin. By enticing him and giving him what she herself had tasted she did not nullify her sin; rather, she repeated it.[18]

Ambrose argues against "many" who say that Eve loved her husband and was afraid that she would be separated from him; her desire to have her partner share her fate, "they say," was, if not excusable, at least understandable. Ambrose disagrees: no extenuating circumstances can excuse Eve's seduction of Adam. Since she ate first, her eyes were opened first, and "she ought not . . . have made her husband a partaker of the evil of which she was conscious. . . . She sinned, therefore, with fore-thought, and knowingly made her husband a participant in her own wrongdoing."[19]

Curiously, Ambrose's treatise on "paradise" is obsessively concerned with the first sin and with woman's place in a fallen world. The woman, who was the first to see that she was naked, must bear the full guilt and responsibility for the fall of the human race. Ambrose goes so far as to assert that Adam "fell by his wife's fault, and not because of his own." How then, Ambrose asks himself, can woman's creation be considered a good? His answer is that "the Lord declared that it is not good for man to be alone, *because the human race could not have been propagated from man alone*."[20] Eve's derivation from Adam's body emphasizes the unity of the first two human beings; that he was created first, however, indicates her inferiority. The entire foundation of her existence and status, then, rests on her undeniably "major import in the process of generation."[21] "Woman is a good helper, even though in an inferior position," Ambrose concludes, illustrating with an example that comes most readily to his mind: "We find examples of this in our own experience. We see how men in high and important offices often enlist the help of men who are below them in rank and esteem."[22]

Yet there are "many" who still argue that since it was Adam who received the command from God not to eat of the tree of the knowledge of good and evil, it was Adam's fault and not Eve's that sin entered the world. Ambrose backtracks to discuss Eve's creation from Adam's rib, pointing to its social implications for all women:

"The rib which God took from Adam he built into a woman." The word "built" is well chosen in speaking of the creation of a woman because a house-hold, comprising man and wife, seems to point toward a state of full perfection. One who is without a wife is regarded as being without a home. As man is con-sidered to be more skillful in public duties, so woman is esteemed to be more adaptable to domestic ministrations.[23]

Another long discussion of Eve's responsibility ensues. Although God's command was given to Adam before Eve was created, it had been duly passed on to her by Adam, who had, for emphasis, supplemented God's injunction not to eat the forbidden fruit with "neither shall you touch it." Although others' opinions should be taken into consideration, Ambrose concludes, "it seems to me that the initial violation and deceit was due to the woman . . . we can discern the sex which was liable first to do wrong. . . . The woman is responsible for the man's error and not vice versa."[24]

The evidence and symbol of the fall into sin was Adam and Eve's recognition of their nakedness. Ambrose distinguished two meanings of nakedness: nakedness before sin, when the prototypical human beings were clothed with the garments of virtue, and nakedness after sin. Before sin, in the "purity of their character," they knew nothing of the bondage of deceit. However, when they lost this primal innocence, their first reaction was to "look for objects made by the hand of man wherewith to cover the nakedness of their minds and hearts." The act of clothing themselves produced the first inordinate gratification experienced by human beings: "They added gratification so as to increase the idle pleasures of this world, sewing, as it were, leaf upon leaf in order to conceal and cover the organ of generation."[25] Adam and Eve experienced nakedness as shame and, in spontaneous response, clothing as gratification; the sense of shame and the act of covering their nakedness directly followed and were initiated by the state of sinful existence. It is for Ambrose still the primary form of sin:

Whoever, therefore, violates the command of God has become naked and despoiled, a reproach to himself. He wants to cover himself and hide his genitals with fig leaves, making use, as it were, of empty and idle talk which the sinner interweaves word after word with fallacies for the purpose of shielding himself from his awareness of his guilty deed.[26]

Ambrose also offers an allegorical interpretation of the story of Adam and Eve: "The serpent is a type of the pleasures of the body. The woman stands for our senses and the man for our minds. Pleasure stirs the senses, which, in turn, have their effect on the mind. Pleasure, therefore, is the primary source of sin."[27] Eve, it appears from Ambrose's interpretation, is simultaneously more guilty and more innocent than Adam. As a figure of sensuality, with a body created from Adam's body rather than from the dust of the ground and the breath of God, she could hardly be expected to exercise the critical judgment that Adam possessed as his birthright. She is also more forthright than Adam, admitting her fault readily rather than shifting the blame to another person or to extenuating circumstances. Her acknowledgement is brief and descriptive, "The serpent deceived me and I ate."[28] Therefore, Ambrose concludes, she was given a "milder and more salutary" sentence: "She was to serve under her husband's power, first, that she might not be inclined to do wrong, and secondly, that being in a position subject to a stronger vessel, she might not dishonor her husband, but on the contrary might be governed by his counsel." [29] Ambrose makes no mention of Eve's condemnation to painful childbearing, finding in her subjection and servitude to her husband the core of her punishment.

Nakedness and clothing play a crucial role in Ambrose's interpretation of the story of the Fall, as they do in the Genesis account. The placement of blame for the first sin and the implications of Eve's responsibility for gender arrangements are also central to his interest in the story. How are these two connected? The clothing of Adam and Eve—their own effort to cover themselves with leaves, and then God's clothing of them in the skins of dead animals—marks their existence in a newly sinful condition. Clothing is also the evidence that Adam and Eve's descendants continue to live in a state of deceit and concealment both in relation to one another and in relation to God. Finally, clothing symbolizes Eve's subjection to Adam; the first gender arrangements occurred simultaneously with the first clothing.

At the beginning of the fifth century, Augustine of Hippo wrote a commentary on the literal meaning of Genesis. While his other interpretations of the Genesis story had emphasized the symbolic and spiritual import of the stories of the creation and Fall, in *De genesi ad litteram* Augustine set himself the task of rebutting those who accused him of excessive spiritualization in his treatment of Genesis. This work, he writes, is to be a historical treatment of the creation of the physical universe, the natural world, and the bodies of animals and human beings, describing "the events that actually occurred and the words that were actually spoken." [30]

Augustine first takes up the question of human creation in God's image, deciding, in book 3, that woman, in spite of "her physical qualities as a woman" and because of her creation as a rational being, was, like man, made in the image of God. Compared to Adam and Eve's bodies as created, their descendants' bodies are "much inferior," since for Adam and Eve's descendants, death is an irreducible entailment of embodiment. The sin of the first couple condemned their descendants to many evils, foremost of which are two pieces of evidence of the Fall: the undifferentiated lust that drives human beings to seek sex, power, and possessions; and death, the dissolution of the bond of body and soul.

Although most Christian authors before Augustine thought that procreation by sexual intercourse was initiated by sin and would not have occurred if Adam and Eve had not sinned,[31] Augustine believed that it would have existed in paradise but would not have been characterized by the compulsiveness that accompanies it after the Fall. In book 14 of the *City of God,* where he gives his most extensive and detailed account of sexuality in paradise, Augustine calls marriage after the Fall, a "legalized depravity."[32] It was, however, originally "worthy of the happiness of paradise." Admittedly lacking experience of unfallen sexuality, Augustine fantasizes that sexual intercourse would have occurred "at the bidding of the will,"[33] "at the appropriate time, and in the necessary degree."[34] He employs an agricultural metaphor to picture the lustless sexuality of the Garden of Eden: "The instrument created for the task would have sown the seed on 'the field of generation' as the hand now sows seeds on the earth."[35]

Apparently feeling that some explanation and support were needed for his suggestion that "the instrument created for the task" could have been moved at the will's behest rather than in the spontaneous and insubordinate way the male organ is presently "moved" to sexual intercourse, Augustine labors to provide an experiential analogy. His explanation affords earnest readers of the *City of God* a rare humorous moment:

For we [presently] set in motion at our command, not only those members which are fitted with bones and joints, like the hands, feet, and fingers, but also those which are loosely constructed of pliant tissues and muscles, which we can move, when we choose, by shaking, which we extend by stretching, which we twist and flex, contract and harden—such parts, I mean, as those of the mouth and face, which the will moves, as far as it can.[36]

The analogy may amuse more than it persuades the reader that paradisaical sex might have enjoyed a different physiology than that of present sexual experience. It is also noteworthy that Augustine does not allow for different experiences of sexual arousal in men and women, but bases his conjectures about sex in pardise on the male body and male concerns.

Augustine's vision of sex in the Garden of Eden was of a calm but blissful activity, initiated by will and motivated by the duty of producing offspring. What role does woman play in this blissful male paradise in which no performance anxiety intrudes?[37] Woman was created by God specifically to help Adam in the work of procreation; Eve was created for and defined by her biological role in childbearing:

Now if the woman was not made for the man to be his helper in begetting children, in what was she to help him? She was not to till the earth with him, for there was not yet any toil to make help necessary. If there were any such need, a male helper would be better, and the same could be said of the comfort of another's presence if Adam were perhaps weary of solitude. How much more agreeably could two male friends, rather than a man and a woman, enjoy companionship and conversation in a life shared together?[38]

In the fallen world of his experience, Augustine could not imagine a condition in which human beings would not need to be in relationships of dominance and subordination. Even if two men undertook to live together in community, Augustine says in the same passage, there would be a threat to "the peace of the household" if one had not been created after the other and derived from the other so that "proper rank" could be maintained. Since "proper rank" was guaranteed by the order of creation, woman was "constructed" by God from the raw material of Adam's rib in order to establish simultaneously the unity of humankind and the precedence of the man.

Augustine discusses the "literal meaning" of the sin of Adam and Eve on the basis of the text of Genesis 2:25–3:24. After taking up many philosophical matters concerning why sin occurred, Augustine narrates the moment of temptation and sin. The words of the serpent, he says, could not have convinced Eve to disobey God "if there was not already in her heart a love of her own independence and a proud presumption of self."[39] Adam also ate, persuaded by seeing that although Eve had eaten the fruit, she was not dead as God had warned. "The eyes of both were opened," not in the literal sense—Augustine demonstrates at length that Adam and Eve had possessed natural vision before the fall—but precisely in noticing "what they had not formerly noticed": "Casting their eyes on their bodies, they felt a movement of concupiscence that they had not known."[40] Shame at their nakedness was the first evidence of tragic loss:

As soon as they had violated the precept, they were completely naked, interiorly deserted by the grace which they had offended by their pride and arrogant love of their own independence. . . . In this man realized with what grace he had previously been clothed when he experienced nothing indecent in his nakedness."

As a result of the fall "their bodies lost the privileged condition they had had" and "became subject to disease and death, like the bodies of animals, and consequently subject to the same drive by which there is in animals a desire to copulate."[41]

Adam and Eve experienced the first result of the Fall as physical change: nakedness as shame and as vulnerability to disease and death. The second result was social and gendered: the subordination of one human being to another, woman to man. Although Augustine says that "even before her sin, woman had been made to be ruled by her husband and to be submissive and subject to him," the former condition was to have been maintained effortlessly and without resentment, whereas after sin, "there is a condition similar to that of slavery."[42] Only because of sin does woman "deserve to have her husband for a master," and "if this order is not maintained," Augustine warns ominously, "nature will be corrupted still more, and sin will be increased."[43]

Some striking dissonances in the passage alert Augustine's readers to his commitment to maintaining the gender constructions of church and society. For example, he quotes Paul's injunction to Christians "Through love serve one another" immediately after stating that the submission of woman to man, wife to husband, was a harsh condition of "slavery," and he adds that Paul "by no means" intended one to have dominion over the other. This appears to prepare the foundation for an argument to the effect that, in Christian communities, human beings might endeavor to overcome the fallen condition of secular gender arrangements and to reinstate, as Paul seems to advocate, a condition of mutuality based on love and the acknowledgment of interdependence. Not so, unfortunately— even disastrously—for gender relations in the Christian West to the present. As though suddenly realizing the potential social implications of Paul's prescription for male-female relationships in a distinctively Christian community, he completes his interpretation of the admonition "Through love serve one another" with a non sequitur: "Hence married persons through love can serve one another," he writes, "but St. Paul does not allow a woman to rule over a man." Apparently Augustine feared that relationships of gender equality would inevitably lead to a simple reversal of present gender relations of domination and submission; he hastily invokes another passage, 1 Timothy 2:12, to undermine the radical implications of Galatians 5:13. Although Augustine cannot be responsible for the acceptance of his ideas of social and sexual arrangements by future generations, his agenda for his own society was clearly to counsel maintenance of gender relations that can, without exaggeration, be simply designated as slavery.[44]

Discussing the exact nature of Adam's sin, Augustine poses the question of how Adam, a "spiritual man," could have fallen for the words of the serpent. His attention turns to Eve; his questions become rhetorical, suggesting more than he can substantiate from the scriptural text:

Was it because the man would not have been able to believe [the transparent lies of the serpent] that the woman was employed [by the serpent] *on the supposition that she had limited understanding,* and also perhaps that she was living according to the spirit of the flesh and not according to the spirit of the mind?[45]

Why, Augustine continues, did Paul not attribute to woman the image of God?[46] Not, he replies, "because she was unable to receive that same image, for in that grace St. Paul says we are neither male nor female," but because "the woman had not yet received the gift of the knowledge of God, but under the direction and tutelage of her husband she was to acquire it gradually." In short, Adam ate the fruit not because he had any fault, but because of his love for and generosity toward Eve: "he did not wish to make her unhappy, fearing that she would waste away without his support, alienated from his affections, and that this dissension would be her death."[47]

Augustine, to his credit, did not attempt to recommend this interpretation as a literal reading of the story of Adam and Eve. He concludes book 11: "But enough of these speculations."[48] The vividness of Augustine's narration, the intuitive rightness of his interpretations in his society and the patriarchal societies of the Christian West, and the authority with which he was invested by future generations have all helped to make his analyses of the origin and inevitability of asymmetrical gender constructions compelling to Christians through history and to the present time. Augustine's description of Eve, the prototype and figure of "woman" as designed and "built" for procreation, limited in rationality, and dangerous to men has also contributed to attitudes toward women. Finally, we should notice that Augustine omitted from his account of creation any vision of the splendid nakedness of Adam and Eve before the Fall, though he was poignantly aware of the fragility, vulnerability, and shame of naked flesh after the Fall.

Augustine's version of creation and the Fall also influenced countless paintings of the Genesis story in the Christian West. In the fifteenth century, Jan Van Eyck's altarpiece *Adoration of the Lamb* (figure 11) reiterates

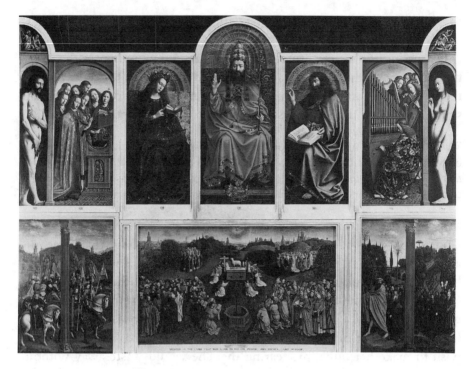

II
—

JAN VAN EYCK
*Adoration of the Lamb* (Ghent Altarpiece), 1432
St. Bavo, Ghent (Art Resource, New York; photo Giraudon)

both Eve's subordination to Adam and Augustine's association of her naked body with sex.[49] Adam and Eve, naked in the outer panels, share the upper range of the painting, the heavenly sphere, with the reigning Christ, the Virgin, John the Baptist, and musician angels. In the lower or earthly register a surreal combination of physical and symbolic realities appears as scenes from Christ's arrest and crucifixion culminates in the center panel, where a large lamb stands on an altar while worshipers and bystanders gather in front of the altar.

Adam and Eve, "the first monumental nudes of northern panel painting"—only slightly less than life-sized—face one another across intervening panels.[50] They stand in dark niches: on Adam's side Cain and Abel offer their gifts of grain and sheep, while on Eve's side Cain clubs his fallen brother to death. Adam's panel is on Christ's right. Eve, created from Adam's left side, is on Adam's left. Adam stares reflectively into the eyes of viewers "whose eye level is below the bottom of the panels,"[51] thus inviting the viewer to acknowledge kinship and empathy with him. Eve's eyes are unfocused in the middle distance, neither engaging the viewer's eye nor looking directly at the figures of the other panels; she has the intent but preoccupied gaze of a sleepwalker. Adam strides, upright and purposeful, his right toes raised in mid-step. Eve's body undulates from the left to the right frames of her niche; her position is unbalanced as her right foot is placed in a forward direction while her left foot points across the altarpiece at Adam.

Both figures are naked, but Adam's erect stance, self-contained posture, and the gestures with which both arms shield his nakedness render him less exposed and vulnerable than Eve. Eve's nakedness, only partially masked by her slight turn away from the viewer and by the leafy twig that covers her genitals, is self-conscious (figure 12). Her rounded and elongated belly indicates pregnancy; it also pleased the "period eye" as a mark of ideal feminine beauty.[52] Eve's body, isolated in her dark niche from the heavenly court on her right and indifferent to the presence of a viewer, displays the sensuous curves that initiated the fall of the human race.

Hildegard, abbess of the Benedictine monastery at Bingen in the last decades of the twelfth century, also retold the story of Adam and Eve. A prolific writer and energetic administrator, Hildegard founded two monasteries, preached throughout Germany, and wrote six books.[53] She also experienced waking visions throughout her life: "What I do not see," she wrote, "I do not know, for I am not educated." Hildegard had a different interpretation of Adam and Eve from that of Ambrose and Augustine. Her contribution to the twelfth-century debate on whether woman was created in the image of God was grounded in her use of the feminine as symbolic of the eternal wisdom of God. For Hildegard, "woman's role as vessel of the Incarnation was the very seal of her creation in the image of God."[54] Because "man signifies the divinity and woman the humanity of the Son of God,"[55] Hildegard found Eve, not Adam, to be the representative human being.

The distinctiveness of her reading of the Genesis story lies in her interpretation of the entrance of sin into the world. Hildegard's Eve is "more sinned against than sinning" and "victimized outright" by Satan's wiles.[56] Her emphasis is on Eve's vulnerability and suffering, not on her

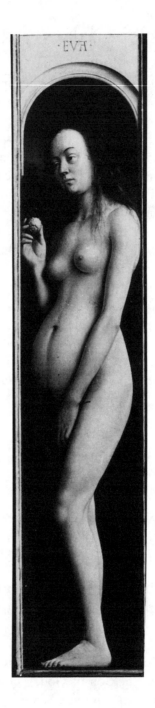

12
___

*Eve*, detail, Ghent Altarpiece
(Photo Giraudon)

instigation of sin. Yet her interpretation of the figure of Eve as simultaneously frail and powerful reflects the ambiguity with which she described
her own abilities and strengths. Aside from the assistance of divine light,
she called herself a "paupercula feminae forma," a poor little womanly
figure.[57] What she had seen, however, empowered her, granted her authority, and allowed her to speak and write with the utmost self-confi-
dence. "She oscillates," Peter Dronke writes in *Women Writers of the
Middle Ages,* "between rapturous praise of womankind—'o femina
forma, quam gloriosa es!'—and a despairing sense of woman's weakness."[58] Barbara Newman has demonstrated, however, that the apparent
contradictions in Hildegard's sense of woman's frailty and "glory" serves
a theological and psychological function. Again, the story of Eve is the
touchstone for her view of woman:

If Adam had sinned before Eve, that transgression would have been so grave and
incorrigible, and man would have fallen into such great, unredeemable stub-
bornness, that he neither would nor could have been saved. Hence, because Eve
transgressed first, the sin could more easily be undone, since she was weaker
than the male.[59]

"The ambiguous frailty of woman makes her more accessible to both
temptation and redemption," Newman comments.[60]

In the *Scivias* Hildegard reinterprets the Genesis account of the creation of Adam and Eve. For Hildegard, as for other authors, Eve was derived from Adam, but not, however, from Adam's body. Rather, Eve's
form was, in a quite literal sense, the distillation of Adam's love: "And
God gave a form to that love of the man, and so woman is the man's
love." Moreover, the fact that Eve was the product of Adam's love meant
something quite specific about gender relations:

When Adam gazed at Eve, he was entirely filled with wisdom, for he saw in her
the mother of the children to come. And when she gazed at Adam, it was as if
she were gazing into heaven, or as the human soul strives upward, longing for
heavenly things—for her hope was fixed in him.[61]

The creation of Eve, as described by Hildegard, provides a foundation
for her retelling of the Genesis account in such a way that mutuality, interdependence, and complementarity modify the hierarchical implications of Eve's "derivation" from Adam. Hildegard's account of the story,
both in language and image, leaves that order open to question or even
reverses it. The illustration[62] (figure 13) that accompanies her narration
of the fall of the human race compresses two temporally distinct events—

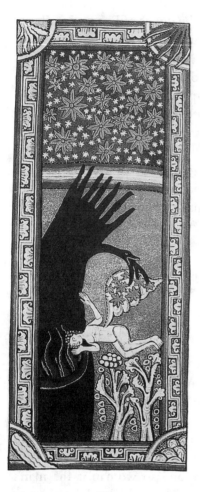

**13**

creation and the Fall—into one scene.⁶³ Under starry skies, and floating above fruited and flowering trees, Adam lies across the center of the picture space, his head at the edge of a flaming pit that emerges from a dark shape, his right hand cupping an ear as he appears to listen to sounds that come from the fiery blackness. A serpent spews forth fingers of "foul smoke." From Adam's side comes a white floral-shaped cloud containing large stars which, Hildegard says in her commentary, represent the bodies of all future human beings, contained in Eve. The black bile that comes from the serpent's throat spills onto this white cloud. Hildegard's commentary reads:

This form breathed forth into a clear region a white cloud which contained a large number of stars in itself and which had *sent forth down through itself* the fair form of a man: this signifies that in this garden of pleasantness, the devil—through the seduction of the serpent—approached Eve in order to get her cast out from the garden. . . . And the cloud *threw the form of the man out of itself:* this signifies that the ancient seducer, expelling Adam and Eve from the seat of blessedness by treachery sent them into the darkness of destruction.⁶⁴

The illustration underscores the text's suggestion that the white cloud that represents Eve produced Adam. After all, the Genesis story reverses the experiential order of human birth. In Genesis 2:18, woman is derived from man, not man from woman. Hildegard's medical interest in reproduction as well as her psychological and theological interest in Eve predisposed her to question the Genesis order of creation. Previous depictions of the creation of Eve show the emergence of Eve from the side of the sleeping Adam, an extension of his body, just as, in Hildegard's illustration, the white cloud emerges from Adam's body. Hildegard's compression of the moments of creation and the Fall, however, create a complex image that supports her insistence on the interdependence of Adam and Eve: "'Woman was created for man's sake,' and man was made for woman's. For as she is from man, so too man is from her."[65]

Hildegard's theology of human sexuality informs her view of the mutuality of Adam and Eve in their prelapsarian condition. Peter Dronke has claimed that, in some passages, Hildegard tries "to project a wholly positive theology of sex."[66] This is certainly true of her treatment of sexuality before the Fall. Sexuality in paradise revealed, more than any other single condition, the mutuality of female and male: "In one activity they perform one act, just as the air and the wind work together. . . . The wind stirs the air and the air enfolds the wind."[67] Without the Fall, in Hildegard's vision, husband and wife would have remained free of lust but would nevertheless have experienced great pleasure as they lay side by side, "gently perspir[ing] as if sleeping." A painless birth would have followed this conception: "Then the woman would become pregnant from the man's perspiration (*sudor*), and, while they lay thus sweetly asleep, she would give birth to a child painlessly from her side . . . in the same way that God brought Eve forth from Adam."[68]

Because both male and female bodies have been physically altered by sin, lovemaking has also changed. "The purity of [man's] blood," writes Dronke, "was turned into another mode, so that, instead of purity, he now ejects the spume of semen."[69] Women suffered even more immediate and dramatic change, according to Hildegard:

When the torrent of greedy desire invaded Eve, all her veins opened into a river of blood. Hence every woman has tempests of blood within her. . . . But all women's veins would have remained intact and healthy if Eve had remained for the full time in paradise.[70]

This contrasts sharply with Hildegard's description of the "sweetness" of sexual intercourse in paradise, where it consisted of the mingling of a "gentle perspiration," a delicate, fragrant essence distilled, as Dronke has written, not from laborious activity, but from "anything that is fertile and beautiful on earth."[71]

The physical changes have led to the loss of mutuality in lovemaking.

Female sexuality after the Fall, Hildegard says, has a different structure from male sexuality:

The man's love, compared with the woman's, is a heat of ardour like a fire on blazing mountains, which can hardly be put out, whilst hers is a wood-fire that is easily quenched; but the woman's love, compared with the man's, is like a sweet warmth proceeding from the sun, which brings forth fruits.[72]

But it was the experience of lovemaking itself that suffered the most deplorable change. Hildegard's profound and nuanced understanding of sexuality, like her extensive medical knowledge, was the result of listening carefully to many contemporary women's descriptions of their physical and sexual experience. Although Hildegard acknowledges that lovemaking after the Fall is still motivated by a powerful and "sweet" passion, it now has a compulsive urgency unrelated in kind—though related in intensity—to the love of Adam and Eve in paradise:

But the great love that was in Adam when Eve came forth from him, and the sweetness of the sleep with which he then slept, were turned in his transgression into a contrary mode of sweetness. And so, because a man still feels this great sweetness in himself, and is like a stag thirsting for the fountain, he races swiftly to the woman and she to him—she like a threshing-floor pounded by his many strokes and brought to heat while the grains are threshed inside her.[73]

Hildegard's image of woman as threshing-floor, passively pounded by the man's repeated thrusts, presents a bleak picture of the prospect of female pleasure in fallen heterosexual sexuality.

In her medical descriptions of sexual intercourse, however, women's pleasure plays an active and essential role. The woman's pleasure is necessary for conception since it is the woman's pleasure that produces the man's orgasm:

When a woman is making love with a man, a sense of heat in her brain, which brings with it sensual delight, communicates the taste of that delight during the act and summons forth the emission of man's seed. And when the seed has fallen into its place, that vehement heat descending from her brain draws the seed to itself and holds it, and soon the woman's sexual organs contract, and all the parts that are ready to open up during the time of menstruation now close, in the same way as a strong man can hold something enclosed in his fist.[74]

The story of Adam and Eve in the Garden gave Hildegard a vehicle for her vision of a prelapsarian sexuality of delight and mutuality; it also provided an explanation for the absence of such sexual and social relationships between men and women in her world of experience.

Despite her esteem for women, their bodies, and their sexuality, Hildegard's allegiance to traditional interpretations of the Genesis story is evident in her treatment of gender roles. As a woman who spent her life as abbess of a Benedictine monastery, Hildegard was necessarily influenced by a literary and social context in which alternative interpretations of Genesis must not openly contradict traditional interpretations. With her passion and intelligence, Hildegard managed to combine rather effectively traditional interpretations that emphasize the hierarchical implications of the story of the creation and Fall of humanity with her own reading that highlighted the interdependence of the first man and woman. Yet it is not surprising that her interpretation did not affect subsequent Christian readings of the story. One reason was that it did not enter the sphere of public discourse but remained isolated in Hildegard's monastery. More importantly, the message of equality did nothing to support, nor was it reinforced by, the social institutions of her society. It could therefore be dismissed by contemporaries as well as by subsequent Christian authors as irrelevant or idiosyncratic, a less compelling reading than interpretations that provided a clear rationalization of familiar gender constructions.

Over a millennium after Ambrose and Augustine wrote their commentaries on the story of Adam and Eve and its social and political implications for the gender arrangements of their own time, another influential Christian leader commented on the story. Martin Luther, instigator of the Protestant reformations of the sixteenth century, retold the story in lectures given at the University of Wittenberg in 1535. By this time the Lutheran reform had reached its greatest geographical extension; it was established in southern Germany as well as many other localities, some of which would, in the next century, return to Roman Catholic jurisdiction. Delivered close to the end of his life, these lectures represent Luther's mature exposition of a story he had often reworked in sermons and treatises, a story that contained, for him, the structure of not only creation and sin, but also salvation.

The condition of Adam and Eve after the Fall anticipates the condition of every human being who would come after them. Recognizing their sinfulness, Adam and Eve attempted to construct pitiful shelters from the all-seeing eye of God, woefully shabby and transparent garments that, even if God were not omniscient, would have informed God that they were feeling guilty about something. In Luther's version of the story, only when those specious shelters are exposed in all their inadequacy by the Word of God do human beings turn, in terror and hope, to God. In the only trustworthy shelter, the covering of Christ's righteousness, the sinner can find real protection from God's righteous intolerance of sin.

Luther's account of the saga of Adam and Eve begins with God's proposal, "Let us make a man according to our image and likeness."[75] Man, "a creature far superior to the rest of the living beings that live a physical life,"[76] was created with both a physical and a spiritual life; he was

not to live without food, drink, and procreation. But at a predetermined time, after the number of saints had become full, these physical activities would have come to an end; and Adam, together with his descendants, would have been translated to the eternal and spiritual life. Nevertheless, these activities of physical life—like eating, drinking, procreating, etc.—would have been a service pleasing to God; we would have rendered this service to God without the defect of the lust which is there now after sin, without any sin, and without the fear of death.[77]

Luther acknowledges that his discussion of the original condition of human beings is a fantasy: "We are speaking of something unknown. Not only have we no experience of it, but we continually experience the opposite."[78] He imagines an original human condition of integrated fulfillment in which Adam and Eve could enjoy God, each other, and the world without fear, pain, lust, or the anticipation of death.

In addition to being naturally superior to all other created creatures, Adam "had greater strength and keener senses than the rest of the living beings,"[79] and he—with Eve—was their ruler: "Adam and Eve became the rulers of the earth, the sea, and the air. . . . The naked human being—without weapons and walls, even without any clothing, solely in his bare flesh—was given the rule over all birds, wild beasts, and fish."[80] Even the natural world was brighter, richer, and more beautiful: "before sin the sun was brighter, the water purer, the trees more fruitful, and the fields more fertile."[81]

Moreover, "in Adam there was enlightened reason, a true knowledge of God, and a most sincere desire to love God and his neighbor, so that Adam embraced Eve and at once acknowledged her to be his own flesh."[82] Absence of gender politics was the hallmark of paradise! Eve was endowed with mental gifts "in the same degree as Adam,"[83] and "her very nature was pure and full of the knowledge of God to such a

degree that she herself knew the Word of God and understood it." Moreover, she was beautiful, if not in herself, at least in the eye of the beholder: "No other beautiful sight in the whole world appeared lovelier
and more attractive to Adam than his own Eve."[84]

Luther constructs a thin line between affirming, against contemporary
and historical detractors, Eve's created worth and insisting on her inferiority and appropriate subordination to Adam, in support of contemporary gender arrangements. Within a single passage he sets up the issue:

If the woman had not been deceived by the serpent and had not sinned, she
would have been the equal of Adam in all respects. For the punishment, that she
is now subjected to the man, was imposed on her after sin and because of sin,
just as the other hardships and dangers were: travail, pain, and countless other
vexations. Therefore *Eve was not like the women of today;* her state was far better
and more excellent, and she was in no respect inferior to Adam, whether you
count the qualities of the body or those of the mind."[85]

Perhaps thinking he may have gone too far in praising Eve, Luther appears to reconsider his earlier statements of Adam and Eve's equal gifts:

Although Eve was a most extraordinary creature—similar to Adam so far as the
image of God is concerned, that is, in justice, wisdom, and happiness—she was
nevertheless a woman. For as the sun is more excellent than the moon (although
the moon, too, is a very excellent body), so the woman, although she was a
most beautiful work of God, nevertheless was not the equal of the male in glory
and prestige.[86]

The reason for Luther's reconsideration of Eve's worth soon appears. His
need to support contemporary gender politics has occurred to him, and
his interpretation of Genesis must concur with his sense of appropriate
gender arrangements. The examples by which he seeks to illuminate the
Genesis story reveals that in fact it is the Genesis story that must rationalize and support present society. The naming of Eve by Adam, Luther
says, indicates Adam's power over her, just as contemporary women,
when they marry, lose their family name and are called by their husband's name:[87]

In the household the wife is a partner in the management and has a common
interest in the children and the property, and yet there is a great difference between the sexes. The male is like the sun in heaven, the female like the moon, the
animals like the stars over which the sun and moon have dominion. In the first
place, therefore, let us note from this passage [Genesis 1:27: "Male and female
He created them"] that it was written that this sex may not be excluded from
any glory of the human creature, although it is inferior to the male sex.[88]

Luther obviously recognized the pivotal role played by the story of Adam and Eve in supporting contemporary social arrangements; he also acknowledged quite openly the male need for female support and help. The gender perspective from which he speaks is apparent in the following statement, though his use of personal pronouns partially disguises his message:

Today, after our [human] nature has become corrupted by sin, woman is needed not only to secure increase but also for companionship and for protection. The management of the household must have the ministration of the dear ladies. In addition—and this is lamentable—woman is also necessary as an antidote against sin. And so, in the case of woman, we [men] must think not only of the managing of the household which she does, but also of the medicine which she is. . . . Therefore, we [men] are compelled to make use of this sex [women] in order to avoid sin.[89]

Having established women's social and sexual necessity for men, as well as women's inferiority, as the justification for this "use," Luther nonetheless argues against scholars and philosophers who claimed, like Plato, that human beings were first created bisexual and then split into two separate beings, or like Aristotle, that woman is a "maimed male," a variety of monster. These conjectures reveal, Luther writes, the inability of reason to discover God's workings.[90] In rebutting these "aspersions against the female sex," Luther showed not only his philosophical training, but also that he was well aware of the contemporary debate, known as the "querelle des femmes," over the nature, status, and roles of women.[91] He carefully took what he considered a nuanced and informed position in this heated debate, a position that affirmed "woman" as she was figured by Eve in her original state of creation, but maintained the social and sexual arrangements he thought of as "necessary."

Inevitably, Luther's discussion moves to the occasion of the Fall of humankind, the point at which his affirmation of Eve finds its limits. Contrasting the idyllic picture of prelapsarian human happiness with the condition of humanity after the Fall, Luther finds that the first, and perhaps the most dramatic and lamentable, effect of sin was the loss of "the glory of our bodies, so that now it is a matter of the utmost disgrace to be seen naked, whereas at that time it was something most beautiful."[92] He calls the loss of nakedness a "wound of nature," like the loss of "our upright will and our sound intellect."[93] Originally, "the fact that Adam and Eve walked about naked was their greatest adornment before God and all the creatures," but "now, after sin, we not only shun the glance of men when we are naked; but we are also bashful in our own presence. . . . This shame is a witness that our heart has lost its trust in God which they who were naked had before sin."[94] Clothing is a constant symbol and reminder of sin: "Whenever they looked at their garments, these were to serve as a reminder to them to give thought to their wretched fall from supreme happiness into the utmost misfortune and trouble."[95]

Faithful to his earlier affirmation that "Adam was not to live without procreation" in his created condition before the Fall, Luther deplores Adam and Eve's covering of their genitals as if they were "something most shameful." In fact, he writes, the genitals are "that part of the body which by its nature was most honorable and noble." "What," he asks rhetorically, "in all nature is nobler than the work of procreation?" The magnitude and horror of sin can be measured by the fact that, because of sin, "the most useful members [of the body] have become the most shameful"[96] (figure 14).

How did this loss come about? Human nature, Luther says, was only as strong as its weakest link, Eve. Indeed, Satan's cleverness was apparent in his attack on

the weak part of human nature, Eve, the woman, not Adam, the man. Although both were created equally righteous, nevertheless Adam had some advantage over Eve. Just as in all the rest of nature the strength of the male exceeds that of the female, so also in the perfect nature the male somewhat excelled the female. Because Satan sees that Adam is the more excellent, he does not dare assail him; for he fears that his attempt may turn out to be useless. And I, too, believe that if he had tempted Adam first, the victory would have been Adam's. . . . Satan, therefore, directs his attack upon Eve as the weaker part and puts her valor to the test, for he sees that she is so dependent on her husband that she thinks she cannot sin.[97]

Eve, according to Luther, sinned because she failed to understand herself as a responsible subject before God and used her husband as shelter, considering her relation to *him* to be the relationship on which her life depended. Having made this amazingly modern—even proto-feminist[98]—assessment of the nature of Eve's self-deception, however, Luther does not pursue its implications for social and sexual arrangements; instead, he returns to discussing Eve's sin and punishment, finding them *prescriptive* for gender roles and expectations.

Eve, because weak, took and ate the forbidden fruit. Adam, however, had a different reason for eating the fruit. "Almost everybody," Luther says, believes that Adam "was not seduced, but sinned knowingly."

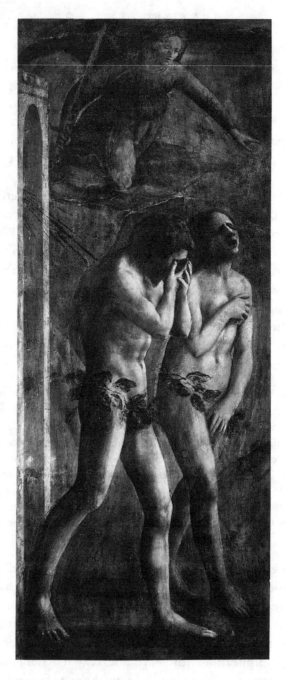

14

MASACCIO
*Expulsion,* 1427
Brancacci Chapel, Santa Maria del Carmine, Florence
(Art Resource, New York)

Adam did not desire the fruit, but ate it out of love for Eve. Although he introduces this interpretation somewhat hesitantly as popular opinion rather than as his own, Luther says that he does "not disapprove" of the argument that Adam's sin had extenuating circumstances: "Adam did not yield to the persuasion of the devil as Eve did; but he was unwilling to cause sadness for his delight, that is, for his wife, and so he preferred his wife's love to God."[99] Although Adam was not deceived by the serpent, "he was deceived by his wife and by himself when he persuaded himself that his deed would not result in the punishment the Lord had said would follow."

Punishment did indeed follow, in the form of mortality. But with that came the hope of the human race for resurrection from the dead. For even though Eve brought about not only her own but also Adam's fall, her punishment, Luther says, is "happy and joyful" because "she is not being deprived of the blessing of procreation, which was promised and granted before sin. She sees that she is keeping her sex and that she remains a woman. She sees that she is not being separated from Adam to remain alone and apart from her husband."[100] And Luther sympathized with women who continue to experience the punishment of Eve. His vivid description of the "severe and sundry ailments" of conception, pregnancy, and childbirth demonstrates, if not accurate medical information, both sympathetic observation and loving engagement:

From the beginning of that time a woman suffers very painful headaches, dizziness, nausea, an amazing loathing of food and drink, frequent and difficult vomiting, toothache, and a stomach disorder which produces a craving, called pica, for such foods from which nature normally shrinks. Moreover, when the fetus has matured and birth is imminent, there follows the most awful distress, because only with utmost peril and almost at the cost of her life does she give birth to her offspring.[101]

Motherhood is, nevertheless an "outstanding glory," which brings with it "other gifts," namely "that we are all nourished, kept warm, and carried in the womb of our mothers, that we nurse at their breasts and are protected by their effort and care."[102] Luther expresses his "great pleasure and wonderment" in the apparent fact "that the entire female body was created for the purpose of nurturing children."[103]

The benefits for men and children are certainly abundant, but Luther can also understand that for women themselves confinement to the home, childbearing, and rearing are not an unmixed blessing. They are, in fact, a blessing that has strong components of punishment; in addition to the pains and sorrows of gestation and childbirth "Eve has been placed under the power of her husband." That means, Luther notes:

The rule remains with the husband, and the wife is compelled to obey him by God's command. He rules the home and the state, wages wars, and defends his possessions. . . . The woman, on the other hand, is like a nail driven to the wall. She sits at home. . . . [She] has been deprived of the ability of administering those affairs that are outside and that concern the state. She does not go beyond her most personal duties.

Luther laments Eve's fall and sees that gender roles need not have been so unequal, for "if Eve had persisted in the truth, she would not only not have been subjected to the rule of her husband, but she herself would also have been a partner in the rule which is now entirely the concern of males."[104]

Well aware that women of his acquaintance were not content meekly to live out Eve's punishment, Luther sees no help for it. He does not question women's confinement to the home but finds it necessary and mandatory. He acknowledges that exclusion from activity in the public sphere is as significant a part of the punishment of Eve's descendants as painful labor and childbirth. In analyzing Eve's punishment as loss of the public sphere, however, he does not seem to notice that this was not a direct part of God's commandment to Eve in the Genesis story. Rather, he finds that enclosure in the home is entailed in female subordination to male rule. The figure of Eve—her volatile, untamed, susceptible "nature"—has more weight and programmatic urgency for Luther than does his experience of actual women, whom he does not accuse of anything more heinous than grumbling and impatience at their confinement. For whatever solace it may provide, he assures readers that the husband too suffers. Because of Adam's sin, a "raging lust kindled by the poison of Satan in his body" compels him to marry and thus become responsible for the support, rule, and instruction of his family, "and these things cannot be done without extraordinary trouble and very great effort."[105]

In the nineteenth century the Danish theologian and philosopher Søren Kierkegaard retold the story of Adam and Eve in *The Concept of Anxiety*. This forefather of existentialist philosophy used the Genesis account as a way to identify the root source of anxiety, the condition of apprehensive dread in which he thought human beings to exist. That Kierkegaard's

Adam and Eve are figures of "man" and "woman" is clear from his use of collective nouns for both. We enter his description at the point at which he says that Eve was more sensuous than Adam: "That woman is more sensuous than man appears at once in her physical structure. . . . The fact that woman's life culminates in procreation indicates precisely that she is more sensuous."[106] Kierkegaard does not discuss this further, but does define woman under two aspects: aesthetically, her "ideal aspect" is beauty; ethically, her ideal aspect is procreation.[107] Aesthetically, the beauty of woman differs from that of man. Since "the spiritual has its expression in the face," and the spiritual is more prominent in the man, "in the beauty of the man, the face and its expression are more essential than in the beauty of the woman." Expression is less important to woman's beauty. The woman's face "must be that of a totality without history." Since "the sleeping state is the expression for the absence of spirit," the child and the woman, like Venus, are more beautiful in sleep than awake. Kierkegaard has said earlier that "awake, the difference between myself and my other is posited; sleeping it is suspended."[108] Thus woman, enclosed in the ahistorical sleep of the spirit, cannot possess either self-aware subjectivity or individuality. Language, the tool of self-definition, also eludes her: "Silence is not only woman's greatest wisdom but also her highest beauty."[109] Ethically, woman's highest ethical imperative is procreation. Her desire is necessarily for her husband, but "although it is true that the husband's desire is for her, his life does not culminate in this desire, unless his life is wretched or lost."[110]

Kierkegaard uses the story of Adam and Eve both as illustration and as rationale for his analysis of woman. He writes:

Eve is a derived creature. To be sure, she is created like Adam, but she is created out of a previous creature. To be sure, she is innocent like Adam, but there is, as it were, a presentiment or a disposition that indeed is not sinfulness but may seem like a hint of the sinfulness that is posited by propagation.[111]

Even in translation, the trickiness of simultaneously claiming Eve's innocence and the existence, *in her original, pre-Fall created condition,* of the "presentiment of a disposition" or "hint" of the sinfulness that is inevitably entailed in propagation is evident. Eve's incipient predilection is, moreover, a physical property, both signaled by and contained in her body. She was designed and created for propagation. The female body, before the Fall, was already precariously tilted, by its aesthetic and ethical functions, toward the Fall that will make her sensuousness sinful.

Representations of nakedness in the moments before and after the fall of the human race reveal a great deal about discourse of sexuality and gender in the societies of the Christian West. Four of the accounts of the story of Adam and Eve in the Garden of Eden we explored are by male authors; one is by a woman. Hildegard of Bingen's account differs in at least one fundamental aspect from the interpretations of Saints Ambrose and Augustine, Luther, and Kierkegaard. Both celibate and married male authors place blame for the entrance of sin into the world squarely on Eve, whose weakness or malicious seduction of Adam initiated the condition of punishment and misery that has haunted the human race ever since. Hildegard, however, understands Eve as victimized by the serpent, as the unsuspecting dupe of *his* deceit. Luther, the married man among the male authors, sympathized in a more urgent, detailed, and lengthy way with Eve's punishment, seeing in woman's confinement to the home, subordination to her husband, and painful childbearing much benefit for the men and children she nourishes, but little for the woman herself except the rather unsubstantial "glory of motherhood."

The problems of fallen sexuality are also formulated differently by the different authors. Hildegard, with her extensive knowledge of contemporary women's experience of menstruation, sex, and childbirth, finds the loss of physiological and psychological complementarity and mutuality in lovemaking to be one of the most intimate and painful evidences of fallen sexuality. Eve's subordination to her husband carries, for Hildegard, the indirect but harsh result that his sexuality—his pace, momentum, and urgency—govern the sexual act just as his psychological and intellectual agenda—his needs, desires, and wishes—rule the public sphere. Hildegard's life in a female monastery and her committed attention to women's medical and emotional experience enabled her to become the conduit for a collective female voice whose reading of the story of Adam and Eve differed greatly from that of the male authors who influenced mainstream Christianity.

Do male authors never describe fallen sexuality as a lack of mutuality? Several of those we reviewed, like Luther, describe a new and problematic relation to the body, signaled by experiencing nakedness as humiliating, or even, like Augustine, display an almost neurasthenic awareness of the embarrassment of uncontrollable sexual responses. Yet their primary and fundamental concerns are different from Hildegard's. The issues for Ambrose, Augustine, Luther, and Kierkegaard revolve much more around the implications of the Fall for gender politics. Even though they envision sex in paradise as pleasurable, they do not permit that vision of an ideal sexuality to inform either an analysis of the inadequacy of contemporary sexual and social arrangements or a proposal for more just and equitable relationships. Instead, accepting the fallen condition as normative for social and sexual relations, they seek to justify the necessity, if not the positive goodness, of contemporary society. To be sure, Hildegard does not advocate the reformation of society or the social equality of men and women. Though she herself expected to act with authority and effectiveness, not only in her monastery but also, as her correspondence reveals, in her dealings with powerful people, in her writings she settles for identifying the spiritual compensations that can alleviate women's subjection. Her solution to the denigration of women and their social and sexual subordination is, in Barbara Newman's phrase, "symbolic exaltation and pragmatic subjection."[112]

Beneath male authors' complaints about Eve's role in bringing evil, sin, and death into the world lies a leitmotif that supplies the rationale for acceptance, or even vigorous reinforcement, of contemporary social arrangements and gender politics. Their proposal that Adam fell into sin because he trusted, loved, and did not want to disappoint his wife carries special significance because it is not so much as hinted at in the Genesis text. For example, Luther, proposing this interpretation of Adam's sin with some diffidence, says that he "[does] not disapprove" of the opinion that Adam ate the proferred fruit because "he was unwilling to cause sadness for his delight, that is, for his wife."[113] Augustine also finds Adam's excessive love for, and attachment to, Eve the primary motivation for his choice. This interpretation carries an implicit warning to men: to maintain the autonomy required for ruling the home and for exercising public responsibility, men must not allow themselves to assume Adam's posture in relation to "their own Eve"; they must not love too much, or permit themselves to enjoy sexual and social relationships of mutuality and interdependence. Indeed, perhaps one of the reasons for the repetition of the story of the woman's disobedience and seduction was the reminder and incentive the story provided to men to separate themselves from seductive intimacy and deny their interdependence with the women they loved.[114]

Although the authors we have explored insist that confirmation of the unity of man and woman was intended by Eve's creation from Adam, each suggests that, in fact, gender hierarchy actually existed, at least latently, in the very creation of Eve. Her body itself was the first and decisive proof of her status in relation to Adam: she was created to help Adam in the work of propagating the human race. Thus, woman was sex object even before the Fall, though in paradise she was not limited to this role. Although Eve's subordination became explicit and deserved after the Fall, it would have existed, albeit spontaneously and without resentment, in paradise.

The perspective of male exegetes is also evident when they discuss the nakedness of Adam and Eve after the Fall and their covering of their genitals. Augustine describes the reason for the "sudden embarrassment at nakedness" as insubordinate "movements" of the flesh. Since female sexual arousal is not visibly apparent, his model is clearly male sexual arousal. Though he protests that the genitals are "honorable" and "useful," they are covered because they have also become shameful. Curiously, however, even if the male sexual organ displays the most visible willfulness—or "mind of its own"—it is the female who is identified with her sexual and reproductive organs.

Differences in interpretations of the Genesis story of the creation of Adam and Eve and the fall of the human race are instructive, not primarily in suggesting that men and women interpret a mythical account of origin from different perspectives. Sex difference alone is not decisive in producing difference of interpretation, even in such intimate matters as sexual relationships. Moreover, women who have been educated to see the world from the perspective of the collective male voice of the public sphere are far more numerous than are women who see differently and express distinctively their vision of the world. Even Hildegard incorporated inherited interpretations of the Genesis story. Rather, what these different interpretations reveal is that the social setting in which authors live—their institutional commitments, personal relationships, and lifestyles—inevitably shape their vision and interpretation. In addition, interpretation is both privileged and limited by the generosity, flexibility, and subtlety with which the author understands her or his own life. It is also dependent on cultural conditions. Finally, whether an interpretation enters and influences the mainstream of a religious tradition is contingent on whether or not that interpretation can claim the authority of a collective voice, constructed in the public sphere.

# 4

## THE FEMALE BODY AS FIGURE

*From a woman sin had its beginning, and because of her we all die.*[1]

*And a sweet melody filled the bright air—*
*   so sweet that I reproached in righteous zeal*
*   Eve's fatal recklessness. How could she dare?—*
*One woman alone, made but a moment since—*
*   all heaven and all earth obedient—to refuse*
*   the one veil willed by High Omnipotence;*
*beneath which, had she stayed God's acolyte,*
*   I should have known before then, and for longer*
*   —those raptures of ineffable delight.*[2]

*The originator of sin was a woman, formed from the side of Adam; but when Jesus came to grant pardon freely to men and women alike, he was pierced in the side for woman's sake, to undo the sin.*[3]

In the last chapter I discussed several influential interpretations of the Genesis story of the creation of Adam and Eve and their fall—decisive for their descendants—into a state of sinfulness. The commentaries of Augustine, Ambrose, Hildegard, Luther, and Kierkegaard, however, were not, in their own time, popular reading matter. Before the advent of printing at the end of the fifteenth century, these texts were inaccessible to all but a few scholars and monks. But their ideas, interpretations, and attitudes circulated widely in sermons, popular devotional texts, religious dramas, and, most importantly, paintings. Eve's culpable flesh, the flesh of every woman, was sculptured in stone on cathedral facades, painted in illustrated gospel books, on church walls and ceilings, and set in delicate mosaic tesserae. Few subjects were as fascinating to medieval and Renaissance people, if we are to understand frequency of treatment as continuing interest, as the flesh of the first woman, the prototypical woman, who was seduced by the insinuating serpent.

Religious visual images, though frequently called the "books of the illiterate" by both historical and modern authors, were a common source of religious instruction for the educated and uneducated, rich and poor, women and men of the Christian societies of the West. Until the Italian Renaissance, when artists began to interpret traditional scenes more boldly and idiosyncratically, artists were skilled craftsmen, conduits of common opinions and interpretations, translators into color and shape of the characters and events most significant for the community. While it is clearly impossible, lacking evidence, to reconstruct what people thought or felt when they worshiped in a church covered with frescoes and mosaics, it is nonetheless possible to identify popularly accessible interpretive tools—scriptural passages, liturgical lectionaries, sermons, and devotional manuals—that told them the meaning of the pictures they contemplated.

The methods by which modern people attempt to reconstruct and understand the past can, if we are not careful, obscure aspects of the past that were evident and pressing to historical people. For example, historians are interested in identifying the distinctive features of historical situations, the particularities of people's construction of reality, and the peculiar needs and pressures that motivated them. This interest in the unique has been important in overcoming historical generalizations and oversimplifications; it has steered historians to evidence that had been ignored. A wealth of practical information has been gleaned from documents and records as new questions prompted investigation of popular belief and culture, women's lives and work, and social, economic, and political arrangements. These studies have immeasurably enriched the discipline of history, both in new knowledge and in the articulation of self-conscious and self-critical methodologies.

Nonetheless, interest in the particular and the unique can lead to neglect of continuities across historical societies in the Christian West. In fact, the religious stories and visual images that were repeated in many geographical locations for centuries not only provided raw material that could, no doubt, be interpreted in various ways according to the interests of communities and individuals, but also carried a continuity with earlier societies that was more than superficial. Generations of people consciously and unconsciously shaped themselves to ideas, attitudes, and social and religious values formulated by their religious heritage and institutionalized in the legal, social, and ecclesiastical structures of their societies. Religious ideas and images produced, across centuries, societies with some astonishingly similar values. Thus, although it is important for historians to assume the dissimilarity of societies and to look for their particularities, rather than to assume "the more things change, the more they stay the same," to place continuities and similarities in the silent background of historical reconstruction is to give the impression that historical people chose and developed "from scratch" their symbolic representations of reality.

In previous chapters we examined some of the practices and textual representations by which the societies of the Christian West maintained and reproduced gender relations. Male dominance and female subordination are characteristic of societies in which men design and administer the public sphere. However, the cohesive force of strong societies is not achieved by the coercion of behavior and belief; rather, "strong power," as Michel Foucault has argued, effectively *attracts* people to the beliefs and behavior necessary for the maintenance of society. If people are to be attracted to certain values, attitudes, and explanatory myths, a variety of methods and media must be employed. Certainly, language plays a large role; stories, admonition, debate and discussion—all verbal exchanges— define, express, and extend common interests. But no society in the Christian West neglected the powerful medium of religious images; even cultures that practiced and advocated iconoclasm proscribed only certain kinds of images.[4] Religious images were central in training religious sensibilities, educating values, and formulating and expressing common interests.

Thus, telling and showing the story of Adam and Eve was not a matter of merely historical or mythical interest in the Christian West. Rather, this story told people something fundamental about human life and relationships in the present. The Genesis story was contemporary in its performative value; it explained, oriented, rationalized, and reinforced the social world as seen and experienced every day, giving an "aura of facticity" to social and sexual arrangements.[5] As I argued in the previous chapter, Eve, more than any other scriptural character, was the basis for a fictional figure of "woman" that allowed men to feel that they understood both the "nature" of actual women and appropriate male roles and responsibilities in relation to women.

Other scriptural women also provided images of women that could structure women's self-images and suggest the roles they should—or should not—fill in the family and in society. Representations of the Virgin formulated the valued and valuable, the obedient, nourishing, empathic and maternal woman; but devotional texts and sermons usually emphasized the contrasts, rather than the similarities, between the Virgin and actual women.[6] Moreover, Mary of Magdala, a composite figure drawn from eight different scriptural accounts, might be seen as the New Testament parallel to Eve. Mary Magdalene, like Eve, was a sinful and repentant woman, bearing her self-imposed penance as Eve bore her punishment, humbly and obediently. In spite of the popularity of the Virgin, Mary Magdalene, and a host of other scriptural women and female saints, however, it was the figure of Eve that defined the nature and potential of all women. Eve stood for—and replaced—the bodies of particular and actual women in the discourse on gender of the societies of the Christian West.[7] For example, the figure Eve explained the significance of women's suffering in childbirth. Women suffer because Eve was the first to sin, hence the learned opinion, often repeated in sermons and theological writings, that the Virgin, the only woman who did not share Eve's sin, did not have physical suffering in bearing Christ.

In this chapter I will examine some representational practices by which woman's "nature" was characterized visually. My discussion of Eve and several other naked women who were the frequent objects of visual representation will not attempt to summarize images of female nakedness in the Christian West. Nor will I identify "positive" and "negative" images of female nakedness in the iconography of the Christian West.[8] Judgments of positivity or negativity tend to reveal much more about the judge and her or his cultural presuppositions than they do about the image in its culture of origin. Rather, by exploring some naked female "figures," I will seek to identify the pictorial strategies or devices by which women's bodies are presented as revealing their "nature." I will show that in the representation of woman as sensual, sinful, or threatening, whether in images of Eve, Susanna, grotesque figures, or witches, the primary pictorial device by which the problem of "woman"—for men— is signaled is female nakedness. Finally, I will compare treatments of male nakedness, especially Christ's nakedness, with depictions of female nakedness in sixteenth-century Renaissance and Reformation central Europe.

Furthermore, I will show that when women's "nature" is presented as the equivalent of women's subjectivity, women can be viewed not only as inherently weak, flawed, and susceptible to error and temptation, but

also as consciously and deliberately malign, sinning not by accidental in-
discretion but by willful design. The purposeful wickedness of woman
was viewed as coming directly from her body, unlike male sin, which, as
Gregory the Great and a host of others insisted, comes from the spirit.[9]
The *Malleus Maleficarum,* a manual on how to identify, interrogate, and
execute witches that was printed and reprinted fourteen times between
1486 and 1520,[10] reported gravely:

[That a woman] is more carnal than a man is clear from her many carnal abominations. And it should be noted that there was a defect in the formation of the
first woman, since she was formed from a bent rib, that is, a rib of the breast,
which is bent as it were in a contrary direction to a man. And since through this
defect she is an imperfect animal, she always deceives. . . . All witchcraft comes
from carnal lust, which is in women insatiable.[11]

As we saw in the preceding chapter, the first theological meaning of
nakedness was the innocence, fragility, and vulnerability of human
bodies as created. In visual images the creation of Adam and Eve follows
the Genesis account in depicting Adam's creation from the dust of the
earth by the breath of God. Eve's creation was from Adam's side; in
paintings, mosaics, and bas reliefs from cathedral facades a vertical Eve
appears to float upward from a slit in the side of the horizontal Adam. In
the earliest Christian painting, in catacombs like that of Peter and Marcellinus, a naked Adam and Eve awkwardly hunch forward to cover their
genitals. Visual interest is equally distributed to Adam's and Eve's bodies
as both appear frontally, of the same size, and with the same lack of detailed articulation (see figure 6).

Depictions of the Fall, however, focus visual interest on Eve and on
her initiative in sin. A fourteenth-century mosaic from Monreale shows
Adam and Eve standing on each side of a stylized tree; Adam points at
Eve, and she points at the serpent. A bas relief from the facade of Notre
Dame du Port foregrounds a naked and corpulent Eve standing next to
the tree; Adam recedes on her right. Adam's foot is positioned on top of
hers, indicating his superiority to her. Medieval people, noticing the figure of a naked woman with pendulous breasts on the facade of the local
cathedral would associate that stone flesh with original sin and with the
fall of the human race.[12]

Scriptural women, some of them minor figures whose recurring appearance in paintings is puzzling, are also repeatedly depicted as naked.
We will examine only one such figure. The apocryphal book Susanna

tells the story of a beautiful ruling-class woman—a daughter, wife, and mother—who was framed by two men, powerful judges in Israel, who tried to seduce her. The Elders, desiring Susanna, hid in the private garden where she bathed and approached her when she had sent her maids away. They threatened to accuse her of adultery if she did not yield to them, but Susanna refused them. The next day they summoned her for trial before the leaders and people of Israel and obtained her condemnation. As she was being led to execution, however, a young man, Daniel, protested her innocence and tricked the Elders into revealing their deceit. The two Elders were put to death and Susanna was vindicated.

There are several points in this literary account that are worthy of notice before we examine some visual treatments of the story of Susanna and the Elders. First, Susanna was utterly passive in the face of an unjust judgment, though she was anything but passive in private when the Elders importuned her to transgress.[13] She did not tell her husband—a man fully as powerful as the Elders—her side of the story. Nor did she speak at her impromptu trial, at which she arrived veiled, as if in shame.[14] She implores God for justice, protesting her innocence, but she is otherwise helpless and passive until Daniel, her unexpected champion, speaks for her. In the story, she is alone in a world of men, without voice. Second, we should notice that in the story the assumptions of the self-righteous community that was ready to execute Susanna without hearing *her* story are never questioned. Wicked leaders are exposed and executed, thereby purging the community of corruption in high places and returning it to equilibrium. The legal, political, and social arrangements within which a woman—even one who belongs to a respected and powerful family—received no human protection from becoming a victim of false accusation and condemnation were not examined. Rather, God, as *deus ex machina,* functioned as guarantor of the justness of Israel's institutions.

As a tale of miraculous deliverance, the story of Susanna and the Elders was depicted in the first Christian art of the catacombs and on early Christian sarcophagi.[15] References to the story were abundant and diverse in patristic and medieval literature. It was not, however, until the sixteenth century that the frequency and vividness of visual renditions indicates a widespread fascination with the story. In the literary account, Susanna is voiceless; in visual depictions, she is naked and her body moves to center stage to occupy the viewer's attention.[16] Judging from the frequency of depictions of the moment in which the Elders spied

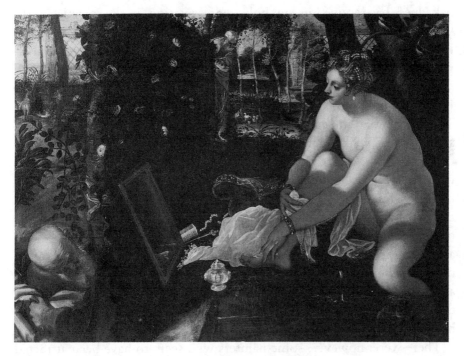

15

TINTORETTO
*Susanna and the Elders*, 1560
Kunsthistorisches Museum, Vienna (Art Resource, New York)

on Susanna at her bath, it seems to have been this aspect of the story
that most captured the imagination of painters and viewers alike. In
Tintoretto's version (figure 15) light fetishizes Susanna's body as the
viewer is placed in the position of the Elders, spying on her, a voyeur,
enjoying her body.

These paintings attempt to reproduce, in the eyes of an assumed male
viewer, the Elders' intense erotic attraction, projected and displayed on
Susanna's flesh. The Elders, placed in crepuscular shadows, do not bear
the weight of communicating the urgency of their active desire; rather,
her body represents that desire. Viewers are directed—trained—by the
management of light and shadow and by the central position of Susanna's
body to see Susanna as object, even as cause, of male desire. In the paintings Susanna's innocence becomes guilt as her body communicates and
explains the Elders' lust. As this visual narration illustrates, female

nakedness has received its symbolic representation, in the societies of the Christian West, from "the Elders." Female nakedness has a range of meanings assigned by voyeurs for whom female bodies represented simultaneously threat, danger, and delight.

Sixteenth- and seventeenth-century paintings of Susanna and the Elders illustrate more than a perennial fascination with female nakedness. They also reveal the existence of a visual culture in which it was impossible to paint a naked female body in such a way that it symbolized innocence. Since the act of vision itself is informed and directed by culturally trained visual associations and by an interpretive lexicon, the possibility of seeing Susanna's nakedness as innocence was blocked by repeatedly reiterated and reinforced associations of female nakedness with Eve and original sin. In addition, most painters of the theme were apparently well aware that female nakedness did not, and perhaps could not, connote innocence; they collaborated with visual convention in fetishizing Susanna's body by using the devices we have noted—Susanna's placement in the picture frame, and lighting that emphasizes the curves and planes of her body.

There were, however, some painters who seem to have been attracted to the theme for the challenge it presented of painting a naked woman as innocent. Rembrandt, for example, perhaps recognized this challenge and struggled to overcome visual associations of female nakedness with sin and guilt. His 1637 *Susanna Surprised by the Elders* depicts a partially draped Susanna whose feet are thrust into baggy slippers. She is simultaneously turning away from the Elders who approach from the background and the viewer standing in front of the painting. Even Rembrandt, however, was not successful in overcoming visual convention, either in the 1637 painting or in a painting on the same theme done in 1647 (figure 16) in which Susanna's unbalanced, shrinking pose from the 1637 painting is repeated exactly, although in the earlier painting she is seated and in the later one she descends steps into the pool. By the later painting Rembrandt apparently surrendered to visual convention; he has eliminated the awkward slippers and has placed Susanna's body in a stronger light in relation to the dark background. In the societies of the Christian West, the story of Susanna and the Elders apparently could not be translated into a visual image that accurately preserved the story's emphasis on Susanna's innocence. In the visual mode, Susanna's nakedness inevitably contradicted her virtue.

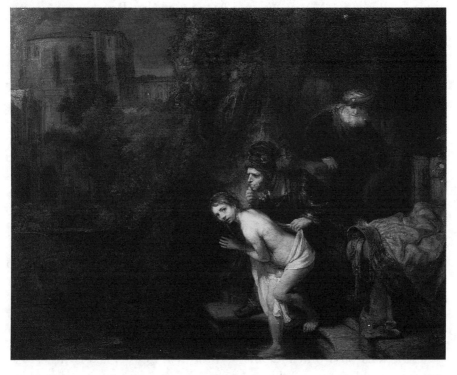

16
—

**REMBRANDT**
*Susanna and the Elders,* 1647
Staatliche Museum, Berlin (Art Resource, New York)

Although, as we have seen, a naked female figure cannot communicate innocence, it easily communicates sin, sex, and evil. A historically located example, a group of images by a single sixteenth-century artist, Hans Baldung Grien, will enable us to examine the convergence of some iconographical motifs and social conditions in which Eve, "woman," and witches symbolize evil and danger. Before examining some images of female nakedness created by Baldung, let us consider the society in which these images appeared. Ever since Joan Kelly-Gadol's article, "Did Women Have a Renaissance?" questioned the use of the term "Renaissance" for describing the situation of women, historians have been adding documentation to her conclusion that women in fact lost significant ground in southern Europe in the period traditionally labeled "the Renaissance."[17] Recently, Merry Wiesner has argued that Renaissance women defined "freedom" as access to the public sphere and showed that it was precisely in this sphere that women were losing traditional roles in professional and commercial life due to increasing legal restrictions. This progressive curtailment of women's economic and social power "continued over centuries," Wiesener writes, "eventually restricting not only upper-class women . . . but middle- and lower-class women as well."[18] Martha Howell came to a similar conclusion from her study of urban women's roles in market production in late medieval cities of northern Europe. Legal changes accompanied loss of labor status by the sixteenth century; concurrently, "women's lives were increasingly centered in a newly constructed patriarchal household."[19] Based on her work on early modern France, Natalie Zemon Davis writes:

Women suffered for their powerlessness in both Catholic and Protestant lands in the sixteenth to eighteenth centuries as changes in marriage laws restricted the freedom of wives even further, as female guilds dwindled, as the female role in middle-level commerce and farm direction contracted, and as the differential between male and female wages increased.[20]

Restrictions on women's ability "to be witnesses, make wills, act as guardians for their own children, make contracts, and own, buy, and sell property" also attest to a dramatically shrinking female sphere. Moreover, in the sixteenth and seventeenth centuries in many areas, women were required to have a male guardian "who was to oversee their financial affairs and appear for them in court."[21] Professional women and craftswomen—female medical practitioners and midwives, weavers, and widows of master craftsmen who continued to administer their husbands' shops after their deaths—frequently brought to court grievances against their guardians as well as grievances relating to the curtailment of their public roles. These court cases were usually individual, not collective grievances, a fact that itself suggests that women had limited access to the public sphere in which collective action might have emerged. As Wiesner argues:

(There were) few women's guilds or other corporate bodies in which women could develop a sense of work identity. . . . Ceremonies which celebrated women's work identity were very rare, in contrast to the huge number of parades, banquets, drinking parties, and festivals in which men participated as members of a craft.[22]

Since restrictions on women's public activity all rested on the distinction between public and private realms, Wiesner writes, women "stressed the connection, not the distinction, between the public and the private spheres, a continuity from the household to the world beyond."[23]

In this context in which women were fighting to define their own public roles, female nakedness became the focus of a newly explicit public figuration. The struggle over whether women would represent themselves in the public sphere or whether they would be forced to retreat from the public sphere occurred at the same time that female nakedness was fetishized in art. While new laws were relegating women to the private sphere and isolating them from collective voice, the female body at its most private and naked was presented as a symbol of specific evil, not the general evil of the fall of "man," but the carefully documented evil of witchcraft. Although he was not the only artist in southern Germany who worked on the themes of female nakedness, Eve, and witchcraft, Hans Baldung Grien created graphic images that reflect public controversies over women and their roles evident in Renaissance literature and society.[24]

Baldung came from a prominent family of educated professionals, mostly lawyers, and was independently wealthy. His brother was a professor of law and his uncle was the personal physician to Maximilian I. Shortly before his death Baldung was elected to serve as a senator on the Strasbourg city council.[25] A Protestant, he worked in Strasbourg for most of his life, where, in 1529–30 Protestant iconoclasm destroyed much of the painting he had done for churches; however, his woodcuts, printed in large editions, as well as paintings for private patrons were not destroyed and they form a sizeable enough collection to provide a rather wide view of his work.

One of the most skillful and innovative artists in Germany in the first half of the sixteenth century, Baldung developed what one of his commentators has called a "heightened awareness of the theology of the Fall."[26] In his work a new and increasingly explicit visual connection is made between Eve, sex, and death.

In a 1514 woodcut (figure 17) depicting the Fall, Adam, Eve, and the serpent pose between verdant trees. A new sensuousness characterizes the idyllic natural surroundings of the first couple: lush growth explodes everywhere. Eve's hair mingles and blends into tree branches and leaves while Adam's curls into hers. Two rabbits, symbols of fertility, gambol

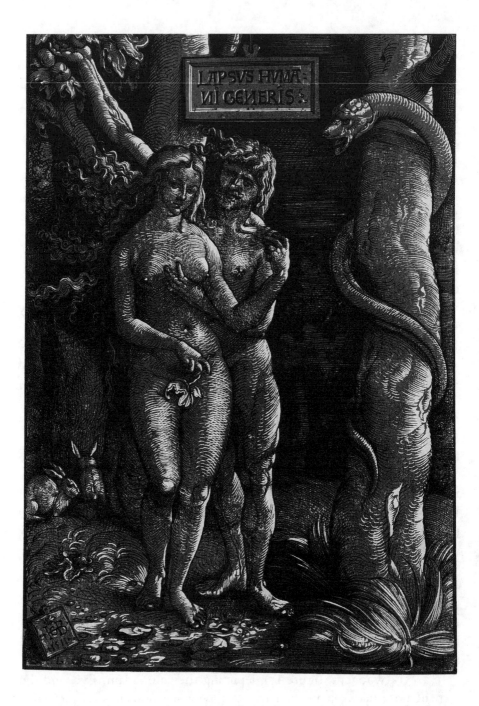

LAPSVS HVMA-
NI GENERIS.

17
HANS BALDUNG
*The Fall,* 1511
Öffentliche Kunstsammlung, Kupferstichkabinett, Basel

nearby. Even the serpent curls sensuously around the tree trunk, directing its gaze and venomous tongue at Eve. Adam's body is modeled with
rippling muscles that are mirrored in the swirls of the tree trunk. Eve,
less muscled but fully fleshed, adopts a demure, unbalanced stance, as she
holds an apple up and backward to Adam. A newly explicit sexuality also
appears;[27] Adam, in a gesture that parallels Eve's offering of the fruit,
offers Eve's left breast to the viewer. Both stare at the viewer in a medi-
tative mood. Adam's genitals are hidden by Eve's body, hers by a twig
she holds. With his left hand, Adam reaches behind Eve to grasp an apple
from the tree, not accepting the one Eve hands him—or, perhaps, implying his simultaneous acceptance of the apple and his offering of it, as
Eve's breast, to the viewer.

In 1515 Baldung painted a couple in a similar posture. *Death and the
Maiden,* a drawing in pen and wash, heightened with white, shows death
presenting a naked woman to the viewer as she turns aside, preoccupied,
to gaze at her reflection in a mirror (figure 18).[28] Like Adam in *The Fall,*
death approaches the maiden from behind. Baldung was the first artist to
personify death as a corpse. But Baldung's corpses are not the properly
coffined bodies of earlier centuries; these corpses could not be more active—ambushing, raping, murdering, and dancing with the living. In
another oil-on-wood painting on the same theme in about 1517, a new
element of horror emerges as Death no longer appears to fondle the
woman (figure 19). Instead, his partially decomposed left hand scratches
her breast deeply while his teeth, in a caricature of a kiss, are poised to
bite into her cheek. Again, the woman is positioned frontally, her robe
falling in a way that emphasizes but still covers her genitals.

Two more of Baldung's paintings of Adam and Eve will occupy us
briefly. *Eve, the Serpent, and Death* (figure 20), an oil on panel painted
early in Baldung's career (1510–12),[29] seems to omit one of the central
characters in the Genesis story—Adam—in order to depict instead
death's first appearance in the Garden of Eden. Eve's body is presented
frontally, exposed to the viewer. She clutches the apple in her right hand,
while Death grips her left arm with his left hand. Death's flesh is flayed in
places to reveal bone, and it hangs in shreds from his knee and shin. Perhaps, however, Adam has not been left out of the painting, but has become the corpse. The focus of the painting lies just above the center and
slightly to the right (figure 21), where a knot of interrelated gestures
presents, in abbreviated form, the whole saga of the Fall: Eve holds—
perhaps strokes—the serpent's tail, while Death grips Eve's left arm in a

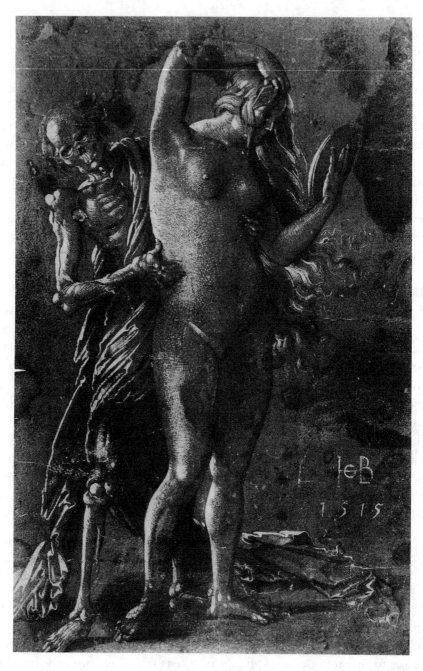

18

HANS BALDUNG
*Death and the Maiden*, 1515
Staatliche Museum, Berlin (Art Resource, New York)

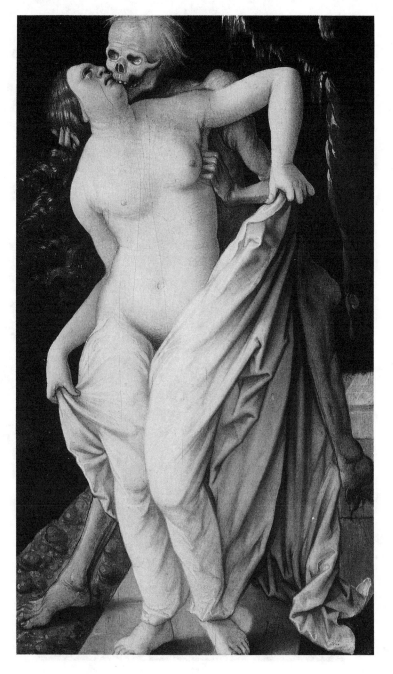

19

HANS BALDUNG
*Death and the Maiden*, 1517
Öffentliche Kunstsammlung, Kunstmuseum, Basel

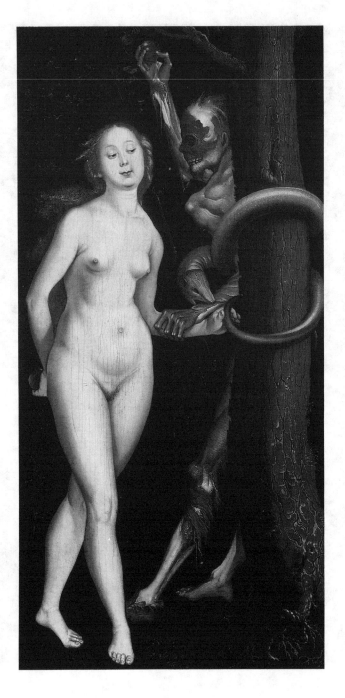

20

HANS BALDUNG
*Eve, the Serpent, and Death*, 1510–12
National Gallery of Canada, Ottawa

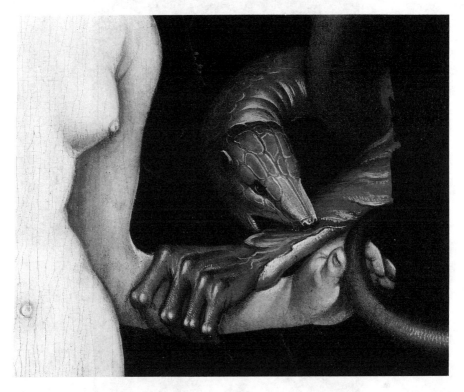

21

Detail, *Eve, the Serpent, and Death*

knuckle-whitening clutch and the serpent bites his/Adam's bony wrist. The viewer's eye is directed from Eve's body to her left arm, by the serpent's circled body to the serpent's head and thereby to Death's/Adam's hand. Eve's body initiates the eye movement just as it initiated the chain of events by which Adam became a walking corpse.

In a painting approximately twenty years later (figure 22), Baldung repeats a gesture in *The Fall* as Adam turns Eve's naked body toward the viewer, cupping her breast and articulating her hip with his left hand. In this painting, Adam has become Eve's impresario, displaying her nakedness to the viewer. He stands behind her in the shadows, framing her, while she stands hypnotized in the foreground. Here no serpent distracts, and Adam has only one conspicuous feature: his left eye leers at the viewer with a lecherous glint. Joseph Koerner explains the "fallen sexuality" of this painting:

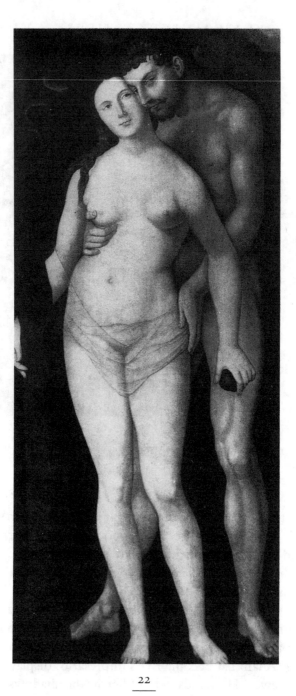

22

HANS BALDUNG
*Adam and Eve, 1536*
Collection of Baron H. H. Thyssen–Bornemisza, Lugano–Castagnola
(Art Resource, New York)

Adam not only gazes out of the painted space toward us, he also looks as if he were regarding himself in a mirror, fascinated by the sight of his own flesh making contact with Eve's body. . . . He wants both to touch Eve and to see himself touching her; thus he turns his head toward her, resting his cheek against hers, while at the same time looking off to the right to see his gesture mirrored. And he takes care to handle her body so that everything remains exposed and yet appears touched by him. We, of course, stand where this mirror would be. Adam's leering eye fixes us in its gaze, making us accomplices in a fallen sexuality.[30]

Baldung, Koerner says, was "the first artist ever to represent the Fall as an overtly erotic act."[31] In the Genesis account, we will recall, fallen sexuality followed—did not cause—the Fall. Moreover, by implying the gaze of an assumed male viewer,[32] Baldung explicitly associates the Fall "with voyeurism, with fallen sexuality as perverted vision, or scopophilia." As a "party to Adam's desires we [that is, male viewers] recognize our true kinship with Adam."[33]

Thus far I have assumed that Baldung's naked Eves and maidens are erotic. I have implied either that they strike the "we" of Koerner's description as erotic or that the artist, knowing his audience, intended that they arouse male desire. But "erotic" is not, after all, a "self-evident, universal category, but a culturally defined concept."[34] That Baldung's Eves were, in fact, erotic images in their own time needs to be shown rather than claimed.

Let us begin by assuming that "erotic" means erotic for heterosexual men.[35] Were Baldung's Eves, then, erotic? They may not seem so to "us," so how can we hope to recover the "period eye"[36] in order to make a judgment about their effect on viewers in their own time?

Anne Hollander has proposed a method for identifying erotic bodies in the visual representations of historical societies. In her book *Seeing Through Clothes,* she argues that fashions exist to produce erotic attraction. In the clothed societies of the Christian West, the object of daily perception is the "body-and-clothes unit." When one looks at a naked body, Hollander claims, the "implied absent clothing" is still associated with the body, providing the body's specific eroticism for the viewer. Clothing has shaped the body as visual socialization has trained the viewer to find certain bodies more beautiful than others.

Renaissance female nudes, for example, exhibit the small high breasts, short waist, and rounded belly that are found in clothed figures of the time. Modish costume required "long, heavy skirts spreading out from below a tiny rib cage, encased in a meagerly cut bodice with high, confining armholes." The belly must "thrust its sexy swell through the fabric" of the skirt; indeed, "in the erotic imagination of Europe, it was apparently impossible until the late seventeenth century for a woman to have too big a belly." Heavy breasts, however, Hollander writes, "are characteristic of ugly women and witches."[37]

Clearly Baldung's nudes fulfilled in their own time the criteria for an erotic female body. They both represented and evoked male desire. That was the point of Baldung's new visual interpretation of the Fall: Eve's body, offered to the sixteenth-century male viewer, did not merely symbolize but effectively reproduced the lust that, in Baldung's reinterpretation, simultaneously caused and resulted from the Fall. But, as I argued earlier, representations do not simply reflect society; they also reproduce cultural attitudes, styles of relationship, and social arrangements.[38] And Eve's naked body also evoked fear by reiterating, in an intensified iconography, the singularly disastrous moment of the doom of the human race. Moreover, a sixteenth-century viewers' association of fear with sex may not have been purely theological. The first epidemic of syphilis to sweep Europe occurred at the end of the fifteenth century.[39] Martin Luther recalled the terror occasioned by this new and dread epidemic in his commentary on Genesis 3: "When I was a boy, syphilis was unknown in Germany. It first became known when I was about fifteen years old. Now even children in the cradle are stricken with this evil. In those days everyone was terrified by this disease."[40]

Baldung's naked Eves and maidens provide an iconographical connection to another part of his artistic work in which the naked female body is even more insistently associated with evil—his paintings and drawings of witches. He was the first fine artist to depict witchcraft with some frequency. Before Baldung other fine artists—like his teacher, Albrecht Dürer—had treated the theme only occasionally, but broadsheets relayed information about the deeds, trials, and executions of witches and were often illustrated with crude woodcuts. Baldung's naked witches bear a striking resemblance to his Eves and maidens. By showing young and old women, erotic nudes and naked crones as equally susceptible to the evil of witchcraft, Baldung painted what the *Malleus Maleficarum* had stated about fifty years earlier, namely that "all women are naturally prone to evil through their weak, corruptible will and their insatiable lust"[41] (figure 23). Baldung's depictions of witches as Eve or as any "maiden" reflected a society in which whole communities—rich and

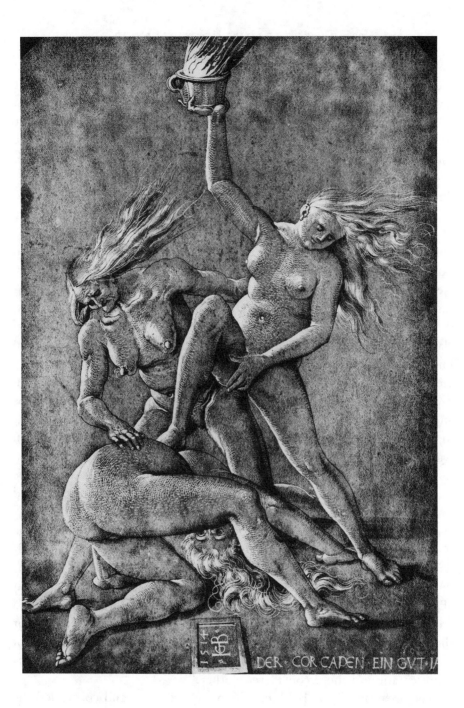

23

HANS BALDUNG
*Three Witches*, 1514
Albertina, Vienna (Art Resource, New York)

poor, educated and uneducated, aristocrat and peasant—agreed that most witches were women and all women were potential witches. The fleshly bodies of these witches, and their frequent placement in a verdant and promiscuous landscape, further reinforce their association with the scene in the Garden of Eden. As Linda Hults has shown, witches were thought of as simultaneously deluded and powerless, ridiculous and evil, deceived and guilty, duped by the devil and morally responsible. Baldung's witches, by their iconographical associations with naked Eves and maidens, imply that witchcraft is nothing more than an extreme instance of endemic female vice and folly.[42]

Does Baldung's identification of the naked female body with sex and sex with witchcraft and death signal an increment of misogyny in six-teenth-century Germany?[43] Could his be an idiosyncratic rather than rep-resentative vision? There are several ways to approach these questions, the most important of which is to insist on caution in making general claims on the basis of the work of one artist. It would also be valuable to know how many of Baldung's woodcuts were printed and to whom they were distributed. Acknowledging the impossibility of demonstrating causal relationships between visual representations and social situations and events should not, however, prevent us making the observation that, in fact, Baldung's work occurred at the same time that witch persecution was scapegoating large numbers of women, and in a geographical region in which more accused witches were burned than in all the rest of Europe put together.[44] It is quite likely that his choice of themes was influenced by his society's current interest in witch burning. One could argue, how-ever, that instead of inevitably reinforcing and helping to reproduce the dominant social attitudes and values, representations may critique, chal-lenge, and reject them or offer alternatives. Baldung's work did not pro-vide a critique of his society's interest in scapegoating women, but aligned its considerable visual force with the physical force that attacked women. It thus illustrates the danger—the literal, physical danger for thousands of women tried and executed as witches—of the projection of a dominant perspective unchallenged either by the artist or by the self-representation of those considered "other."

Have men like Hans Baldung Grien, who created and controlled the public sphere, consciously and willfully misrepresented women? Al-though this may sometimes have been the case, it is more likely that they simply represented women from their own perspectives, uncorrected by women's self-representations. In the visual arts, for example, women painters were not admitted to the academies in which figure drawing from models was taught until the end of the eighteenth century. Even when women were given access to training in artistic skills, they did not—for many social reasons—enter these fields in large enough numbers to construct alternatives to traditional representations of women.

But what of the myriad positive images of women that could be marshalled from this era? "Positive" images of women—that is, images of socially approved women, "good" women from the perspective of the governing male collective—often function not as "rewards" for women, but as prescriptive messages. Positive images define what female "goodness" looks like and urge women to imitate the qualities of these images. Positive images of women, then, play a very important role, even, or especially, in the most misogynist societies. Similarly, misogynist literature consistently pictures and praises good women; frequently an unrealistically inflated sense of women's superiority justifies the author's attack on women who fall from this ideal as most women inevitably must.[45] Praise for the "superiority" of women therefore can operate to justify vilification of women.

Indeed, figures of the ideal woman—like the Virgin—played as important a role in shaping real women's subjectivity and socialization as negative female images that formulated what women must avoid. Together, "positive" and negative figures defined the range of acceptable appearance, attitudes, and behavior prescribed for women. In the Italian altarpiece *The Madonna of Humility with the Temptation of Eve* (figure 24), for example, images of the "good woman" and the "evil woman" are juxtaposed in the same visual field. The Madonna is heavily shrouded in dark clothing that covers her from her neck down except for her hands, which shield the nursing child, and one round breast that juts awkwardly from her right shoulder to feed him. Guarded by angels holding weapons, the Virgin sits without visible support, her head surrounded by a sparkling nimbus while stars and a sun reflect her brilliance. Depiction of the Virgin's body is limited to parts directly in the service of bearing and nourishing the child. Her head tilts protectively over him, and the ear is exposed by which, according to popular tradition, he was conceived.

A flowered frame separates the picture plane occupied by Mary from that in which Eve reclines, apparently pressed by the frame into a space less than a third the size of that occupied by the Madonna and Child.

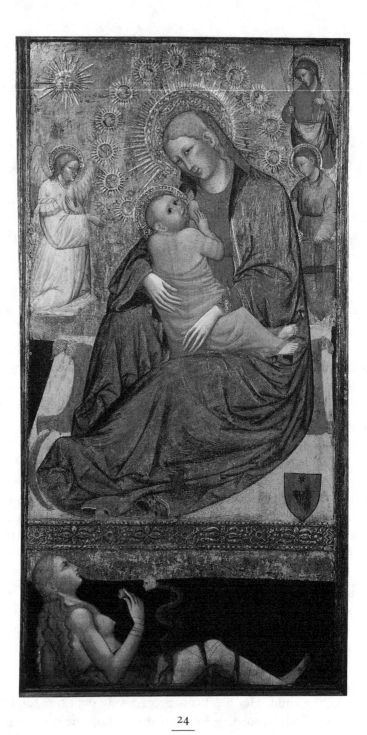

CARLO DA CAMERINO
*The Madonna of Humility with the Temptation of Eve,* late fourteenth century
Cleveland Museum of Art, Holden Collection, 16.795

Naked, Eve balances awkwardly on her elbows as a dark snake curls around her legs, its head raised to stare at a half-eaten apple she holds.

Female good and female evil are clearly identified in these contrasted figures. Despite her monumental bulk, Mary is disembodied, placed in a heavenly setting, with only enough body to protect and nourish the infant Christ. Eve, on the other hand, *is* body. Her plane is earth; plants grow at her eye level as she stretches to see above the dark grave in which she lies. Her naked body—her realistic breast, so different from the Virgin's breast above; her flowing, wavy hair and shapely thigh—signals her sinfulness, just as the Virgin's lack of body reveals her goodness.

It is impossible to identify with precision the social effect on historical women of representations of the female body as literary figure and artistic device. Religious figures like Eve, the Virgin, Susanna, and Mary Magdalene have acted as figures in a male discourse rather than as female subjects. Certainly, there were pockets in Western societies—like female monasteries—in which women's religious subjectivity was cultivated. That there were unusual individual women who were able to enter the male public arena and even to exercise some power and skill in tht arena is also to be acknowledged. But women did not collectively organize social arrangements or define how women were to be publicly represented; both were instead "provided" for women by male collectives. We need simultaneously to admire the ability of some unusual historical women— like Saint Hildegard of Bingen—to conceptualize alternative ways to construe women, the world, and Christianity *and* to recognize that because most women with powerful ideas were restricted in their expression of, and audience for, those ideas, their visions did not become part of a cumulative collective interpretation of Christianity in Western culture.[46]

One way to approach an understanding of the ways representations of female nakedness functioned in the societies of the Christian West is to reconstruct visual representations of male nakedness and its meanings and then to ask if it parallels the treatment of female nakedness. Although we can treat male nakedness only in summary, to do so will help to give us perspective.

Jerome's statement "nudus sequi nudum Christum" (naked to follow a naked Christ) became the basis for an iconographical motif that was frequently used in Renaissance painting, though earlier instances exist.[47] For

example, in Michelangelo's Doni tondo *Holy Family,* in the foreground
the Virgin passes the naked Christchild over her right shoulder to Joseph,
who is seated behind her. In the middle ground naked or stripping male
figures prepare to begin a race symbolic of their commitment to the athletic exercise of asceticism.[48] Similarly, in the *Adoration of the Magi,*
painted by Fra Angelico and Fra Filippo Lippi, small naked figures in
the upper register cavort in athletic exercise. Michelangelo's David, like
Donatello's young David, also displays male nakedness as expressive of
a moment of self-awareness and self-definition.[49] Since antiquity male
nakedness has been used to represent "physical strength as a symbol of
extraordinary spiritual strength."[50] Heroic struggle against temptation, a
sense of personal choice, and single-minded, undistracted pursuit of an
athletic crown characterized spiritual "athletes." Male nakedness represented spiritual discipline and physical control and order—the body as
perfect vehicle and expression of the difficult and committed work of the
creation and cultivation of religious subjectivity.

Other theological meanings cluster around male nakedness, the most
startling of which was explored by Leo Steinberg in *The Sexuality of
Christ in Renaissance Painting and in Modern Oblivion.*[51] Steinberg's thesis is
that in Renaissance imagery the genitals of Christ became the focus of a
new pictorial presentation of the Christian doctrine of the Incarnation.
Paintings of the infant Christ, the crucified Christ, the dead Christ, and
the resurrected Christ have, Steinberg says, "an emphasis on the genitalia
of Christ that is assertive and central." He argues against naturalistic interpretations of depictions of Christ with uncovered genitals. It is not
enough, he insists, to claim that paintings of the infant Christ simply display an unclothed baby. In Renaissance painting, in which every detail of
the painting carried strong visual associations, it is not possible that the
inclusion of Christ's genitals was accidental or haphazard. Rather, Steinberg notes, the nudity of Christ carried a specific doctrinal message: "To
profess that God once embodied himself in a human nature is to confess
that the eternal, there and then, became human and sexual. . . . The evidence of Christ's sexual member serves as a pledge of God's humana-
tion."[52] Supporting his interpretation with a group of sermons delivered
at the papal court between 1450 and 1521, Steinberg argues that a new
attention to the Incarnation prompted this increment of visual specificity:

The Incarnation of the Trinity's Second Person is the centrum of Christian orthodoxy. . . . This much Christendom has professed at all times. Not so Chris-

tian art. . . . For those Western Christians who would revere the Logos in its human presence, it was precisely an "admixture of earthly realism" that was needed. . . . And because Renaissance culture not only advanced an Incarnational theology . . . but evolved representational modes adequate to its expression, we may take Renaissance art to be the first and last phase of Christian art that can claim full Christian orthodoxy. . . . It became the first Christian art in a thousand years to confront the Incarnation entire, the upper and lower body together, and not excluding even the body's sexual component.[53]

Steinberg's illustrations are as startling as is his explanation of their theological import. Christ is repeatedly depicted with deliberately featured genitals in paintings of the Epiphany and circumcision, in paintings and sculptures of Christ on the cross, in depositions and lamentations, and in resurrected glory. In scenes treating the years of Christ's ministry, however, nakedness is absent; Steinberg reasons that during this time in Christ's life, his sexuality "matters in its abeyance: Jesus as exemplar and teacher prevails over concupiscence to consecrate the Christian ideal of chastity."[54]

Although Steinberg's claim that only the exposed male genitals of Christ fully supported Christian orthodoxy is overdrawn, his evidence reveals the existence of a new focus on the unclothed male body in the Renaissance. Prior to the Renaissance the full humanity of Christ had been demonstrated and supported by reference to his birth from a human mother, the "second Eve," who gave her flesh to the redeemer of the first Eve and her descendants. As a continuous stream of late classical and medieval theologians insisted, she was "the great proof of Christ's true humanity."[55] It was her "pure blood" that supplied his flesh, it was she who gave the Word a body. By the Renaissance the pivotal role of Mary in the Incarnation had repeatedly been visually articulated. Medieval paintings and icons show her presenting Christ to the world, his body surrounded by her body and sometimes enclosed in an egg-shaped casement that signified her womb. The bare feet of the infant Christ also signified his human vulnerability in an established iconographical device.[56]

Nevertheless, Steinberg's visual evidence establishes the existence of the phenomenon he noticed: in the Renaissance Christ's nakedness did become a vehicle for showing his humanity, vulnerability, and strength in weakness. The heroic male nakedness of athletic asceticism adds visual associations to Christ's nakedness, constructing a richly complex visual symbol in which strength and weakness, triumph and vulnerability are resolved.

Were female bodies represented as the site of heroic spiritual struggle in the Christian West? One might immediately think of depictions of the Annunciation as a transformative moment for a female subject, a moment when Mary recognized her role in the saga of redemption. Similarly, pietás seem an especially vivid rendering of a woman's inner anguish over the brutal murder of her son. However, several points must be considered. First, and most obviously, these depictions do not parallel treatments of heroic male nakedness by representing female nakedness as the site and symbol of subjective event. Clothed female figures can, of course, signal a transformative subjective event by facial expression or gesture. The clothed body, however, is not as expressive as the naked body, in which subjectivity is written in the lines of the whole body. In Western Christian representations of women, the unambiguously good woman is a clothed woman, a fully socialized woman.[57] But, someone may object, a naked woman is necessarily too erotic to portray heroic spiritual struggle. Exactly! The female body has been, in the societies of the Christian West, so thoroughly "mastered" in representation that viewers' most immediate reaction is to see female nakedness as an object of male desire. In short, there is no iconographical tradition in the Christian West that identifies spiritual struggle or the cultivation of a centered religious self with the female body.

As we have seen, Eve was simultaneously the mother of all human beings and the first sinner. Her naked body was an iconographical device that associated female nakedness with fecundity and evil, sexual desire and death. But female scriptural figures and saints were not the only public representations of the female body. We turn, in the next chapter, to some literary and visual evidence that suggests that female bodies, from the perspective of male fears and fantasies, are not only sinful and dangerous but quintessentially grotesque.

# 5

---

# "CARNAL ABOMINATIONS": THE FEMALE BODY AS GROTESQUE

*The most ridiculous thing of all will be the sight of women naked in the palaestra, exercising with the men.*[1]

*[A woman] is more carnal than a man, as is clear from her many carnal abominations. And it should be noted that there was a defect in the formation of the first woman, since she was formed from a bent rib, that is, a rib of the breast, which is bent as it were in a contrary direction to a man. . . . And all this is indicated by the etymology of the word; for* femina *comes from* fe, *and* minus, *since she is ever weaker to hold and preserve the faith. . . . What else is a woman but a foe to friendship, an inescapable punishment, a necessary evil, a domestic danger, a delectable detriment, an evil of nature, painted with fair colors.*[2]

*A body is docile that may be used, subjected, transformed, and improved.*[3]

One of the most popular travelogues of the later medieval period recounts the prodigious marvels Sir John Mandeville witnessed in his journeys to exotic lands. Sir John reported not only what he claimed were firsthand experiences, but also stories he had heard in the course of after-dinner gossip, introduced by a phrase like "some men say." The land of Amazonia, for example, "is all women and no man . . . because the women will not suffer no men amongst them to be their sovereigns." Sir John records their wondrous relations with men and children:

When they will have any company of man, then they draw them towards the lands marching next to them. Then they have their loves that use them and they dwell with them an eight days or ten, and then go home again. And if they have any knave child, they keep it a certain time and then send it to the father . . . or else they slay it. And if it be a female, they do away with that one pap with an hot iron.[4]

The women of Amazonia were marvels primarily because they had devised a way to be independent of men without relinquishing the prerogatives of childbearing and rearing. They also eliminated one breast to make wielding the weapons of war easier—the left if they carried a shield, the right if they were trained to the crossbow—so that they could resist intruders and maintain their way of life. The Amazons fascinated and terrified medieval readers, but they were far away; no one claims actually to have seen them. They were a fantasy.

The daughter of Hippocrates was another female prodigy described in Mandeville's *Travels*. She had been "changed and transformed from a fair damsel into the likeness of a terrifying dragon by a goddess." She required only to be kissed by a young man in order to return permanently to her human form. Unfortunately, the brave knights who undertook this task consistently died. The damsel still waits: "When a knight cometh that is so hardy to kiss her, he shall not die, but he shall turn the damsel into her right form and kindly shape, and he shall be lord of all the countries and islands abovesaid."[5]

A third group of marvelous women represents yet another fantasy: these women wear no head coverings so, Mandeville says, men and women are indistinguishable, except for married women, who "bear the token upon their heads of a man's foot in sign that they be under man's foot and under subjection of man." Furthermore, the wives dwell not together but every of them by herself, and the husband may lie with whom of them that he liketh."[6]

These three kinds of women represent the range of medieval male fantasies of women: the totally independent woman, capable of crimes against nature in order to maintain her autonomy; the woman who initially appears terrifying and horrendous, but who needs only a man's love to be transformed into a beautiful and tractable woman; and the completely colonized woman, wearing her docility on her head at all times for all to witness, uncomplaining when her husband flits from woman to woman at whim.

These women are all "prodigies," however; the text presents them as outside experience, exotic. How are they related to the actual women medieval men lived with and loved? Most of them lack the standard features of grotesqueness: gargantuan size, a mixture of the body parts of different species, inversion, or unanticipated transmogrification. These women's lack of grotesqueness, in a text that specializes in titillating its readers with weirdness, suggests that it is not merely that some women were thought of as grotesque in socially defined, culturally specific ways, but that an element of the grotesque is present in every woman. As the women in Mandeville's *Travels* illustrate, the creature closest to the male subject, but innately, disturbingly different, is ultimately more grotesque than are exotic monsters. "The grotesque world does not constitute a fantastic realm of its own," Wolfgang Kayser has said, "the grotesque world is—and is not—our world."[7] That which is familiar but alien is finally the most confusing and troubling, and it requires figuration that reassures by indicating how the disturbing figure can and should be managed.

In Western Christianity the primary opportunity for figurations of the grotesque has been verbal and visual descriptions of hell. In paintings of the Last Judgment, the blessed arrange themselves in neat rows on the right hand of Christ while the damned, with twisted, elongated bodies, stream downward and mix with the bodies of others (figure 25). At the lower edge of such paintings, attacked by demons who stab, burn, and pull them apart, they often lose all configuration and integrity. In S. Francesca Romana's fifteenth-century vision, hell was "a lurid and rotting uterus," where perjurers, blasphemers, magicians, doctors who hastened death by their ineptness, people who had made inadequate confessions, adulterers, and cheating shopkeepers, all endured inventive and horrible torments.[8] Particular crimes were punished in prescribed sequence of tortures, according to many medieval authors. The damned were tortured particularly in the organs involved in their sins; for example, "the breasts and abdomen of the lustful woman are sucked out by toads and repulsive serpents"[9] (figure 26). For medieval people, hell was grotesque for all human integrity, physical and social, was overwhelmed by chaos.

In this chapter I will first examine several definitions of the grotesque in order to identify the components of grotesque figuration. I will then argue that, because of woman's affiliation with the quintessentially grotesque events of birth, sexual intercourse, and death, from the collective male perspective of the public sphere, the most concentrated sense of the grotesque comes, not from exotic but distant monsters, but from the figure "woman." I will then explore several devices by which a familiar world can become grotesque, asking how women's bodies and behavior,

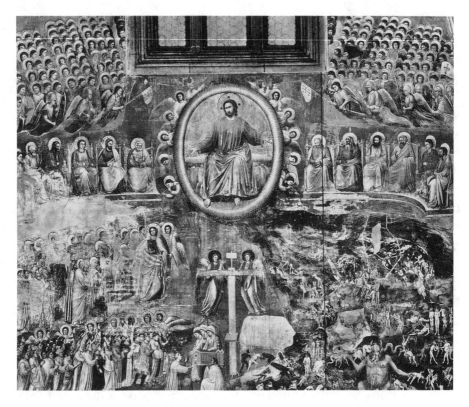

25

GIOTTO
*The Last Judgment,* c. 1305–8
Arena Chapel, Padua (Art Resource, New York)

as represented in historical societies, related to these literary and pictorial devices. Finally, using several different genres of sixteenth-century literature, we will explore an example of the social function of figuring "woman" as grotesque.

The grotesque is notoriously difficult to define. In a recent study of the grotesque, Geoffrey Galt Harpham begins with this elusive definition:

Grotesqueries both require and defeat definition; they are neither so regular and rhythmical that they settle easily into our categories, nor so unprecedented that we do not recognize them at all. They stand at a margin of consciousness be-

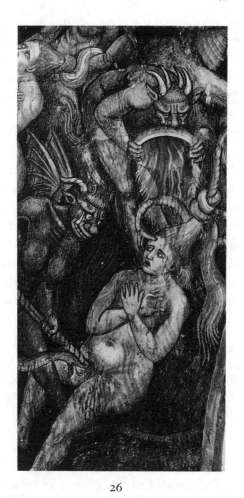

26

*Lust,* detail from *Inferno,* San Gimignano, Italy, 1396
(Photograph: Katherine J. Gill)

tween the known and the unknown, the perceived and the unperceived, calling into question the adequacy of our ways of organizing the world.[10]

This definition is as loose and baggy as the grotesque creatures it attempts to classify. Confusion is intrinsic to the grotesque, and, as Harpham acknowledges, "it is always difficult to think clearly about confusion."[11] Both Harpham and his predecessor, Mikhail Bakhtin, interpret confusion positively, however. Harpham criticizes Bakhtin for his uncritical embrace of the grotesque: "Reading Bakhtin, we may be encouraged to feel that by embracing the grotesque we can regain fullness of meaning, purity of being, and natural innocence, lying breast to breast with the cosmos and with our fellow creatures."[12] But his own more measured appreciation maintains that "confused things lead the mind to new inventions [and] lie at the heart of all scientific discoveries of a revolutionary character."[13] "The grotesque implies discovery," Harpham concludes in the last paragraph of the book, "and disorder is the price one always pays for the enlargement of the mind."[14] Finally, the grotesque can be defined only in relation to an ideal, standard, or normative form; a grotesque figure is "an entity—an image, object, or experience—simultaneously justifying multiple and mutually exclusive interpretations which commonly stand in a relation of high to low, human to subhuman, divine to human, normative to abnormal, with the unifying principle sensed but occluded and imperfectly perceived."[15]

Bakhtin gives an example of grotesque conversion of the "high," or intellectual, to the "low," or physical. In a scene from the Italian *Commedia dell'arte,*

a stutterer talking with Harlequin cannot pronounce a difficult word; he makes a great effort, loses his breath, keeping the word down in his throat, sweats and gapes, trembles, chokes. His face is swollen, his eyes pop: it looks as if he were in the throes of childbirth. Finally Harlequin, weary of waiting, relieves the stutterer by surprise; he rushes head forward and hits the man in the abdomen. The difficult word is "born" at last.[16]

Bakhtin comments:

A highly spiritual act is degraded and uncrowned by the transfer to the material bodily level of childbirth, realistically represented. . . . The gaping mouth, the protruding eyes, sweat, trembling, suffocation, the swollen face—all these are typical symptoms of the grotesque life of the body; here they have the meaning of the act of birth.[17]

Unremarked by Bakhtin, the debasement of the act is brought about by a gender inversion, by the simple placement of the production of a word in a reproductive body. Thus the "highly spiritual act" is that of a man, while its conversion to the comic occurs—must occur?—in the body of a woman. The transfer to the material, corporeal, and sexual requires woman's body as the catalyst of the conversion. The association of the female body with materiality, sex, and reproduction makes it an essential—not an accidental—aspect of the grotesque. The socially constructed *différance* which means that male and female bodies are not only physically different, but also hierarchically arranged and asymmetrically valued underlies the literary use of woman's body as the primary figure of debasement.

Grotesque figuration of the female body might be seen as benign or merely descriptive if we fail to notice another feature of the grotesque. In subverting order, rationality, and "reality" as socially represented, it signals the insidious omnipresence of evil, the confusion of an orderly creation by an irreducible undertow, a bleeding of "high" into "low" which is both achieved and demonstrated by erratic matter's insubordination to form. The theological significance of grotesque form was supplied for learned medieval literati by a late classical author, Boethius. Early in the sixth century Boethius extrapolated from Christian neoplatonism a description of the genesis of grotesque forms:

Anything which turns away from goodness ceases to exist, and thus . . . the wicked cease to be what they once were. That they used to be human is shown by the human appearance of their body which still remains. So it was by falling to wickedness that they also lost their human nature. Now, since only goodness can raise one above the level of humankind, it follows that it is proper that wickedness thrusts down to a level below humankind those whom it has dethroned from the condition of being human.[18]

Certainly, in the best known instances of the grotesque, from the Paleolithic caves of southern France, to medieval manuscript illumination and cathedral facades, to Rabelais, Jonathan Swift, *Alice in Wonderland,* and Aubrey Beardsley, male as well as female bodies are subjected to grotesque figuration. Yet it was women's bodies, permanently implicated by Eve's sin, that symbolized the fact that humanity exists in a state of sinfulness and punishment. Furthermore, when they become grotesque male bodies take on precisely the characteristics regularly attributed to female bodies; they lose form and integrity, become penetrable, suffer the addition of alien body parts, and become alternately huge and tiny. Like women's bodies, the grotesque male body is no longer "clearly differentiated from the world, but transferred, merged, and fused with it."[19]

Several social factors also ensure the centrality of women's bodies in the category of the grotesque. Grotesques, like other artistic figurations, were formulated and circulated in the public arena by a male collective. Women did not represent themselves in this arena, but their cooperation in reproducing both human beings and society was essential. Needing women to play their social and reproductive roles, yet resentful of their dependence on women, the male collective sought a variety of ways to secure women's support. Not the least effective method for establishing women's dependence on men—a simple reversal of their dependence on women's support for a public realm women had little share in designing—was to construct women collectively as the figure "woman," object in relation to the male subject. As Biddy Martin has written:

If women have been marginal in the constitution of meaning and power in Western culture, the question of woman has been central, crucial to the discourse of man, situated as she is within the literary text, the critical text . . . and social texts of all kinds as the riddle, the problem to be solved, the question to be answered.[20]

The female, from the perspective of the collective male public, is constantly and frustratingly mobile between poles of similarity and alienness. As we have seen in earlier chapters, women's ability to overcome the limitations of their sex and achieve intellectual and spiritual accomplishments—to "become male"—was emphasized in the literature of martyrdom and asceticism in the early Christian churches. Women's difference from the normative male was, however, far more frequently noted in medieval Christianity. Male authors wondered whether women have souls; women often seemed, to the men who represented them, to lack the subjectivity they associated with having a soul.

Figured as Eve, the perversely bent rib, every woman was seen as essentially grotesque, though the revelation of her hidden monstrosity could be prevented by her careful adherence to socially approved appearance and behavior. The function of this figuration was to identify, define, and thus to stabilize a feared and fantasized object. Grotesque figuration contributes the bonus of laughter, permitting relief of tension; the simultaneously feared and desired object becomes comic. For women, in societies in which they were defined as "Eves," the perpetual threat was that their "true nature" would emerge. Only by constant labor could women establish and maintain their identification with images of the "good" woman, the docile, nurturing, obedient woman. Since the grotesque threatened to bleed into public view at any moment, constant vigilance was required, primarily by women, but also by the fathers and husbands responsible for them.

Even with the most careful self-scrutiny and male surveillance, however, women harbored an irreducible element of monstrosity.[21] For it was

not only female behavior—loquaciousness, aggressiveness, stubborn-
ness—that could at any moment reveal a woman's identity with Eve, but
her body itself. Some women were seen as personifications of the grotesque; prostitutes, for example, epitomized the penetrable body, the
body shaped by lust, the permeable body that produces juices and smells.
The prostitute's body was described as the opposite of the closed, self-
contained, controlled male body,[22] and the opposite of that of some
virtuous women, especially of virgins, who were called "gardens
enclosed."[23]

One of the most prominent features of the grotesque is sexuality and
the sexual organs,[24] and female reproductive functions, as we will see,
were in the medieval period the quintessential terror that must be "conquered by laughter."[25] Bakhtin identifies the three main acts in the life of
the grotesque body as "sexual intercourse, death throes, and the act of
birth."[26] "Birth and death are the gaping jaws of the earth and the
mother's open womb,"[27] he writes, reminding us that Rabelais's hero
Pantagruel emerged triumphantly from the body of his mother by kill-
ing her, "for he was so wonderfully great and lumpish, that he could not
possibly have come forth in the light of the world without thus suffocat-
ing his mother."[28] Pregnancy and birth provide images of "natural" grotesqueness. "Woman with child is a revolting spectacle," Jerome wrote in
the fourth century, a judgment with which countless medieval authors
concurred.[29] Pregnancy, like menstruation, reveals that woman's body is
not the "closed, smooth, and impenetrable" body that serves as the symbol of individual, autonomous, and "perfect" existence. In menstruation, sexual intercourse, and pregnancy, women's bodies lose their individual configuration and boundaries. "The grotesque body," Bakhtin
writes, "is a body in the act of becoming. It is never finished, never completed; it is continually built, created, and builds and creates another
body." The grotesque body, in short, "outgrows its own self, transgress-
ing its own body."[30]

In Christianity conception, birth, and sexual intercourse have frequently focused doctrinal or practical debates. Several brief examples
will suffice here. Despite some Christian gnostics' frequent use of female
figures, like Eve, in positive religious symbolism,[31] others balked at the
idea that God could have entered the human realm as a helpless infant,
born like other human beings, from a woman's body. At the beginning of
the third century Tertullian taunted his squeamish opponent, Marcion,

with the physical details of Christ's fully human birth. Two centuries later one of Jerome's many panegyrics on virginity celebrated the fact that virginity reestablishes the order of creation, before the Fall. Although virgins are conceived from men's semen, he said, men are not born from virgins, just as Eve was created from Adam, not Adam from Eve: "A virgin owes her being to a man, but a man does not owe his to a virgin."[32] Similarly, proscriptions on abortion throughout the Christian tradition reveal not only religious conviction or concern for patriarchal control of women's bodies, but also male identification with the helplessness and dependency of the fetus.[33]

Women's "natural" affiliation with the body has also been accused of creating other problems for men. As we saw earlier, in Augustine's discussion of fallen sexuality in book 14 of the *City of God,* impotence—not sexual activity or even promiscuity—provided Augustine with an example of the male sexual organ's "insubordination" to the will. A different kind of text, the sixteenth-century witch persecution manual, the *Malleus Maleficarum,* lists first among the powers of witches the ability to cause impotence. With their customary precision, the authors define the kind of impotence caused by witches: "When the [male] member is in no way stirred, and can never perform the act of coition, this is a sign of frigidity of nature; but when it is stirred and becomes erect, but yet cannot perform, it is a sign of witchcraft."[34]

Moreover, perennial accusations concerning the "insatiability" of women, though they may relate to an ancient belief that sexual intercourse is enervating and potentially damaging to men,[35] may also expose male anxiety. Both Jerome and the authors of the *Malleus Maleficarum* insisted that it was not only the flamboyantly grotesque woman, the prostitute, who is insatiable, but all women. Jerome wrote that "it is not the harlot or the adulteress who is spoken of; but woman's love in general is accused of being ever insatiable; put it out, it bursts into flame; give it plenty, it is again in need; it enervates a man's mind and engrosses all thought except for the passion which it feeds."[36] It seems at least worth considering whether men whose female sexual partners were not pleased with sex[37] may have projected on women their unwillingness or inability to give pleasure as evidence of female "insatiability."[38] In any case, women's identification with the body in the patriarchal societies of the Christian West resulted in the apparently contradictory charges that they both caused impotence and were tirelessly lustful.

Three major rhetorical and pictorial devices contribute to grotesque presentation: caricature, inversion, and hybridization. Each of these devices has a specific connection to women, their bodies, and their behavior. The special affiliation of the female body with the grotesque is founded on the assumption that the male body is the perfectly formed, complete, and therefore normative body. By contrast, all women's bodies incorporate parts (like breasts, uterus, and vagina) and processes (like menstruation and pregnancy) that appeared grotesque to the authors and artists who represented women.[39] The female body is inherently volatile, the "source of change, disruption, and complication."[40] Twentieth-century analysts of the grotesque—Kayser, Bakhtin, Harpham—fail to notice the gender assumptions embedded in grotesque art and literature, with the effect that they ignore a structural feature of the genre.

Ultimately, the function of gender in grotesque art and literature can be understood in detail only when its culturally specific interpretive associations—social and sexual arrangements, and class affiliations—are accurately identified. Gender roles and expectations within the society must also be taken into account. A rhetorical or pictorial device applied to a male figure may take on a very different meaning and value when applied to a female figure. In societies, for example, in which women are considered beautiful only if they are small, thin, and fine-boned, caricature featuring monstrous size has quite different connotations when applied to male or to female figures. Associated with men, monumental size, whether of the total body or of particular parts of the body, commands both respect and admiration. Thus the "magnificent" and hugely proportioned codpiece of Rabelais's hero, Pantagruel, carried a very different social meaning from that of the yawning vaginas of medieval sheelas. Massive male sexual organs are figures of pride, self-assertion, and aggression; massive female genitals, however, are likely to represent women's dangerous propensities for threatening men's self-control, autonomy, and power.[41]

Caricature, as we began to notice in the previous chapter, often reveals, with economy and clarity, social consensus on what is to be avoided. The extreme example inevitably discloses what it is that socialization aims to prevent. Caricature isolates and fetishizes parts of the body. In theological and medical discourse as well as in the popular arts of the Christian West, the breasts, vagina, and uterus have frequently been objects of caricature, in both explicit and covert ways.[42] Perhaps the least obvious caricature of the uterus appears in paintings and writings in which hell is represented as uterus-shaped. Similarly, the vagina appears covertly in icons and paintings as the mouth of hell. The frontispiece of John Climacus's *The Ladder of Divine Ascent,* for instance, shows monks climbing the ladder to God while tiny demons attempt to pull them off the ladder. Some of the monks fall into an open, sucking mouth/vagina on the earth's surface. Women's mouths, tongues, and speech have also frequently been correlated with the vagina—open when they should be closed, causing the ruin of all they tempt or slander.[43] The association of garrulousness with wantonness was part of a well-established polemic against women across many societies of the Christian West.

More than a millennium after Christian martyrdom virtually ceased in the West, texts like Jacobus da Voragine's *Golden Legend* and myriad visual images supplied the popular interest in women's body parts. Devotional texts like the *Golden Legend* graphically describe women martyrs, and such texts are often accompanied by pictures of their torture, dismemberment, and executions. Indeed, religious pornography featuring at least partially naked women increased through the Renaissance and Reformation periods; pornography did not become secular until well into the modern period. In figure 27, the legendary Saint Barbara is depicted being tortured before her execution. One burly executioner beats her with a knotted cord while another slices off her left breast. Another legendary woman, Saint Agnes, suffered a similar fate and became a frequent subject of paintings: her breasts were cut off, and she was often depicted carrying her large, firm breasts on a platter.[44]

Popular culture shared with learned theological discourse a fascination with and horror of female breasts and genital organs. Female grotesques and sheelas, often on the facades of churches, displayed their splayed vaginas (figure 28), reminding viewers of the dangerous power of female sexual organs. Jørgen Andersen has documented the development of the sheela motif from French Romanesque corbels and capitols to its extensive use in England and Ireland during the later Middle Ages. It evolved from naked female figures, "aggressively displaying their genitals," to horrific figures with skeletal ribs, skull-like heads, and a large genital hole in frontal exhibition. Commenting on the use of sheelas in religious architecture, Andersen shows his unwillingness to explore gender assumptions—his own or those of the societies in which sheelas were used in public church architecture—when he writes, "Devotion does not shrink away from showing the things that drag men down, grotesque

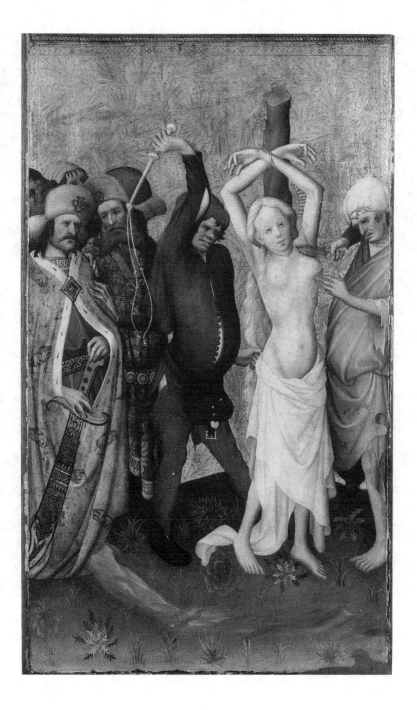

27

**MASTER FRANCKE**
*Martyrdom of Saint Barbara,* fifteenth century
National Museum of Finland, Helsinki

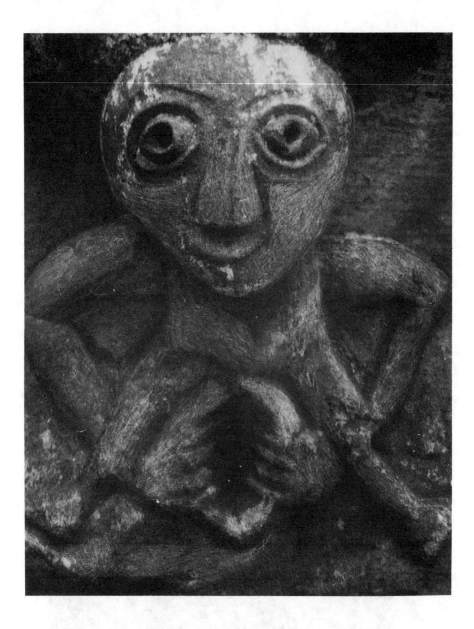

28

*Sheela-na-gig,* Corbel, Church of Saint Mary and Saint David, 1140s
Kilpeck, Herefordshire, England
(Royal Commission on the Historical Monuments of England)

shapes, frightening and ludicrous."[45] The "frightening, evil-averting influence of the *vulva*,"[46] according to Andersen, lies behind the continued
use of these female figures for about three hundred years; the sheela was
a "demonic figure yielding protection against the demons."[47] These
figures were often placed above doors to repel intruders.[48] Male fear of
the vagina is evident, at least in Andersen's explanation and, if his explanation of sheelas' popularity is correct, in the Christian societies in
which sheelas were portrayed: "Like the frontal face, [the vagina] has the
power to ensnare the viewer's glance and hence capture his subjectivity or
selfhood."[49]

The second device employed in grotesque presentation is that of inversion. Inversion refers to the reversal of an expected and pleasing appearance to produce a disturbing image. As medical historians have shown,
women's genitalia and reproductive organs were thought to be the precise inversion of men's.[50] Thomas Laqueur's article "Orgasm, Generation, and the Politics of Reproductive Biology" in *The Making of the
Modern Body* reproduces illustrations by Leonardo and Vasalius that seek
to demonstrate the homologies of female and male reproductive organs.
These drawings were prompted by arguments going back to the earliest
Greek treatises on female physiology. According to Aristotle's account,
woman "is characterized by deprived, passive, and material traits, cold
and moist dominant humors and a desire for completion by intercourse
with the male."[51]

Aline Rouselle has discussed the origins of this construction of reproduction and female sexuality in Greek medical treatises like the *Hippocratic Collection*.[52] She writes, "Male doctors who had no knowledge of
female anatomy or physiology, but fantasies only, used logical reasoning
to construct a male science of the female body."[53] The vocabulary with
which female genitals were described demonstrates the assumption of
the normativity of the male body. With the exception of the uterus and
the cervix, the female reproductive system was described as the inverted
equivalent to the male: "The ovaries were testicles and the Fallopian
tubes, which they described perfectly, were a *vas deferens*. They even
spoke of female sperm. . . . [Male doctors] explained that 'the internal
genital organs surround the neck of the womb just as, in men, the fore-
skin grows around the glans.'"[54] Galen wrote: "Turn outward the
woman's, turn inward, so to speak, and fold double the man's, and you
will find the same in both in every respect. . . . You could not find [in
the female] a single male part left over that has not simply changed its

position."[55] In short, female sexual and reproductive organs are male organs turned outside-in.

Physiological homologies, however, seem only to dramatize the difference and asymmetrical value of male and female bodies. Women lack the necessary heat, Galen says, to turn the sexual organs outward. Lacking heat, female physical organs cannot achieve the perfection of the male body. Moreover, relative heat defines one's ontological value: "Humans are the most perfect of animals, and men are more perfect than women by reason of their 'excess of heat.' . . . The male is a hotter version of the female, or, to use the teleologically more appropriate order, the female is the cooler, less perfect version of the male."[56]

Moral consequences also attend the inverted female body. In the sixteenth century an Italian anatomist, Prospero Borgarucci, acknowledged the traditional thesis of female physical inferiority. He denied it, however, saying that women's physical equality with men was guaranteed by their inverted sexual organs. Nevertheless, physical equality, he said, did not imply moral equality. Rather, because of women's moral inferiority, he wrote, they should remain in ignorance of their physical equality:

Woman is a most arrogant and extremely intractable animal; and she would be worse if she came to realize that she is no less perfect and no less fit to wear breeches than man . . . I believe that is why nature, while endowing her with what is necessary for our procreation, did so in such a way as to keep her from perceiving her sufficient perfection. On the contrary . . . to check woman's continual desire to dominate, nature arranged things so that every time she thinks of her supposed lack, she may be humbled and shamed.[57]

Different accounts of generation by various ancient, medieval, and Renaissance authors explain female lack in various ways. All, however, compare the female to the normative male and find the female body and/ or "nature" deformed and defective. The uterus, which has no counterpart in the male body, was thought to be woman's most important sex organ as late as the nineteenth century.[58] Thus, women's ills—from lack of appetite to hysteria—were diagnosed as attributable to malfunctioning of the uterus. Sex difference was usually reduced to biological difference, and biological difference was made to account not simply for female inferiority, but also for female evil. Evidence that men found women different and dangerous is abundant throughout the history of Christianity.[59]

Clearly, woman was seen as inferior, but was she seen as monstrous? Theologians, philosophers, and medical authors discussed the question of whether woman is a "monstrous creation." Although Aristotle had said in the *Metaphysics* that women are not of a different species than man, his description of the birth of females as an incomplete generative act furnished grounds for inferring the inferior status of women. Thomas Aquinas, in one text, casually assimilated individual women, to "other monsters of nature," though he says that "in the general plan of nature" women are not monstrous.[60] That the question could be raised and discussed at all—that the monstrosity thesis could be posed and argued in serious debate—may be astonishing. It perhaps becomes less so when we remind ourselves that it is the figure "woman," not the actual women of everyday experience, that was under discussion. Nevertheless, women in Christian societies were not unaffected by the public representation of "woman" as defective in body and mind. A perennial open question as to whether women were human beings with souls, surfacing repeatedly in learned debate and popular caricature, cannot have failed to generate hostility toward women and, for women themselves, problematic self-images.

A third device for producing grotesque figuration is that of hybridization. The German artist Albrecht Dürer wrote, "If a person wants to create the stuff that dreams are made of, let him mix freely all sorts of creatures."[61] The grotesque body is a random combination of disparate parts, without functional integrity. Hybridization typically isolates organs and appendages of humans, animals, fish, and birds to reconnect them to other bodies at random. Some grotesques, however, "are not true hybrids at all in the sense that, in them, generic lines are not crossed." Bakhtin discusses one such instance, some terra-cotta figures of laughing, senile, pregnant hags. These figures, rather than conflating the parts of different bodies, conflate "the poles of the biocosmic cycle."[62] In other words, they exhibit the different stages or periods of woman's life, with pregnancy and senility in one figure, they represent birth and death simultaneously.

The female body, even without the usual device of hybridization, appears to be innately and simultaneously fascinating and terrifying. In the twentieth century as in the sixteenth century, interest in isolated body parts is evident in advertising images as well as in pornography; in contemporary communication media, women are still encouraged to think of themselves as parts that must be evaluated, judged, and altered separately: big thighs, small breasts, or skinny legs.

Finally, a figure that deserves the label "grotesque" must be perceived as such by someone. To be grotesque, to paraphrase Berkeley's famous aphorism, is to be perceived as such. No set of features, or lack of features, automatically qualifies a figure as grotesque. As Kayser notes, "the grotesque is experienced only in the act of reception. . . . it is entirely possible that things are regarded as grotesque even though structurally there is no reason for calling them so."[63] Men, who wielded the power of creating public representations of women, perceived the female body as quintessentially grotesque, and when they made the male body grotesque, they did so by giving it female characteristics.

In the Middle Ages Aristotle's doctrine of woman as a misbegotten and deformed male crossed easily into Christian speculation about Eve and her secondary and derivative creation.[64] The literary and pictorial presentation of the figure "woman," as we have seen, carried remarkable continuity across medieval societies and appears to have relied very little on what actual women were doing. It is, in fact, very important to differentiate the figure Eve/woman from actual women in order to grasp the staying power of a figure that must have contradicted the experience of many men and most women. At the end of the medieval period, the sheer cumulative weight of "woman" ensured that this figure survived the sixteenth-century social, ecclesiastical, and political upheavals. Although "woman" was never a completely monolithic image, it continued to be the focus of an intense discussion, a discussion that, at the end of the sixteenth century, renewed the approximately two-hundred-year-old "querelle des femmes."

In 1595 a debate on the subject of "woman" was initiated by an anonymous German tract, "A new disputation against women, in which it is proved that they are not human beings." The satirical tract was refuted and rebutted by various authors, and the debate became widespread in intellectual circles; the tract was repeatedly republished and published in translation. In Roman Catholic circles, the question of whether woman has a soul was still sufficiently unsettled to require discussion and a pronouncement—in affirmation that women have souls—at the mid-sixteenth-century Council of Trent.

To understand the sex/gender system invoked in such discussions, it will be helpful to explore what Ellen Messer-Davidow has labeled the "metaphorical congruence" of rhetoric about "woman" in several genres of sixteenth-century literature. Devotional literature, sermons, manuals of manners, and satirical works all exhibit the "structural congruence" that indicates an agreement of the public culture on "woman."[65] These writings also reveal the identification of the grotesque female body with the figure "woman" and prescribe a governance of actual women appropriate to "woman's" characteristics.

Beginning in the sixteenth century it becomes possible for historians to estimate the popularity and probable influence of particular books on the reading public. With the invention of printing presses at the end of the fifteenth century, information about the number of books printed and sold is often available. One of the most popular devotional manuals of the sixteenth century, Erasmus of Rotterdam's *Enchiridion militis christiani* (*Manual of the Christian Soldier*), uses "woman" as a rhetorical figure with which to contrast the commitment, training, and courage of the Christian soldier. This book was published in thirty editions in the first twenty years after its initial publication in 1503; there were dozens more publications and six translations before the end of the sixteenth century.[66] Erasmus called his manual "a kind of hand dagger," a "little blade,"[67] that would help the reader to recognize that "mortal life is nothing but a kind of perpetual warfare."[68] Throughout the manual, he says, he uses "woman" as a cipher for sensuality, doubt, and cowardice; "man" and "manly" designate courage.[69]

According to the *Enchiridion,* lust is the most debilitating vice the soldier can indulge: "no evil attacks us earlier, pricks us more sharply, covers more territory, or drags more people to ruin." When "filthy sensuality" inflames the mind, the "weapons" of certain thoughts should prevent the soldier from succumbing: "First of all, think how foul, how base, how unworthy of any man is this pleasure which reduces us from an image of divinity to the level, not merely of animals, but even to that of swine, he goats, dogs, and the most brutish of brutes."[70] The soldier should also think how transient and spurious sexual pleasure is, and how unworthy of the male body, the "temple of God." Contemplating the loss of his reputation should be his next "weapon" against lust. Examples of those who have resisted, moreover, should help the soldier to "stiffen [his] continence." But the primary device by which the Christian soldier can resist lust is to picture the female body as grotesque: "How unworthy and disgraceful it is to touch the disgusting flesh of a whore . . . to handle loathsome filth."[71] Erasmus's vivid language paints the prostitute's body as monstrous, a "stinking hog wallow of lust."[72] The ancient fear that sexual intercourse can damage health, Erasmus writes, can also help to steel the soldier against lust; the fear that, as we noticed in the previous chapter, had fresh content at the beginning of the sixteenth century because of the virulence of the syphilis epidemic. Erasmus equates sexual activity with venereal disease: "[Lust] destroys at the same time the vigor and attractiveness of the body. It damages health and produces countless ailments, all of them disgusting."[73] Finally, the soldier must consider how he must look to others:

And imagine to yourself just how ridiculous, how completely monstrous it is to be in love: to grow pale and thin, to shed tears, to fawn upon and play the beggar to the most stinking tart, to croak and howl at her doors all night, to hang upon the nod of a mistress, to endure a silly woman's dominating you, flying at you in rage, and then to make up with her and voluntarily offer yourself to a strumpet so she can play upon you, clip you, pluck you clean! Where, I ask you, in such behavior is the name of a man? Where's your beard? Where is that high mind fashioned for the most beautiful things?[74]

Once you have "proffered your miserable neck to Dame Lechery," Erasmus warns, "you will cease to be your own master." Clearly, Erasmus's representation of the female body as an enemy, if not *the* enemy, of male self-possession plays a key role in his construction of male power and autonomy. Throughout the *Enchiridion,* female figures—Eve, Dame Lechery, and nameless prostitutes—signal potentially fatal enemies of the Christian soldier. The *Enchiridion* knows only two types of women: "tarts" and wives. Erasmus's instructions on how to love a wife, like admonitions against consorting with other women, do not suggest that women have either subjectivity or unique personality characteristics. Warning against loving one's wife "only because she provides you with sexual pleasure," Erasmus urges instead that "you love her most deeply because in her you have seen the likeness of Christ, that is to say, goodness, modesty, sobriety, chastity." Only then will the reader "love her now not in herself but in Christ [and] in reality you love Christ in her; and so at last you love in a spiritual sense."[75] It is difficult to tell from these brief instructions whether Erasmus imagines that the repeatable traits of character which, he says, ought to be the object of love are Christian virtues that can appear in many people, or whether the woman is to be valued and loved as a unique configuration of these virtues.[76] There is not, in any case, any suggestion that heterosexual relationship might provide a format for mutual learning and growth; sex, even within Christian marriage remains problematic at best:

If you are married, think how admirable a thing is an undefiled bed, and try as hard as you can to make your marriage resemble the most holy wedlock of Christ and his Church, whose likeness it bears. That is to say, see to it that it has as little lewdness as possible, and as much fruitfulness, for in no status of life is it not most abominable to be a slave to lust.[77]

In religious literature like the *Enchiridion*, the female body, from the perspective of the male author, is a dangerous provocation for male lust. In the *Praise of Folly* Erasmus evoked the supreme authority of Plato for an egregious misreading of *Timaeus* 91a: "Plato seems to doubt whether woman should be classed with brute beasts or rational beings."[78] If we look in other contemporary literary genres, the "woman problem" appears in similar configurations. Exploring the composite image of woman in books of manners, sumptuary laws, and sermons, Peter Stallybrass has found the public image of the female body in the sixteenth and seventeenth centuries to be what he calls a "naturally grotesque body" that requires constant surveillance. According to such legislators of social order, woman's tongue, like her body, must be strictly governed, and there is no surer sign of a woman who is sexually loose than that her speech is unrestricted, both as to quantity and to its exercise in the public sphere. "The signs of the 'harlot,'" Stallybrass says, "are her linguistic 'fullness' and her frequenting of public space."[79] Barbaro, in a treatise *On Wifely Duties,* warned that "the speech of a noble woman can be no less dangerous than the nakedness of her limbs."[80]

Stallybrass shows that a complex discourse surrounded the use of woman's body as the paradigm and site of the well-being or betrayal of the family, economy, and state. "'*Covert,*' the wife becomes her husband's symbolic capital; 'free,' she is the opening through which that capital disappears."[81] By means of surveillance, education, and, if necessary, force, woman can become the exemplar of the well-governed state—orderly, silent, submissive, and closed. Ancient metaphors of woman's body as (re)productive earth[82] are, in this early modern discourse, extended to liken women's bodies to enclosed, cultivated, controlled properties, colonized terrain, the potentially valuable property of a father or husband.[83] However, in Kenneth Burke's words, "property fears theft because it is theft[84];" thus a constant anxiety pervades this discourse of ownership, control, and training, especially since both medical and theological discourse of the time identified women with irrationality and irresponsibility,[85] voracious sexuality and heretical subversiveness.

The grotesque, "unfenced" or wild, female is repeatedly painted in lurid terms as both opposite of the "closed and enclosed" woman and cause of the financial and moral ruin of her male owner.

Sixteenth-century perceptions of the dangers of the wantonly open, permeable, and unconfined body of woman must be seen in the light of the contemporary interpretation of such characteristics. Until the present century, "openness" has not been seen as a praiseworthy attribute of either the individual or society. Rather, in societies in which cultivated earth was rarer and thus more valued, the unfenced, uncultivated, and wild did not suggest a desirable lack of constraint. In twentieth-century North America and Western Europe, the frontier has long vanished and heavily appropriated earth predominates over wilderness. By contrast, in the context of a preponderance of wilderness, patriarchal societies used the female body to represent frighteningly unconquered, ungoverned wilderness. Woman, precisely because she was thought to be so naturally averse to enclosure, needed to be firmly domesticated. Through ceaseless surveillance and cultivation, woman's psyche and body could be shaped by patriarchal virtues. Agricultural metaphors described the necessary pruning, discipline, and hard labor by which women could train themselves, and be trained by their societies, to accommodate to physical and mental enclosure. She could then be recognized in the public sphere as a valuable property.

Restraint of the female body was not only metaphorical; modish women's clothing of the sixteenth century demonstrates the literal confinement of women's bodies. Stylish Renaissance dress "requires long, heavy skirts spreading out from below a tiny rib cage, encased in a meagerly cut bodice with high, confining armholes."[86] Sandra Clark, examining a literature similar to that used by Stallybrass—sermons, pamphlets, and books of manners—found a sustained polemic against women who were apparently wearing men's clothing, thereby enjoying greater freedom and ease, but also, according to these contemporary authors, threatening the very order and stability of society itself.[87] The 1620 anonymous pamphlet *Hic Mulier* (*The Man-Woman*) reveals the connection between confining dress and the woman who is "closed," impenetrable to males other than her own jealous guardian. The pamphlet finds cross-dressing the "symptom of a more general social decadence" in that sexual differentiation in clothing was considered "natural" and "God-ordained." Predictably, the time-honored allegations that women who transgress the restrictions placed on them by patriarchal societies do so in order to indulge their unlimited sexual appetites are reiterated by *Hic Mulier*. The author characterizes the behavior of women who wear men's clothing as "eyes wandering, lips bylling, tongue inticing, bared breasts seducing, and naked arms imbracing."[88] By contrast, the "chaste and impregnable exterior" presented by the virtuous and well-guarded woman is described in the metaphor of a locked house, which has "euery window closed with a strong casement, and euery Loope-hole furnisht with such strong Ordnance, that no vnchaste eye may come neere to assayle them."[89]

A similar evaluation of woman appears in a very different sixteenth-century literary genre. Rabelais's satire caricatures the vagina by attributing to it monstrous size. In *Pantagruel* he reveals the combination of horror, fascination, and ridicule with women's genitals we have noticed in the earlier period. Rabelais tells of a lion who, on seeing a woman's genitals, cries out, "O poor woman, who hath thus wounded thee?" Conferring with his friend the fox about this prodigy, the lion explains: "They have hurt this good woman here between the legs most villanously. . . . See how great a wound it is, even from the tail up to the navel, in measure four, nay five handfulls and a-half. This is the blow of a hatchet, I doubt me, it is an old wound."[90] Rabelais combines standard devices of the grotesque—exaggeration, anthropomorphized animals—with the implicit assumption that the male genitals are normative while female genitals are grotesque. Horror is kept at bay by its debasement to ridicule. Ian Maclean concludes his description of the sixteenth-century discussion of whether women are monstrous with the observation that the number of refutations of the female monstrosity thesis is itself significant, indicating, if nothing else, the intensity of the debate.[91]

Patriarchal cultures, in spite of their many dissimilarities, share a common need to preserve male control that is thought of simply as "order." A central component of maintaining and reproducing social order is the management of women, and a powerful strategy for controlling women is their public representation. Given the similar project of all patriarchal societies, namely, exclusively male design and administration of the public sphere, it is not surprising that images of and attitudes toward women's bodies show continuity across centuries. These continuities should not be attributed solely to literary influence. Metaphors of woman as earth, real estate—house, garden, or field—for example, function within, and are intimately connected to, economic and political situations, as Peter Stallybrass and Page duBois have demonstrated for vastly different societies.[92]

Moreover, the texts that relay these figures of "woman" testify to their recognized capacity for directing women into the precise social locations in which they most adequately contribute to the reproduction of society—cultural and economic as well as literal reproduction. Figures of woman can effectively incite both women and men to adopt certain self-images, attitudes, and behavior, even when the texts in which representations of woman appear are not addressed to women at all, but rather to men. Male power and authority in the public sphere are constructed and maintained by defining the female body as men's opposite and a potential threat. Men must receive coordinated cumulative information about woman's nature and body if they are to manage women with the confidence that they thoroughly understand the reasons for male and female familial and social roles. In patriarchal societies, it is men who must supply the education or, if education fails, the force that insures that actual women will accept these roles. The tract Hic Mulier, for example, ended by calling upon men to "assert their superiority by withholding 'necessarie maintenance' from their womenfolk until they behave themselves and recover their proper sense of duty."[93]

The use of gender as a category of analysis makes noticeable the fact that literary and artistic works that emerge from the public collective male perspective find women's bodies innately grotesque. Gender constructions play a crucial role in constructing the category of the grotesque and therefore must be a part of any analysis of what constitutes grotesqueness. To render gender invisible is to miss the social significance of one of the most important functions of the grotesque, that of converting the terrible into the comic. Men's fear of women comes from the socially constructed but intimately felt need to control a puzzlingly similar-but-different being. And women are felt to be unknown, mysterious, because they do not represent themselves in the public sphere and thus do not reveal and articulate a collective female subjectivity that would both limit the projection of male fears and longings and, ultimately, reassure men that, in Calypso's words, "The heart within me is not of iron, but yearning, like yours."

# 6

---

# NAKEDNESS, GENDER, AND RELIGIOUS MEANING

*My body knows unheard-of songs.*[1]

*The female image in all its variations is the mythical consequence of women's exclusion from the making of art. It is arguable that, despite her ubiquitous presence, woman as such is largely absent from art. We are dealing with the sign "woman," emptied of its original content and filled with masculine anxieties and desires.*[2]

*For me the real crux of chauvinism in art and history is that we as women have learned to see the world through men's eyes, and learned to identify with men's struggles, and men don't have the vaguest notion of identifying with ours. One of the things I'm interested in is getting the male viewer to identify with my work, to open his eyes to a larger human experience.*[3]

I have argued that female bodies, in the societies of the Christian West, have not represented women's subjectivity or sexuality but have, rather, been seen as a blank page on which multiple social meanings could be projected. My point throughout the book has not been to accuse men, who have created and administered the public sphere, of consciously and willfully creating religious practices in which women's socialization was reinforced rather than challenged. Nor do I claim that men consistently and purposely misrepresented women. Male artists and authors have sometimes represented women with sensitivity and empathy. Such theses would, in any case, be helplessly vulnerable to contrary opinions and counterinstances. My point, rather, is that because women have not enjoyed the conditions necessary for formulating the self-representations that could have informed collective male views of women, men have usually created representations of women out of their fears and fantasies.

Men have figured "woman" as a frightening and fascinating creature whose anger and rejection could deprive them of gratification, delight, and, ultimately, of life and salvation. The damage of such unlimited projection has been felt by Western communities as a whole; issues surrounding representations of women are not "women's issues," but common concerns.

"Political power entails the power of self-description."[4] Perhaps the most accurate test of whether a social group has political power is to ask whether that group enjoys the power of self-representation. People who do not represent themselves live under conditions in which their subjective lives—their feelings, concerns, and struggles—are marginalized from public interest; they also live in constant danger of misrepresentation. If women have suffered the effects of a misogyny deeply embedded in the representational practices of the Christian West, can we envision the possibility of more equitable public images of women?

Let us approach this question by considering further the conditions needed for representation. First, adequate representation of women must be self-representation. This is not to deny that one can learn something from "seeing ourselves as others see us." It is, nevertheless, arguable that, in societies that have represented women rather than providing conditions for their self-representation, women cannot begin by paying further attention to collective male representations of women. Since all women introject, to a greater or lesser degree, public representations of women, however, it is important to analyze what those representations circulate as the truth about women in order to understand some of the components of women's subjectivity. We *do* see ourselves as others see us. "In contemporary patriarchal culture," Sandra Bartky writes, "a panoptical male connoisseur resides within the consciousness of most women."[5] Self-representation, then, will require both identification of the public images that have become women's self images and the search for alternatives. Obviously, women's public representation by women cannot merely reverse men's representations of women by using the male body to signify female desire, sexuality, and power.

Secondly, the work of self-representation must occur in public, in the institutions and arenas in which the discourse that both reflects and shapes society takes place. Women must begin to gather the institutional power necessary to correct the male concerns and styles of interaction that have characterized public affairs. Until recently, the isolation of women from public engagement resulted in the privatization of women's

talents and energies. Excluded from public discourse, most women legitimately felt reluctant to accept responsibility for society and politics
and concentrated their attention on their families. As we have seen, con-
certed rhetorical and pictorial campaigns have, at various times and
places in the Christian West, encouraged—if not compelled—them to do
so. Limiting public power to male leadership has meant not only that
women were deprived of public roles, but also that societies have suffered the loss of the contribution women might have made.

If women are to achieve a different public representation than that of
the male collective, we must develop a power base of leadership positions
in public institutions. But we must also imagine and construct a different
dynamic relationship between representation and power. Collective,
public male power has tended to accumulate and congeal in relatively
small power elites. Collective female power must be maintained and revised in continuous circulation; it must resist coagulation. Women's
power, if it is not to reproduce the structure and dynamics of male
power, must be understood as the mutual empowerment of people previously disempowered—ethnic, class, and age groups—and not as power
over others. Women's power must be redistributed among people previously excluded from power as quickly as it is gathered. Instead of being
represented as "other" or alien, these misrepresented people can use self-
representation as an important strategy for maintaining power in suspension and circulation. Self-representation requires power, but it is also an
instrument for producing empowerment.

The third requirement for adequate representation of women is the
construction of a collective voice. Individual perspectives, valuable as
they are within a female collective, cannot command public attention
sufficiently to make a difference in politics, the media, public institutions, or social and sexual relationships. If women are to escape public
categorization under the rubrics of standardized female figures, a collective female voice that parallels and challenges the one-sidedness of the
collective male voice will be necessary. "Collective voice" does not,
however, imply that all women must agree on priorities, theory, or
agenda. Diversity, particularity, and the disagreements they inevitably
create are especially important to maintain and encourage—and even to
find essential and delightful—*within* a female collective voice.

"Unity," the ancient slogan of patriarchal order, is not the hidden
agenda of collective voice. Unanimity, even though it has been a goal
rather than an achievement of male collectives, has yielded representa-

tions of women that are amazingly constant over two millennnia and across a broad geographical area—"woman," the object of male fear and longing, who, in revealing her body, is said to have revealed "herself" (figure 29). In fact, representations of women may be the cultural artifact on which men find most unanimity. Women's self-representations, on the other hand, can seek and delight in the diversity among women, can endeavor to articulate difference rather than sameness. Whatever is common to women or similar about women must emerge from a multitude of self-representations of difference rather than from coercion, however subtle, to demonstrate "unity." Differences within the discourses that create women's collective voice are "a resource rather than a threat."[6] The Enlightenment project, the overcoming of dissent by rationality grounded in a transcendental subjectivity, cannot be the goal of female collective voice.

Collective voice is also central to the process by which women can move toward self-representation. Only a collective voice contains the resources and support necessary for self-criticism and self-correction; individuals in isolation, or even in small groups, cannot consistently identify the myriad ways by which women serve societies without a critical examination of the effects of their support. Women's collective self-representation in the public sphere ultimately has the task and responsibility of deciding both what is to be said about women as women and creating the imagery and language to say it.

The task, no doubt, is enormous. But it is already launched. In courts of law, work places, churches, public media, and academic discourse, the process of achieving the conditions for women's collective self-representation has been going on for at least a century, and with gathering momentum for several decades. The question is not whether women can and should represent themselves but how, at any particular moment, this can most fruitfully be accomplished. An accurate analysis of the present public situation, then, is preliminary to any determination of what kinds of self-representations will both formulate women's self-understandings and effectively challenge and change the public sphere.

What characterizes women's present position in late-twentieth-century North American public culture? The anthropologist Bryan Turner has argued that, although most feminists still use the term, "patriarchy" no longer adequately describes the dominant culture of Western Europe and North America. The notion of patriarchal power, he says, "cannot be uncoupled from the existence of the patriarchal household and . . . the

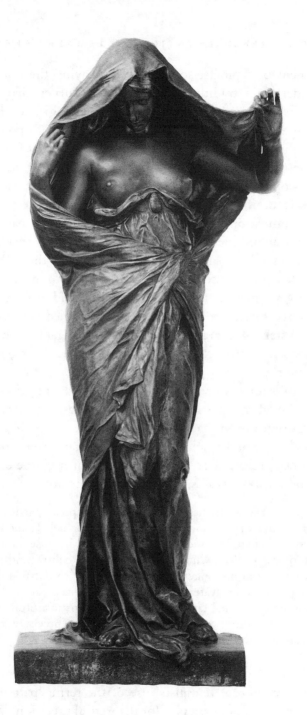

29

LOUIS-ERNEST BARRIAS
*Nature Revealing Herself to Science,* late nineteenth century
Allen Memorial Art Museum, Oberlin College; Gift of John N. Stern, 82.98

development of capitalist society, by destroying the traditional household, undermines traditional patriarchy."[7] Turner characterizes patriarchy as the existence of (1) a legal system that legislates the subjugation
of women as well as their economic exploitation, (2) political authority
based on the use of the father's role in the patriarchal family as a model
for divine-right absolutism, and (3) an ideology of male superiority.
Though women, he acknowledges, "still experience second-class citi-
zenship, closure from elite professional positions, everyday sexism and
petty discrimination," he maintains that "they also have much of the
legal, political and ideological machinery by which that discrimination
can be successfully challenged." As an ideology, then, "patriarchy is a
defensive reaction in a society where marriage and the marriage contract
no longer give [men] dominance in the household or in the market."[8] As
an "objective social structure which is maintained and constituted by a
complex system of legal regulations, political organization and economic
arrangements," patriarchy, Turner concludes, no longer exists in the
Western world.[9]

Turner calls for a "new conceptualization of the position of women," a
condition he labels "patrism." Using race relations theory as a parallel
analysis of oppression, he distinguishes between sexism as a "collection
of prejudicial attitudes" and sexism as a "social system in which certain
social groups are suppressed and exploited through the operation of the
market, political structures, and the law."[10] He notes:

The collapse of patriarchy has left behind it widespread patrism which is a culture of discriminatory, prejudicial and paternalistic beliefs about the inferiority
of women. . . . Patrism is expanding precisely because of the institutional
shrinkage of patriarchy, which has left men in a contracting power position.
Men as a whole can no longer depend on the law to buttress their dominance
within the public and private spheres. Institutionalized patriarchy has crumbled
along with the traditional family unit and the patristic attitude of men towards
women becomes more prejudicial and defensive precisely because women
are now often equipped with a powerful ideological critique of traditional
patriarchy.[11]

Turner's critique of feminists' use of the term "patriarchy" without
definition of its content is a plea for theoretical precision. Wrong or inadequate theory is theory that doesn't work—that doesn't illuminate and
that doesn't point the way to effective action. His proposal for the term
"patrism" as a more accurate designation of the contemporary situation
also has the advantage of recognizing that the women's movement,

coupled with the dramatic decrease in the hegemony of the nuclear family, the "rise of individualistic values, the transformation of traditional authority, and the disenchantment of religious values,"[12] has made substantial advances in dismantling patriarchy. The concept of "patrism," Turner claims, both defines the contemporary situation more accurately and reveals more pointedly the exact nature of the stresses involved in society's transition away from "patriarchy."

Despite the advantages of his theory, there are, I think, fundamental problems with Turner's analysis. While it would perhaps be encouraging to believe that patriarchy is in a state of collapse and that it presently occupies a "contracting power position," it is, in fact, not the case that equal distribution of social and institutional power exists among women and men. As long as the top administrative positions in social, political, legal, and ecclesiastical institutions are dominated by men, one cannot speak of "an institutional shrinkage of patriarchy." Furthermore, women who are "equipped with a powerful ideological critique of traditional patriarchy" are limited largely but not entirely to educated middle-class white women. This critique, even for such women, often fails to be effective when they turn from teaching and writing to problems of family and personal relationships.

Turner's analysis does, however, point to some features of contemporary Western society that should not be ignored. In the first place, alternatives to male objectification of women have become possible in a society in which some legal and social constraints against women's voices and activity in the public sphere have been—and are being—lifted. Furthermore, if, in fact, an obstacle women face in their effort to build a public sphere to which they have equal access is men's anger and sense of threatened privilege, might it not be a critical time for women to formulate and present "what women want"?

Suppose, for example, that women were to represent themselves as human beings embarked on a quest for carnal knowing, a self-knowledge that is not the same as the male hero's but that does, like his journey, require the public sphere and collective voice. Calypso's reminder to Odysseus offers a paradigm: "The heart within me is not of iron, but yearning, like yours." I am not your enemy, seeking to destroy your accomplishments and prevent the actualization of your longings, Calypso says, but someone with my own needs, journey, and dreams. Willingness to articulate and reveal one's own developing subjectivity can sometimes produce understanding and support instead of a response directed not to an actual woman, but to a female figure of the collective male imagination. Frequently middle-class men who are either hostile or indifferent to feminist issues suddenly begin to understand and respect these concerns when their daughters—women whose motivating longings and delights they have known over the course of their lives—find that a profession, an institution, or a career is inaccessible or difficult because they are women. Suspect as such conversions rightly are in feminist eyes, they nevertheless suggest that collective self-representation could, in the public arena, accomplish what individual self-revelation has frequently done in private, namely, convince men of the justice of women's demand for a society in which women, like men, are encouraged to take the active and chosen risks that produce embodied self-knowledge.[13]

I do not mean to imply, however, either that women should accept the model of the male culture hero as normative or that women should appeal to men's sense of fairness in order to gain access to the "smoke-filled rooms" in which decisions that determine the quantity and quality of communal life are made. Both the privatization and the individualization of the male hero must be resisted; the solitary enlightenment of the autonomous hero cannot be women's goal.

If women's self-representation seems urgent, the next question to be considered is this: Can the female body be a usable symbol for women's articulation of themselves as subjects? The fruitfulness of the female body for women's self-representation seems dubious for two reasons. First, women have been so continuously and insistently identified with the body in the Christian West that to appear to accept that identification seems counterproductive, even in a post-Christian era. Second, female nakedness has not suffered from a lack of representation, but has, as we have seen, received the constant attention of male authors and artists; female nakedness has been heavily invested with social and religious meanings. Vision, the activity of seeing, does not occur independently of the associations provided by public meanings. And the female body which has played such a central historical role in the circulation of meaning in the Christian West is perhaps too assimilated to the male gaze to permit inscription with new meaning, with a female-defined sexuality and subjectivity. Female nakedness is, after all, at least as vigorously appropriated to the male gaze in twentieth-century media culture as it ever was.

Female nakedness and its corollary, the disengaged male gaze—scopophilia—are systematically woven into the routine expectations of a media culture. The freight and weight of public representations of female bodies cannot be quickly overcome by women who wish to use the female body to represent and symbolize women's subjectivity.

Edwina Sandy's *Christa* (figure 30) illustrates the danger of appropriating the naked female form to present women's experience. Here a crucified woman droops on an implied cross, thus occupying what is perhaps the position of greatest honor in centuries of Christian depictions of Christ's redemption of the world. The image startles; it makes vivid the perennial suffering of women. As a private devotional image it may have great healing potential for women who have themselves been battered or raped. Yet as a public image, placed for some time in the Cathedral of Saint John the Divine in New York City, there are fundamental problems with the image. The *Christa,* by its visual association with the crucified Christ, glorifies the suffering of women in a society in which violence against women has reached epidemic proportions.[14] Equally disturbing is its association with pornography, which similarly fetishizes suffering women. The naked and tortured female body has been appropriated by a media culture and cannot therefore be arbitrarily assigned religious meaning. The *Christa* cannot communicate religious meaning in twentieth-century Western culture any more than sixteenth- and seventeenth-century paintings of Susanna and the Elders could effectively communicate Susanna's innocence in societies in which, for centuries, female flesh had symbolized sin, sex, and the fall of the human race.

Nor is the problem simply that the female body is assimilated to the male gaze. In an important article, "The Esthetics of Power in Modern Erotic Art," Carol Duncan has argued that "the nude in her passivity and impotence [sic] is addressed to women as much as to men," for "far from being merely an entertainment for males, the nude as a genre is one of many cultural phenomena that teaches women to see themselves through male eyes and in terms of dominating male interests."[15] Women, whose visual training by the communication media has been virtually identical to that of men, have, like men, a subjectivity that is "crucially constituted by relations of looking."[16] Women, like men, acquire "a sense of subject set off against objects through active looking," so that women, insofar as they develop subjectivity, do so by occupying "the position of the male gaze."[17] The complex dynamic in which subjectivity belongs to the one who looks, and objectivity to the one looked at, will be difficult

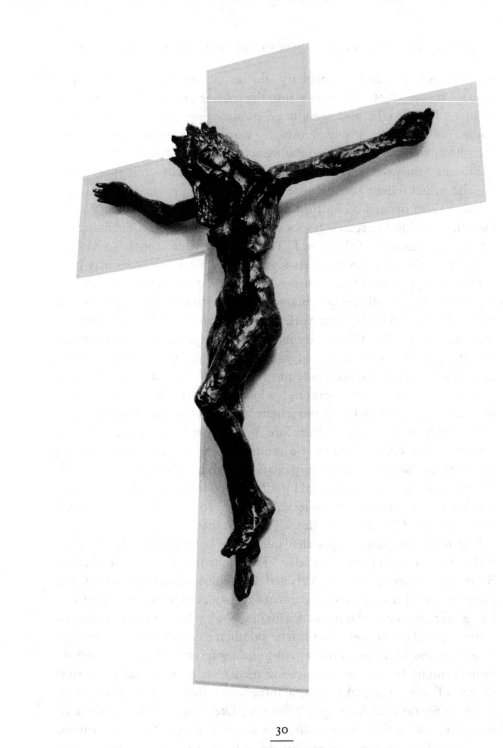

EDWINA SANDYS
*Christa*, 1983
Collection of the artist

for women to change, not only in society, but in our own visual practices.

Another condition identified by feminists as necessary for the effective representation of female nakedness as an expression of women's sexuality and subjectivity seems unlikely to be achieved in the foreseeable future. Men must relinquish the figure of the naked female as a format for the representation of male sexuality and must learn to represent themselves in more direct and honest ways. As Hélène Cixous has said:

Men still have everything to say about their sexuality and everything to write. For what they have said so far, for the most part, stems from the opposition activity/passivity, from the power relation between a phantasized obligatory virility meant to invade, to colonize, and the consequential phantasm of woman as a "dark continent" to penetrate and to "pacify."[18]

Certainly, when a new idiom for male sexuality replaces the use of the female body as a cipher for male desire, the female body, divested of its status as "occupied territory,"[19] will be more readily available to women's art and literature.

An intricate debate, which I will not reproduce here, has converged around issues related to the use of the female body in women's self-representation.[20] It is significant that, as Craig Owens writes, "few [women artists] have produced new 'positive' images of a revised femininity" and that "some refuse to represent women at all, believing that no representation of the female body in our culture can be free of phallic prejudice."[21] And Lisa Tichner has said that in the present "inherited framework" in which women artists work, "women's body art is . . . to a large extent reactive, basically against the glamourous reification of the Old Master/Playboy tradition, but also against the academic convention in so far as that, too, continued to see the female body as a special category of motif."[22] French feminists like Hélène Cixous, Luce Irigaray, and Julia Kristeva have urged women to "write the body," to formulate subjectivity as physical experience and in so doing to repossess the female body.[23] Visual artists have also experimented with a variety of presentations of the female body, but feminist critics like Lucy Lippard have been less certain of the effectiveness of female body images in a society in which these are easily accommodated to the established visual dynamic of the male gaze and the female object.

Is there a "women's art" arising from a distinctive female biology, experience, or sexuality?[24] The question has evoked different responses from women artists and feminist critics. Twentieth-century artists like Georgia O'Keeffe and Judy Chicago, to name only the best known, have used vaginal imagery extensively. They have, however, interpreted their use of female body imagery differently. O'Keeffe refused to think of or present herself as a "woman artist," finding that designation oppressive in an art world dominated by male artists and critics. Judy Chicago, on the other hand, insists on being understood as a woman artist; she established the first feminist art collective and wanted her work to be seen "in relation to other women's work, historically, as men's work is seen."[25] Chicago has also claimed that women artists share a common preoccupation with the female body, a characteristic "female imagery," a claim denied by other women artists and critics.[26]

More recently, the work of Sherrie Levine and Cindy Sherman illustrates the painful difficulty postmodern women artists experience in attempting to develop artistic forms that belong to women and express their subjectivity. Levine's work, from about 1978 to 1984, refused to use the female body as an expressive medium. Instead, she appropriated the imagery of other artists. She rephotographed the photographs of Edward Weston, Eliot Porter, Walker Evans, and others, and she created collages from cut-up reproductions of paintings and watercolors by such artists as Van Gogh, DeKooning, Kirchner, and Matisse. According to the critic Douglas Crimp, Levine did this to insist that art is "always a *re*presentation, always-already-seen."[27] Her work can thus be seen as "a radical critique of the most hallowed of art historical principles: the originality and expressiveness of the artist."[28] Levine's extreme self-effacement as artist, however, while it may dramatize the absence of women from public self-representation, has not suggested directions for the future of women's art.

Cindy Sherman works quite differently with the question of what a woman artist can represent. Although her photographs are usually of herself and/or objects intimately associated with her body (sunglasses, clothing, blood, vomit), Sherman "claims not to be present" in photographs of herself. Rather, her "presence" is that of "a series of stock personalities"[29] belonging to the object "woman." Sherman has been criticized for the way her self-images accept and invite the conventional male gaze. In several photographs she poses in bra and panties on a bed; others show her cringing from the gaze of the male spectator. Though visible, her body reveals only the absence of Cindy Sherman as subject. Like

Levine, Sherman dramatizes the exclusion of women from public self-representation but fails to suggest visual strategies that would permit women to present themselves as subjects in their art.

Essentialist versus social theories of sex and gender (see Appendix) reappear in these debates about women's self-representation in art and literature. For example, Elaine Showalter has argued against essentialist understandings like Cixous's in which women are urged to "write the body." While acknowledging the potential importance of female body imagery in women's literature, Showalter concludes that "there can be no expression of the body which is unmediated by linguistic, social, and literary structures." She proposes a theory of women's culture that "incorporates ideas about women's bodies, language, and psyche, but interprets them in relation to the social contexts in which they occur."[30] If there is any agreement among adherents of social and essentialist theories, however, it is in finding that too great a loss and deprivation for women is entailed in deciding that the female body has been irretrievably appropriated to male agenda.

Lisa Tichner has outlined two courses of action presently open to women artists: "one is to ignore the whole area as too muddled or dangerous for the production of clear statements; the other is to take the heritage and work with it—attack it, reverse it, expose it, and *use* it for their own purposes."[31] Tichner recommends that women artists reclaim the female body from masculine fantasy and "authenticate and reintegrate 'lost' [that is, unrepresented] aspects of female body experience." This reintegration will require, Tichner says, a "de-colonizing" and "de-eroticizing" of the female body.[32]

To begin that enterprise, women must first identify the techniques men use to colonize and eroticize the female body and then devise alternatives. In the last chapter of her study of representations of the female body in Victorian literature, *The Flesh Made Word,* Helena Michie concludes that "full representation of the body is necessarily impossible" in a language that depends for meaning on absence and difference. Nonetheless, she identifies—helpfully for our purposes—a device characteristically employed in male representations of female bodies that directly undermines representation of wonen as subjects. Fetishization of parts of the body—breasts, legs, vulva, uterus—she says, transgresses the body's integrity as subject. Underlying her analysis is the principle that "the recreation of the female body with its many zones of pleasure and playfulness depends on a respect for its integrity."[33] This suggests that the female body must be represented in ways that visually focus the whole body equally. In other words, it is a "naked," not a "nude," body that is able to bear the weight of women's self-representation.[34] The nude body, is, in Kenneth Clark's magisterial definition, passively positioned for the male gaze with its greater interest in some parts of the female body than others.

Women artists should also avoid encouraging a voyeuristic gaze in self-representations that use the female body as a symbol of subjectivity. For, as Iris Young notes:

Voyeuristic looking takes a distance from the object of its gaze, from which it is absent and elsewhere. From this distance the object of the gaze cannot return or reciprocate the gaze; the voyeur's look is judgmental, holding power over the guilty object of the gaze by offering punishment or forgiveness.[35]

Like men, women will need the commitment and self-discipline requisite to learning a new response—in the face of an inadequate response that has become habitual—if we are to look at a representation of a naked woman not with an appraising patriarchal eye, but with an eye that identifies with the person represented. This identification is a necessary preliminary step toward noticing and understanding the visual clues that make that person's interior life accessible.

New visual skills are difficult, even painful, to learn. It is not easy to discern the presence of a subject in visual images in which formerly an object has "caught the eye." Because of this difficulty, not many people will undertake to retrain themselves visually. Thus, a new discipline of seeing cannot be proclaimed as a panacea, a correction for the exclusion of women as subject in Western art and literature. But when feminist artists and authors "paint the body" and "write the body" as the perfect expression of female subjectivity, this art begins to create a new kind of "spectator" a viewer whose aesthetic experience is more like making an acquaintance than like surveying an object.[36]

One of Suzanne Valadon's self-portraits provides an example of female nakedness presented as symbol and site of a woman's subjectivity (figure 31). Her 1932 *Self-Portrait,* painted when she was sixty-seven, shows her naked upper body. Upright—seated or standing—the figure meets the viewer's eye directly. Filling the picture frame, she seems uncomfortably close to the viewer, thereby resisting the distanced eye of the voyeur. *Her* gaze seems to replace or overwhelm that of the viewer. The bottom edge

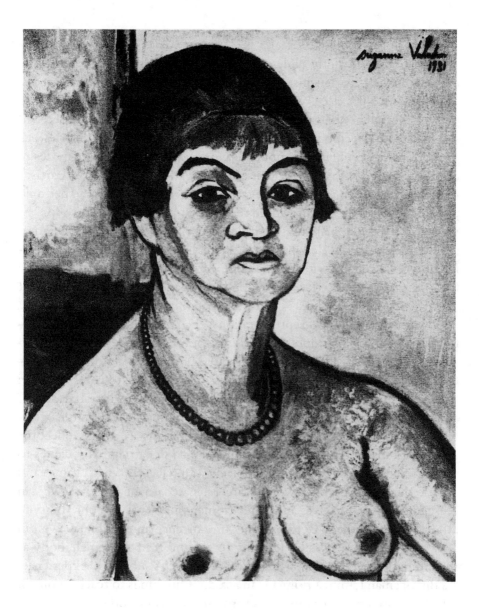

31

SUZANNE VALADON
*Self-Portrait*, 1932
Galérie Pétridès, Paris

of the painting abruptly elides the woman's right breast just under the nipple, refusing the fetishist's pleasure in seeing the shape of the breast. "Dressed" in a necklace, with combed hair and made-up face, the figure presents herself as she wishes to be seen. She appears self-possessed and self-conscious, her body herself, who she is, indifferent to the viewer's projections, and deliberately not endeavoring to attract the gaze or desire of a male viewer. It is not accidental that Valadon, a professional artist's model for about ten years,[37] chose to present herself as subject in her own painting. Filling the picture space reserved in patriarchal culture for the young, attractive female nude with an older woman who stares, rather than attracts stares, Valadon effectively challenges the patriarchal identification of "woman" with female flesh. She repossesses the female body for a woman's subjectivity, "showing [a woman's] nakedness as an effect of particular circumstances . . . differentiated by age and work."[38]

In women's public self-representations, the female body must *look* different from the way it does as the expression of male desire. As in Valadon's *Self-Portrait,* different visual strategies can create a different relation between image and viewer. Perhaps for some time to come, women artists and authors will need to experiment with images, material, styles, and media for self-representation. But women must also learn to *see* differently if their collective public self-representations are not to reflect the introjected male gaze. Women, visually trained in patriarchal societies to see ourselves and other women as objects, can reject the visual values and artistic devices by which women are relegated to objectivity. We can cease to evaluate ourselves and other women on the basis of our ability to attract and hold the gaze that grants us existence and visibility. We can alter our visual practices by learning to see and read the female body as the intimate reflection and articulation of women's subjective experience. As the German feminist Frigga Haug said, "Our aim is to reach a point at which we no longer see ourselves through the eyes of others."[39]

Much of the content of this book has revolved around religious practices and representations of female nakedness in the Christian West, yet the conclusions I have drawn thus far have focused exclusively on the contemporary concerns of secular feminists. What relevance do the gendered practices and representations of women of historical Christan societies have for a contemporary culture frequently characterized as post-Christian?

The central project of Christianity, I suggest, has been subverted by the representational practices of the Christian West. That project, formulated doctrinally as the incarnation of God in human flesh, is carnal knowing, embodied knowledge. It is experiential understanding that is aware and respectful of the particular and concrete conditions in which all learning occurs, whether that learning is named as socialization, religious orientation, or subjectification. In Christianity, however, the flesh has largely been scorned, the body marginalized, in the project of a "spiritual" journey. Christian doctrinal affirmation of human bodies is unambiguous; doctrines of creation, the incarnation of Christ, and the resurrection of the body clearly posit a faith in which bodies are integral. Yet faith, knowledge of self and world, and spiritual progress came to be seen as abstract; at best, the energy and vitality of the body could be usurped for the creation and cultivation of a religious self. Counterinstances can certainly be found to disparagement of the body; one of them, naked baptism, I discussed extensively in chapter 1. My goal in that chapter was not only to describe Christian baptism as gendered, but also to explore the thoughtful, systematic inclusion of bodies in the essential initiation of all Christians.

Why did "the flesh" become marginalized in Christianity? It was not, as has often been charged, Christianity's self-identification with philosophy that most decisively created the view that knowledge at its best is free of the flesh, spiritual rather than carnal, unaffected by the intimate and concrete circumstances of the human being to which it belongs as knowledge. It was, rather, the sexism of Christian societies, revealed most clearly in representational practices that created this view and fatally undermined the Christian project of integrating the flesh. By identifying men with rationality and "woman" with body, *and* by rhetorical and pictorial practices that denigrated women in relation to men, Christian societies effectively ghettoized the flesh, undermining even the strongest doctrinal ratifications of "the body."

In Christianity the body scorned, the naked body, is a female body. Ironically, the contemporary feminist concern for recovering the female body lies at the heart of the ancient Christian project. To represent the female body, not as erotic—as "erotic" has been culturally constructed—not as the object of fascination and scorn, but as revelation and subjectivity is to correct and complete the Christian affirmation of body. It is to present the flesh, not made word, but given voice to sing its own song.

# Appendix

## THE POWER OF REPRESENTATION— PRODUCTIVE OR REPRESSIVE?

A social theory of the subject is necessary for an accurate understanding of the power of representation. Social theories understand socialization as a process in which subjectivity is created and informed by relationships and by the symbolic provisions of culture; they then analyze how that process is carried out in particular societies. Social theories oppose essentialist theories in which, for example, "masculine" or "feminine" traits are seen as innately connected to a person's gender.[1] Essentialist theories posit an essential womanhood, usually based on female biology or sexuality, and advocate the articulation of a female subjectivity rooted in this essential feature. Accordingly, the task envisioned by feminist essentialists is the stripping away of social conditioning in order to arrive at a pure, uncolonized female subject. According to social theories, however, sexualization, the organization of desire toward particular objects, is also a part of socialization, so that to posit an "authentic" female sexuality that precedes socialization is to miss the productive power of both social practices and representations.

Michel Foucault has also challenged the essentialist project, calling attention instead to the *productive* effect of a power that is diffused throughout society by which sexual desire is created rather than repressed, formed rather than appropriated.[2] The productivity hypothesis, in opposition to theories emphasizing women's repression and oppression, suggests that people individuate by selecting from cultural offerings, rejecting some and incorporating others. Individuation is described as a process in which an individual learns socially accepted theories of the self and "practices" the skills of self-presentation, a discipline which is itself "invested with pleasure."[3]

The social construction of the body and sexuality produces what Foucault has called the "docile body," bodies whose desires match the sort of labor and pleasure necessary for the perpetuation of the society. In a capitalist economy, individuals must both be willing to contribute labor and desire consumer goods. But the "docile body" is a gendered body. Women must be attracted to the enormous physical labor and emotional expense of childbearing and rearing. More cultural inducement must be given to women to attract them to giving birth and nurturing children than is necessary to attract men to productive labor. Social rewards for male productivity are both more immediate and more measurable than are rewards for female reproductivity. Unless women are masochists—and Paula Caplan has recently argued convincingly that they are not—it is important to examine the ways by which women are highly and positively rewarded for the inevitably (partially) self-sacrificial behavior required for pregnancy, childbirth, and the nurturing of children.[4]

Thus, to understand people as socially constrained or repressed is seriously incomplete without a simultaneous hypothesis about the social production of motivation, desire, and pleasure. Bodies do not become docile by a "simple process of prohibition"; female social conditioning is not solely something *done to* women. The simultaneous and complementary processes of socialization, sexualization, and subjectification are also invested with learning and the development of competencies—in short, of pleasure "arising from the activity of learning itself."[5] The gratification of progressively learning how to engage, control, and reap the rewards of the social order are inextricably linked to women's "insertion into the social order."[6] For women, sexualization has taken the form of learning the complex arts of attraction, the delicate techniques of presenting themselves as simultaneously seductive and "ladylike," erotic and unapproachable.

Formation by attraction, or the creation and direction of the individual's desire, is effective, economical, and problematic because particular forms of socialization appear to be chosen and pursued rather than imposed as external requirements. Foucault has described "control by stimulation" as "strong power," in contrast to "weak power" that operates by the threat or exercise of physical force. Strong power has no need to repress. Sexualization, by which women are directed to heterosexual desires, is intimately and centrally involved in control of stimulation.[7] Sexualization has thus become a central focus of feminist analysis.

An advantage of the productivity hypothesis is that it refuses to construe male and female sexuality as absolute and unchangeable. It does not appeal to "a form of essentialism in which 'male sexuality' is associated with violence, lust, objectification, and a preoccupation with orgasm, and 'female sexuality' with nurturance, reciprocity, intimacy, and an emphasis on non-genital pleasure."[8] If sexualization is learned rather than intrinsic to one's gender, it can be modified or relearned. In addition, the productivity hypothesis presents a more complex and coherent understanding of women's engagement in patriarchal societies than does the repression hypothesis; it identifies the rewards and advantages for women of learning to work with their cultural provisions. It does not insist that women are masochists who permit and enjoy their exploitation, but sees two kinds of rewards awaiting the woman who is "virtuous" in the eyes of her culture: forms of learning that are intrinsically pleasurable, and the respect and esteem of her community.

This book has discussed a range of practices and representations relating to women that can be seen as a continuum from productivity to repression. Gendered baptismal practices in the early Christian churches, for example, may be closer to the productivity end of the continuum in that women seem to have received—simultaneously with reinforcement of their secondary status in relation to men—resources for choosing a self-identity distinct from any they might have been offered in secular culture. It is not enough, however, to observe that many women managed to work creatively with their options; we must also do our best to evaluate whether the price women paid for respect and esteem was damaging to them, and whether that price was significantly greater than that required of males in the same culture. Medieval women's asceticism may seem to us to lie somewhere around the center of the continuum since it gave women both alternatives to marriage and childbearing *and* often exacted from them harsh renunciations. Martyrdom, while it allowed women to be seen as heroic, also required what most twentieth-century people would consider an incommensurate sacrifice. It is, however, a serious anachronism to assume that women became martyrs in order to win their community's esteem. Even if it is difficult for modern people to understand martyrdom as the self-liberating act that contemporary accounts describe, it can be acknowledged that martyrdom represented a chosen self-identification with religious values. In chapter 5, however, I discussed some representational practices that accompanied unrelieved oppression—the most literal, massive, and severe repression of women in the history of the Christian West.

There are, however, two problems with any attempt to assign places along a continuum from productivity to repression to practices and representations. First, such designations are limited by necessarily imperfect historical understanding, not only in that we do not possess all the relevant factual knowledge, but also because historians' own interests and concerns inevitably limit the extent to which the complex values and loyalties of historical people can be reconstructed. Second, Foucault has argued that socialization and force lie along a single continuum. People who are judged by their societies to exhibit criminal or insane behavior are incarcerated or executed. Socialization is anticipatory force in that it attempts, by training people to docile behavior, to forestall the necessity of coercion. Thus, no clear line can be drawn between persuasion to attitudes and behavior and the force that will be brought to bear if this "education" is not effective. The productivity thesis, then, must be modified by acknowledging the intimate connection of socialization and coercion, of productivity and repression.[9] In short, the repressive thesis is needed in order to recognize the real oppression of woman in patriarchal societies; the productivity thesis is also needed, however, to acknowledge the fact that women are rewarded for learning the skills associated with subordination.

A productivity hypothesis, therefore, cannot replace a repressive hypothesis, but balances it by imagining a continuum along which female sexualization, socialization, and subjectification occurs. At one end is the pleasurable sensation of empowerment by self-discipline and achievement; at the other end are the forceful and painful forms of women's incorporation into society—domestic and other forms of violence against women, restriction of women's activities and prerogatives, and public and private ridicule and vilification of "woman." In isolation from the repressive hypothesis, the productivity thesis fails to acknowledge the gendered power relations that govern social and sexual arrangements, religious provisions, and representational practices. It does not recognize or call attention to women's actual legal, social, and religious oppression.

# ABBREVIATIONS

ANF     Ante Nicene Fathers

ACW     Ancient Christian Writers

CCLS     Corpus Christianorum, Series Latina

CSEL     Corpus scriptorum ecclesiasticorum

DACL     *Dictionnaire d'Archéologie chrétienne et de Liturgie,* ed. F. Cabrol and H. Leclercq (Paris: Librairie Letouzey et Ane, 1903–50)

FOC     Fathers of the Church

LW     Luther's Works

NPN     Nicene and Post-Nicene Fathers

# NOTES

## PREFACE

1. Barbara Duden, *Geschichte unter der Haut: Ein Eisenacher Arzt und seine Patien-tinnen um 1730* (Stuttgart: Klett-Cotta, 1987), 172.
2. Although I usually avoid the emotionally charged word "patriarchy," it does accurately describe the male-designed and administered societies of the Christian West. Thus it is important to say at the outset what I mean by "patriarchy," whether I use the word itself or a synonymous phrase. I use the concept of patriarchy "thickly"; minimally, it is descriptive, indicating that Western Christian and post-Christian societies are and have been designed and administered by men. By "patriarchal," however, I also mean that the formal and informal institutions of these societies are designed to embody and support the agenda of male psyches. Freud described the psychological roots of patriarchal domination in the relationship of the male infant to the mother, especially in the dual and contradictory need of the infant, on the one hand, for recognition by the (m)other, and on the other hand, for independence from the (m)other. Classical psychoanalysis formulated individuation as a difficult and dangerous process of creating a self–other distinction, a development in which "merging was a dangerous form of undifferentiation, a sinking back into the sea of oneness." The infant's task, according to Freud, was to strive for omnipotence and control. The little girl, since she can grow up to be "like" the mother, need not, like the boy, struggle to "have," to possess, the mother. On the level of society, patriarchal institutions reflect the psychic agenda of the male infant—domination and control. See Jessica Benjamin, *The Bonds of Love: Psychoanalysis, Feminism, and the Problem of Domination* (New York: Pantheon, 1988), 81–84.

## INTRODUCTION

1. Gayatri Spivak, quoted by Helena Michie, *The Flesh Made Word: Female Figures and Women's Bodies* (New York: Oxford University Press, 1987), 7.
2. Luce Irigaray, *Speculum of the Other Woman*, trans. Gillian C. Gill (Ithaca: Cornell University Press, 1974), 13.
3. Ibid., 133.

4. Susanne Kappeler, *The Pornography of Representation* (Minneapolis: University of Minnesota Press, 1986), 52–53.

5. Jacques Derrida, "Sending: On Representation," *Social Research* 49:2 (Summer 1982): 325.

6. *The Epic of Gilgamesh*, trans. N. K. Sanders (Baltimore: Penguin, 1960), 99.

7. "Siduri," however, means only "young woman."

8. Craig Owens, "The Discourse of Others: Feminists and Postmodernism," *The Anti-Aesthetic: Essays on Postmodern Culture,* ed. Hal Foster (Port Townsend, WA: Bay Press, 1983), 66.

9. Ibid., 57.

10. Ioan P. Culianu, *Eros and Magic in the Renaissance* (Chicago: University of Chicago Press, 1987), 5.

11. Culianu notes (ibid., 5) that "The *sensus interior,* inner sense, or Aristotelian common sense, which had become a concept inseparable not only from scholasticism but also from all western thought until the eighteenth century, is to keep its importance even for Descartes and reappear, perhaps for the last time, at the beginning of Kant's *Critique of Pure Reason.*"

12. See also Augustine's description of *phantasia* and *phantasma* in *The Literal Meaning of Genesis;* CSEL 2, 128, n. 98, and 285, n. 100.

13. This is Hans-Georg Gadamer's term; see *Truth and Method* (New York: Crossroad, 1984). The "effective history" of an idea is the account of its interpretation and application in different social and intellectual contexts.

14. Culianu, *Eros and Magic,* 19.

15. *Poeti del Duecento,* ed. G. F. Contini (Milan and Naples, 1960), vol. 1, 49; quoted by Culianu, 22.

16. Immanuel Kant, *Critique of Judgment,* trans. J. H. Bernard (New York: Macmillan/Hafner, 1951), 37.

17. Ibid., 38.

18. Augustine, *Enarrationes in Psalmos* 132.10; trans. H. Chadwick, *Augustine* (London: Oxford University Press, 1986), 46.

19. Kappeler, *Pornography of Representation,* 55.

20. Francis Barker, *The Tremulous Private Body: Essays on Subjection* (New York: Methuen, 1984), 101.

21. See Craig Owens's discussion of classical, modern, and postmodern theories of representation in "Representation, Appropriation and Power," *Art in America* 70:5 (May 1982): 9–21.

22. Owens, "Discourse," 66.

23. Ibid.

24. Jacques Derrida and others have advocated a distribution of the process of critical judgment, pointing out that socially located perspective always influences—and largely determines—critical judgments. See ibid., 58–59.

25. Ibid., 61. Though decentering or destabilizing the subject has been a project of postmodernism, it has been, according to Owens, "scandalously indifferent"

to feminist critique of the masculine subject of representation. It is important to note, however, that destabilizing the subject is a project that can be undertaken only by those whose subjectivity is supported and privileged by existing social arrangements and institutions. It is a project for white, educated, male Westerners. Having no institutionalized subjectivity to decenter, women and minorities can deconstruct only the female or minority object constructed in male-designed and -administered societies. To identify the social location of a task, however, is not to devalue it or to diminish its significance. The importance of the destabilization of the subject in postmodern critical theory is that it indicates the awareness of at least a few men in positions of intellectual, institutional, and cultural leadership of the bankruptcy of the Western intellectual tradition. Modernism's part in this awareness was to formulate the claim to a universalizing mastery of reality by defining discourse in such a dramatic way that the blindness of such claims could become clear.

26. See also *A Lexicon of St. Thomas Aquinas,* vol. 1, ed. Roy J. Deferrari and Sister M. Inviolata Barry (Washington, D.C.: Catholic University of America Press, 1948), 133; *Lexique Philosophique de Guillaume D'Ockham; sapientia, scientia,* ed. Leon Baudry (Paris: P. Lethielleux, 1958), 236–44; *Latin Dictionary: carnalis, sapientia, scientia,* ed. Lewis and Short (Oxford: Clarendon Press, 1962), 293, 1629, 1642.

27. New Testament authors used the word "carnal" to emphasize the contrast between spiritual and material (2 Corinthians 10:4; Romans 7:14; 1 Corinthians 3:3). Human nature under the domination of "lower" impulses was called "carnal." Like New Testament authors, patristic authors usually used "carnal" as a synonym for sin. As a technical theological term, however, "carnal" did not mean physical, nor was the human body necessarily devalued. Rather, the *psyche* was responsible for sin, using the body as a tool for the accomplishment of its agenda.

28. George Lakoff, *Women, Fire, and Dangerous Things: What Categories Reveal about the Mind* (Chicago: University of Chicago Press, 1987), 7.

29. Tertullian, *On the Resurrection of the Flesh* xv; ANF 3, 555.

30. Subjectivity as a cultural artifact has been discussed by philosopher of science Rom Harré, who writes: "The fundamental reality is a conversation, effectively without beginning or end, to which, from time to time, individuals may make contributions. All that is personal in our mental and emotional lives is individually appropriated from the conversation going on around us and perhaps idiosyncratically transformed. The structure of our thinking and feeling will reflect, in various ways, the form and content of that conversation." *Personal Being: A Theory for Individual Psychology* (Cambridge: Harvard University Press, 1984), 20.

31. Ruth Hubbard, "Constructing Sex Difference," *New Literary History* 19:1 (Autumn 1987): 131.

32. Michele Montrelay, "Recherches sur la femininité," *Critique* 278 (July 1970).

33. Barker, *Tremulous Private Body,* 62–63; see also Michie, *Flesh Made Word,* passim.

34. Christine Buci-Glucksmann, "Catastrophic Utopia: The Feminine as Allegory of the Modern," in *The Making of the Modern Body,* ed. Catherine Gallagher and Thomas Laqueur (Berkeley: University of California Press, 1987), 227.

35. Ellen Messer-Davidow, "The Philosophical Bases of Feminist Literary Criticism," *New Literary History* 19:1 (Autumn 1987): 82.

36. Annette Kuhn, *The Power of the Image: Essays on Representation and Sexuality* (London: Routledge and Kegan Paul, 1985), 96; also Griselda Pollock, "Women, Art, and Ideology: Questions for Feminist Art Historians," *Women's Art Journal* 4 (Spring/Summer 1983).

37. Messer-Davidow, "Philosophical Bases," 73.

38. Nancy Chodorow has written: "I argue that the sex/gender system is a social, psychological, and cultural totality. We cannot identify one sphere as uniquely causal or constructive of the others. You cannot understand the social organization of gender apart from the fact that we are all psychologically sexed and gendered, that we do not have a self apart from our being gendered." "Reply," in "On *The Reproduction of Mothering:* A Methodological Debate," *Signs* 6:3 (Spring 1981): 502.

39. Ellen Messer-Davidow's article "The Philosophical Bases of Feminist Literary Criticism" outlines a method for identifying and exploring sex/gender systems. First, *particularization* specifies the individual voices from which statements and images originate; the cohesiveness of society is not assumed, but variables like gender and social location are critical to understanding the statement. Second, *contextualization* examines the culture in which the representation occurs. The relevant question here is: What cultural work did a particular representation do in its historical situation? The analyst should be on the alert for "structural congruence," the appearance of "the same sex/gender ideas in one instance of a medium (a novel), several instances of a medium (novels), or several instances of different media (novels, criticisms, manners, laws)." *Metaphorical congruence,* the repetition of the same metaphors across disciplinary discourses or media of representation, reveals the operation of rhetorical devices so grounded in cultural "common sense" that they can be counted on to move an argument or to persuade. Finally, *influence* can be traced in the circulation of ideas related to sex/gender from author to text and from reader-authors back to other authors and texts: "Discerning congruence and tracing influence are methods suited to analyze the middle ground of a complex system; they treat the entities and the relations that subsist among them. Enlarging these analyses synchronically and diachronically, and weaving in the variables of race, class, affectional preference, and other cultural specificities, feminist literary critics can approximate the sex/gender system" (87).

40. For a detailed discussion of the extreme food practices of medieval women, see Caroline Walker Bynum, *Holy Fast and Holy Feast: The Religious Significance of Food to Medieval Women* (Berkeley: University of California Press, 1987).

41. Kenneth Clark, *The Nude: A Study in Ideal Art* (London: John Murray, 1956), 3, 4.

42. Ibid., 1. Compare Clark's unawareness of the male-gendered perspective that informs his evaluation of "Correggio's women," whom he calls "ravishing creatures" because "they have a self-surrender that has never been depicted elsewhere"; *Feminine Beauty* (New York: Rizzoli, 1980), 18.

43. Clark, *The Nude*, 6; Clark's equivocal use of "ourselves" in this sentence is revealing. The passive naked body that is recognized as "ourselves" and the spectator who feels an active wish to perpetuate "ourselves" are surely not the same person.

44. Kuhn, *The Power of the Image*, 11.

45. Clark, *The Nude*, 17.

46. Ibid., 18.

47. Ibid., 18–19.

48. Augustine, *The Literal Meaning of Genesis* 3.22; ACW 41, 99.

49. Ibid.

50. Even this limited but clear acknowledgment of women's rational capacities has not always been forthcoming. Though, admittedly, one cannot expect to find affirmation of women in the literature of witch persecution, the *Malleus Maleficarum* is especially emphatic on the issue of women's lack of rationality: "For, as regards intellect, or the understanding of spiritual things, [women] seem to be of a different nature than men. . . . Women are intellectually like children. . . . She is more carnal in nature than a man, as is clear from her many carnal abominations." *The Malleus Maleficarum,* trans. Montague Summers (New York: Dover, 1971), 44.

I
---

CHRISTIAN BAPTISM IN THE FOURTH CENTURY:
THE CONVERSION OF THE BODY

1. John Calvin, *Commentary on Isaiah* 8.7; quoted in William J. Bouwsma, *John Calvin: A Sixteenth-Century Portrait* (New York: Oxford University Press, 1988), 140.

2. Caesarius of Arles, *Sermon* 42; CCSL 32, 537.

3. H. Leclercq, "Nu dans l'art chrétien," DACL 12, 2 (1936), cols. 1782–1808.

4. Hubertus Manderscheid, *Die Skulpturenausstattung der Kaiserzeitlichen Thermenanlagen* (Berlin: Gebr. Mann, n.d.).

5. Werner Heinz, *Romische Thermen* (Munchen: Hirmer, 1983), 75; Erika Brodner, *Die Romischen Thermen und Das Antike Badewesen* (Darmstadt: Wissenschaftliche Buchgesellschaft, 1983), 113–15.

6. Paul Ableman, *Anatomy of Nakedness* (London: Orbis, 1982), 64.

7. For arguments that Christians are indistinguishable from other citizens of the

empire in external matters, see the *Epistle to Diognetus* 5.1.4: "Christians cannot be distinguished from the rest of humanity by their country, language, or clothing. . . . They conform to local custom in the matter of food and daily life." See also Augustine, in *The City of God* 19.19: "It is completely irrelevant to the Heavenly City what dress is worn or what manner of life adopted by each person who follows the faith that is the way to God, provided that these do not conflict with the divine instructions."

8. See my essay "Patriarchy as Political Theology: The Establishment of North African Christianity," in *Civil Religion and Political Theology,* ed. LeRoy Rouner (South Bend, IN: University of Notre Dame Press, 1986): "The confusion and disagreement evident in early Christian authors about what a Christian's appearance and behavior should be in the secular arena indicate that it was not at all easy to sort out which parts of life were directly relevant to the Christian life, requiring Christians to look and act differently from other people. Whether Christians should serve in the army, which professions Christians might follow, and how Christian women . . . should look, as well as many other questions are addressed very differently at different times and in different locations by Christian authors. It was not clear which areas of life required distinctive Christian behavior" (174–75).

9. *Apostolic Constitutions* 1.vi; ANF 7, 393.

10. Ibid., 1.ix; see also Clement of Alexandria, *Paedagogus* 3.5; ANF 2, 279.

11. Cyprian, *On the Dress of Virgins* 2; ANF 5, 430.

12. Jerome, *Epistle* 107.11; NPN 6, 194.

13. Ibid., 108.20; 206.

14. Augustine, *Epistle* 211.13; FOC 31, 94.

15. As Samuel Laeuchli has demonstrated in *Power and Sexuality* (Philadelphia: Temple University Press, 1972, 89), the regulation of sexuality was a major power issue in the fourth-century Christian churches. Regulation of sexual practices was a way to inject the authority of church laws and leaders into the intimate and daily relationships of Christians. Analyzing the canons of the Council of Gangra in AD 309, Laeuchli found that 46 percent of the eighty-one canons were concerned with sexual relationships and practices.

16. See P. de Puniet's discussion of *renuntiare saeculo* in North African baptismal formulae, and his citation of patristic authors on the topic in "Baptême," DACL, cols. 310–25. See also Stevan L. Davies's discussion of early apocryphal *Acts* (c. 160–225 AD), in *The Revolt of the Widows: The Social World of the Apocryphal Acts* (London: Feffer and Sons, 1980), esp. 35. This popular Christian literature takes the attitude that secular social life represents an impediment to Christian life. In these works, itinerant Christian "apostles" model the view that "virtue stems from freedom from the entanglements of social life." Condemning not only judicial authority and structured social obligations, but even "productive activity" in society, the *Acts* stress renunciation of social, familial, and marital responsibilities.

17. Augustine, *Sermon* 198; FOC 38, 58.

18. See, for example, Frederic van der Meer's misleading interpretation of catechumens' feeling about naked baptism: "There is no embarrassment, for they have all been accustomed from childhood on to the freedom practiced in the baths, and at home they invariably sleep naked under the bedclothes." *Augustine the Bishop* (London: Sheed and Ward, 1961), 367.

19. Tertullian, *On the Resurrection of the Flesh* viii; ANF 3.

20. See my *Augustine on the Body* (Missoula, MT: Scholars Press, 1979) for a discussion of Augustine's theological and philosophical ideas of the relationship of body and soul.

21. Galatians 3:28.

22. For example, Palladius's story of Alexandra, a former maidservant who has "shut herself up in a tomb and received the necessities of life through an opening, seeing neither women nor men face to face for ten years." Asked why she chose this extreme life, Alexandra explained, "A man was distressed in mind because of me and, lest I should seem to afflict or disparage him, I chose to betake myself alive into the tomb rather than cause a soul, made in the image of God, to stumble." *The Lausiac History of Palladius,* 5.1, trans. W. K. Lowther Clarke (London: SPCK, 1918), 53.

23. See Michel Foucault, "Sexuality and Solitude," in *On Signs,* ed. Marshall Blonsky (Baltimore: Johns Hopkins University Press, 1985), 367: ". . . techniques which permit individuals to affect, by their own means, a certain number of operations on their own bodies, their own souls, their own thoughts, their own conduct, and this in a manner so as to transform themselves, modify themselves, and to attain a certain state of perfection, happiness, purity, supernatural power. Let us call these techniques the technologies of the self."

24. Ibid., 369.

25. Ibid.

26. A. Dondeyne calls the examination of candidates for baptism a "ceremony of humiliation" composed of exorcisms, prayers, and renunciations of Satan; see "La discipline des scrutins dans l'église latine avant Charlemagne," *Revue d'histoire écclesiastique* 28:2 (January 1932): 18.

27. Did Christian initiation always achieve fundamental change of life? Augustine repeatedly deplored the noticeable imperfection of the *corpus permixtum* that was the church: "If one has been reborn, where is his new life? If he is one of the faithful, where is his faith? I hear the name; let me recognize the reality. . . . If you do not find what you may imitate, then be what somebody else may imitate." *Sermon* 228; FOC 38; 200.

28. Ibid.

29. See R. J. O'Connell's discussion of *fovere caput* in *St. Augustine's Early Theory of Man* (Cambridge: Harvard University Press, 1968), 65ff.

30. Frederic van der Meer, *Augustine the Bishop* trans. B. Battershaw and G. R. Lamb, (London: Sheed and Ward, 1961), 358.

31. Augustine, *Confessions* 9.2. Augustine's rejection of his profession as a rhetorician was voluntary but was based on a desire to commit his life to more con-

centrated study and prayer than would have been possible while pursuing a secular career. People who held some occupations and professions, however, were not permitted baptism until they had renounced their profession: actors, stage managers, pimps, prostitutes, gladiators, etc. Lists of banned professions differ at different times and across the Roman Empire; Tertullian adds "idol-makers" to the list he gives in *On Idolatry* vi; ANF 3, 64; cf. *Apostolic Constitutions* 8.xxxii; ANF 7, 495.

32. Davies, *Revolt of the Widows,* passim.

33. Ibid.

34. Van der Meer, *Augustine the Bishop,* 350.

35. Ibid., 356.

36. Tertullian, *On Baptism* 18, trans. Ernest Evans (London: SPCK, 1964), 40–41; *On Repentance* vi; ANF 3, 661–62.

37. Augustine, *On the Gospel of St. John* 44.2; NPN 7, 245.

38. Van der Meer, *Augustine the Bishop,* 352.

39. Tertullian, *On Repentance,* vii; ANF 3, 664.

40. Van der Meer's paraphrase of a sermon collected by Frangipane, *Sancti Aurelii Augustini Hipponensis Episcopi Sermones X,* in *Augustine the Bishop,* 150.

41. *The Apostolic Tradition of Hippolytus,* ed. Burton Scott Easton (Cambridge: Archon Books, 1962), 46.

42. Cyril of Jerusalem, *The Mystagogical Lectures,* FOC 64, 161.

43. Trans. adapted from R. Tonneau and R. Devreesse, *Homélies catéchétiques de Theodore de Mopsueste* (Rome: "Studi e Testi," 1949), 417; Jonathan Z. Smith, "The Garments of Shame," *History of Religions* 5:2 (Winter 1966): 224.

44. *The Ecclesiastical Hierarchy,* in *The Complete Works of Pseudo-Dionysius,* trans. Colm Luibheid (New York: Paulist Press, 1987), 202.

45. Smith, "Garments," 235; Mabillon-Germain, *Museum Italicum* 1:2 (Paris, 1687), 71–72.

46. Narsai, Homily 22, "On Baptism," trans. R. H. Connolly, *The Liturgical Homilies of Narsai Translated into English,* Texts and Studies, vol. 8 (Cambridge, 1909), 39.

47. J. B. de Rossi, "Insigne vetro, sul quale è effigiato il battesimo d'una fanciulla," *Bulletino d'archeologia cristiana,* ser. 3, 1 (1876): 7–14 and plate 1.

48. See J. Heckenbach, *De nuditate sacrisque vinculis* (Giessen, 1911); F. Pfister, "Nackheit," in Pauly-Wissowa, *Real-Encyclopadie* 16:2, cols. 1541–49; Smith, "Garments," 218–19, footnote 6 lists other discussions of cultic nudity in Greco-Roman society.

49. Smith, "Garments," 219.

50. Ibid.

51. Smith, ibid., 220 n. 12, lists texts that describe baptismal nakedness.

52. Colossians 3.9, 10; Ephesians 4.22–24; quoted by Cyril of Jerusalem and many other authors.

53. Cyril of Jerusalem, "Second Lecture on the Mysteries," FOC 64, 161.

54. Smith, "Garments," 235.

55. Cyril of Jerusalem, "Second Lecture on the Mysteries" 4; FOC 64, 165.

56. Augustine, *Sermon* 228.1, FOC 38, 199.

57. Smith, "Garments," 227.

58. For a discussion of "Becoming Male and Making the Two One" in Gnosticism and early Christianity, see Dennis R. MacDonald, *There is No Male or Female* (Philadelphia: Fortress Press, Harvard Dissertations in Religion, 1987), 98ff.

59. Smith, "Garments," 237 n. 70; Hippolytus, *Refutations* v.8.44; ANF 5, 59.

60. MacDonald, *No Male or Female*, 67ff.; also Smith, "Garments," 235 n. 69 for sources on stripping off the body in gnostic literature.

61. Quoted by MacDonald, *No Male or Female*, 53; also Wayne A. Meeks, "The Image of the Androgyne: Some Uses of a Symbol in Earliest Christianity," *History of Religions* 13:3 (February 1974): 189ff.

62. The following description is dependent on van der Meer's detailed account in *Augustine the Bishop*.

63. Ibid., 349: "Particular importance attached to secrecy around the year 400." Compare the practices of catechetical instruction in North Africa at the end of the fourth century with those at Jerusalem as described by Cyril and John of Jerusalem and by Egeria, a traveler from western Europe to Jerusalem: FOC 64 passim; *Egeria's Travels* 45.1ff., trans. John Wilkinson (London: SPCK, 1973).

64. Van der Meer (*Augustine the Bishop,* 355) says that, although there are references to the sacrament of salt, "nowhere is there a full explanation of it."

65. In *Sermon* 210; FOC, 38, 97, Augustine says that in spite of the fact the Christ fasted *after,* not before his baptism, catechumens must fast before baptism instead. Christ's fasting related not to the baptism of John, he writes, but to his temptation, so that Christians must follow his example in fasting when temptation comes, and the devil's attacks are strongest just before baptism, when he attempts to break the *competens'* resolve to be baptized.

66. Van der Meer, *Augustine the Bishop,* 358.

67. Augustine, *Sermon* 224.2–3; FOC 38, 186–87.

68. Ibid.; see van der Meer, *Augustine the Bishop,* 635 n. 61 for references to the physical examination of candidates for baptism.

69. Theodore of Mopsuestia, *Commentary of Theodore of Mopsuestia on the Lord's Prayer and on the Sacraments of Baptism and the Eucharist,* trans. A. Mingana (Cambridge: Woodbrooke Studies, vol. 6, 1933), 32–36; see also Augustine, *Sermon* 216.10–11; FOC 38, 160, for allusions to the "garments of skin." MacDonald (*No Male or Female,* 61) suggests that the earliest meaning of the "garments of skin" was not repentance for one's past sins, but "the body which one treated with contempt by trampling it prior to baptism."

70. Augustine, *Sermon* 214.1; FOC 38, 130.

71. Ibid.

72. Augustine's sermons 56–59 and 212–16, along with *De catechizandis rudibus*, describe the prebaptismal preparation of candidates in North African churches.

73. Augustine, *Sermon* 222; FOC 38, 181.

74. Van der Meer, *Augustine the Bishop*, 365.

75. Cyril of Jerusalem, *The Mystagogical Lectures* 2; FOC 64, 162.

76. Van der Meer, *Augustine the Bishop*, 367.

77. Augustine, *Sermon* 216.1, 7; FOC 38, 150; 156–57.

78. White robes are first attested in the fifth century; A. J. Klijn, "An Early Christian Baptismal Liturgy," in *Chariskai Sophia. Festschrift for Karl Rengsdorf . . .* (Leiden: Brill, 1964), 216–18.

79. Tertullian, in *De corona* 3, wrote that after baptism, "we taste first of all a mixture of milk and honey, and from that day we refrain from the daily bath for a whole week"; initiates in the Roman cult of Attis were also given milk and honey at their initiation to signify their newborn status. See M. Legay, *Saturne africain, Histoire* (Paris, 1966), 389.

80. Augustine, *Sermon* 216.2 FOC 38, 152; see also the account of the conversion of the late-fourth-century prostitute Pelagia of Antioch in which Satan, as a scowling man, berates Pelagia for her baptism: "Is this my due, Pelagia? Didn't you belong to me and I to you up to just now?" in Sebastian P. Brock and Susan Ashbrook Harvey, *Holy Women of the Syrian Orient* (Berkeley: University of California Press, 1987), 54.

81. Augustine, *Sermon* 216.6; FOC 38, 155–6.

82. Speaking of the unbaptized, Augustine wrote: "When we ask a catechumen whether he believes in Christ, he says, 'Yes, I believe,' and crosses himself. . . . but if you ask him, 'Do you eat the body and drink the blood of the Son of Man?' then he has no notion what all that is about;" van der Meer, 357; *On the Gospel of St. John* 11.3; NPN 7, 75; also *Sermon* 227; FOC 38, 196: "You have read or heard this in the Gospels, but you did not know that this Eucharist was the Son himself."

83. Augustine, *Sermon* 272; quoted by van der Meer, *Augustine the Bishop*, 372.

84. Augustine, *Sermon* 227; FOC 38, 196.

85. Ibid.

86. Stephen Benko describes practices of ritual cannibalism known to later Roman people; he also discusses allegations that Christians practiced cannibalism. See "The Charges of Immorality and Cannibalism," in *Pagan Rome and the Early Christians,* (Bloomington: Indiana University Press, 1986); see also Benko's article, "The Libertine Sect of the Phibionites according to Epiphanius," *Vigilae Christianae* 21 (1967): 103–19.

87. *Tertullian's Treatise on Baptism* 20, ed. and trans. Ernest Evans (London: SPCK, 1964), 41.

88. Augustine refers to the exhaustion of the candidates and their instructors in his Easter Sunday *Sermon* 228.1; FOC 38, 198.

89. Wayne A. Weeks notes that in the sources that give information on fasting

from the early church, "it appears that fasting was never consciously practiced for the purpose of producing ecstatic states." "Fasting and Prophecy in Pagan and Christian Antiquity," *Traditio* 7 (1949–51): 60. Among Gnostics and Montanists, however, there is evidence that fasting was done for this purpose; Tertullian, in his Montanist period, speaks of revelations "wrenched" from God by xerophagies: "revelationes xerophagiis extorquere," *On Fasting* 12; ANF 4, 110.

90. Using contemporary experimentation and observation to draw inferences from the past is called "regressive history." See Emmanuel Le Roy Laudurie, "Famine Amenorrhoea," in *The Biology of Man in History* (Baltimore: Johns Hopkins University Press, 1975), 165.

91. *The Biology of Starvation,* ed. Ancel Keys et al. (Minneapolis: University of Minnesota Press, 1950).

92. Herbert Musurillo, "The Problem of Ascetical Fasting in the Greek Patristic Writers," *Traditio* 2 (1956): 1–64.

93. Athanasius, *On Virginity* 7; see also Abbot Nilus of Ancyra: "It was the desire of food that spawned disobedience; it was the pleasure of taste that drove us from Paradise. Luxury in food delights the gullet, but it breeds the worm of license that does not sleep. An empty stomach prepares one for watching and prayer; the full one induces sleep. The mind is sober when it has a dry diet; a liquid one plunges the mind into the depths. The prayer of him who fasts flies up like the eaglet; but the prayer of the dissipater, weighted down with satiety, drags along the ground. The mind of the faster is a brilliant star among the heavens; the mind of the dissipater is concealed in gloom. Just as a fog obscures the sun, so a heavy quantity of food darkens the mind." *Tractatus de octo spiritibus malitiae,* trans. by Musurillo, "Fasting," 16.

94. Augustine, *Sermon* 207.1, FOC 38, 89.

95. *Apostolic Constitutions* 7.xxii; the earlier *Teaching of the Twelve Apostles* vii, compiled about AD 120, states simply that the candidate for baptism must fast "one or two days."

96. *Apostolic Constitutions* 5.xix; for information on Pascal fasts in different parts of the empire, see Wayne A. Meeks, "Fasting and Prophecy," 42.

97. *Apostolic Constitutions* Canon 69; ANF 7, 504: "If any bishop or presbyter or deacon, or reader, or singer, does not fast the fast of forty days, or the fourth day of the week, and the day of Preparation, let him be deprived, except he be hindered by weakness of body."

98. Tertullian, *On Fasting* 17; ANF 4, 113: "Appendages . . . of appetite are lasciviousness and voluptuousness"; also Jerome, *Epistle* 55.2; NPN 6, 110: "For excess in eating is the mother of lust." See Rudolf Arbesmann, *Das Fasten bei den Griechen und Romern* (Giessen, 1929), 21ff.

99. Basil of Ancyra, *De vera virginitatis integritate* 6–7; quoted in Musurillo, "Fasting," 14.

100. See Musurillo, "Fasting," 17 n. 43, for a list of patristic references to this "Adam-motif"; an interesting later comparison is Martin Luther's interpretation of Adam's reason for eating the unauthorized fruit. Adam ate, Luther says, not

because he desired the fruit, but because "he was unwilling to cause Eve sadness." *Lectures on Genesis;* LW 1, 90.

101. Cyril of Jerusalem, *Procatechesis* 9; FOC 61, 77.

102. Van der Meer, *Augustine the Bishop,* 354.

103. Cyril of Jerusalem, *Catachesis* 13.36; FOC 64, 28.

104. Tertullian, *Apology* xxiii; ANF 3, 37.

105. As David Sabean has recently shown, "What is common in community is not shared values or common understanding so much as the fact that the members of a community are engaged in the same . . . discourse, in which alternative strategies, misunderstandings, and conflicting goals and values are threshed out. What makes community is the discourse." *Power in the Blood, Popular Culture and Village Discourse in Early Modern Germany* (New York: Cambridge University Press, 1984), 29.

106. Galatians 3:28, cited in Wayne A. Meeks, "The Image of the Androgyne: Some Uses of a Symbol in Earliest Christianity," *History of Religion* 13:3 (February 1974): 180.

107. Cyril of Jerusalem, *The Mystagogical Lectures* 2; FOC 64, 162; see also Smith, "Garments," 237: "Being naked and without shame is both a practical requirement stemming from the minister's anointing of nude women in a public ceremony and a typological return to the state of Adam and Eve before the Fall."

108. R. H. Connolly, trans., *Didascalia Apostolorum* (London: Oxford University Press, 1929), 146-47. It is interesting to note the gendered division of labor in administering baptism in the Syriac churches in which deaconnesses were ordained: "Let a woman deacon, as we have already said, anoint the women. But let a man pronounce over them the invocation of the Divine Names in the water" (3.12). Women minister to the body ("And you have need of the ministry of a deaconness for many things; for a deaconess is required to go into the houses of the heathen where there are believing women, and to visit those who are sick, and to minister to them in that of which they have need, and to bathe those who have begun to recover from illness"), while men retain the privilege of language. Similarly, the *Apostolic Constitutions* (the first six books of which follow the *Didascalia Apostolorum* closely) did not permit deaconesses to teach in church (3.6) or baptize (3.9). Thus "to baptize" must have been understood as essentially "the invocation of the Divine Names." "A deaconess does not bless, nor perform anything belonging to the office of presbyters or deacons, but only is to keep the doors, and to minister to the presbyters in the baptizing of women, on account of decency." *Apostolic Constitutions* 8.28; ANF 7, 494.

109. *Apostolic Constitutions* 3.15, 16; Epiphanius also mentioned deaconesses in connection with baptizing. See Jean Laporte, *The Role of Women in Early Christianity* (New York: The Edward Mellen Press, 1982), 111.

110. Smith, "Garments," 222; see also the Epitaph of Aquila, "which clearly depicts a nude girl being baptized by two men," in J. B. Rossi, "Insigne vetro sul

quale è effigiato il battesimo d'une fanciulla," *Bulletin d'archeologia cristiana,* ser. 3, 1 (1876): 7–14; pl. 1.

111. John Moschus, *Prat. spir.,* trans. in M.-J. Rouet de Journal, *Le Pré spirituel* (Paris, 1946), 48–50.

112. Smith, "Garments," 222 n. 21.

113. *Apostolic Constitutions* 3.9; Elizabeth A. Clark, *Women in the Early Church* (Wilmington, DE: Michael Glazier, Inc., 1983), 180.

114. John Chrysostom, *Homily on Ss. Bernice and Prosdoce;* Clark, *Women,* 175.

115. Tertullian, *Prescription Against the Heretics* 41 ANF 3, 263; Meeks, "Androgyne," 198 n. 144.

116. *Apostolic Constitutions* 3.9; Clark, *Women,* 180 (my italics).

117. Tertullian, *On Baptism* 1 and 17. Twentieth-century interpreters of patristic author's teachings on women's roles in Christianity are often as painful—or humorous, depending on what frame of mind one is in—as the patristic comments themselves. Following his comment that Tertullian's treatise on baptism was prompted by "a certain woman teacher, apparently of gnostic or Marcionite connections, and perhaps an adherent of the Cainite sect, who had argued against the sacrament of baptism," Ernest Evans, translator and editor of *Tertullian's Treatise on Baptism,* puzzlingly remarks: "It is possible to make too much of this woman's importance. Christian institutions commonly call for explanation, or even defense: and a wise preacher conciliates by reference to current interests, however temporary and insignificant" (xi, n. 5). See also Tertullian's *The Veiling of Virgins* ix ANF 4, 33: "It is not permitted for a woman to speak in the church; but neither is it permitted her to teach, nor to baptize, nor to offer, nor to claim to herself a lot in any manly function, not to say in any sacerdotal office."

118. *Apostolic Tradition,* 45.

119. W. C. Van Unnik, "Les cheveux défaits des femmes baptisées, un rite de baptême dans l'ordre ecclesiastique d'Hippolyte," *Vigilae Christianae* 1 (1947): 80.

120. *The Martyrdom of Ss. Perpetua and Felicitas,* in *Acts of the Christian Martyrs,* ed. Herbert Musurillo, S.J. (Oxford: Clarendon Press, 1972), 129.

121. Weeks, "Androgyne," 179.

122. Galatians 3:28; J. Duncan Derrett, "Religious Hair," *Studies in the New Testament I: Glimpses of the Legal and Social Presuppositions of the Authors* (Leiden: Brill, 1977), 171.

123. Ibid., 172.

124. *Shepherd of Hermas* 15.

125. Tertullian, *The Veiling of Virgins* 16, ANF 4, 37. Pelagia, the Antiochean prostitute, is described as riding, before her conversion, "with head uncovered . . . as though she were a man." Brock and Harvey, *Holy Women,* 43. *The Apostolic Tradition,* 43, further stipulates that women catechumens must cover their heads with an opaque rather than a transparent veil.

126. Numbers 5:18.

127. Van Unnik, "Cheveux défaits," 96–98.

128. Ibid.

129. MacDonald, *No Male or Female*, 94–95, also 83; for North African conflict over women's hair, see Tertullian, *The Apparel of Women*, 1.1; *Against Marcion* 5.8; *On Prayer* 22.

130. Elisabeth Schüssler Fiorenza has argued that an increasingly strict definition and surveillance of women's place in Christian groups followed a period of countercultural incorporation of women's talents and commitment into the missionary movement of the early Christian churches. See *In Memory of Her* (New York: Crossroad, 1983).

## 2

### "BECOMING MALE": WOMEN MARTYRS AND ASCETICS

1. Abbess Sarah, in *The Sayings of the Fathers,* trans. Owen Chadwick, in *Western Asceticism* (Philadelphia: Westminster, 1968), 121.

2. Augustine, *Sermon* 282.

3. John Chrysostom, *Life of Olympias, Deaconness* 13, trans. Elizabeth Clark, *Women in the Early Church* (Wilmington, DE: Michael Glazier, Inc., 1983), 129.

4. Paulinus of Nola, *Epistle* 29.6, To Sulpicius Severus; CSEL 29, 251.

5. Frigga Haug, ed. *Female Sexualization,* trans. Erika Carter (London: Verso, 1987), 59.

6. Ibid., 172.

7. Ibid., 88.

8. Ibid., 277.

9. Ibid., 173.

10. John Bugge argues that forms of spirituality distinctive to men and women cannot be dated before about 1150, when the first vernacular writing done for women appeared; see *Virginitas: An Essay in the History of a Medieval Ideal* (The Hague: M. Nijhoff, 1975), 2.

11. Palladius, *Lausiac History,* Prologue 5, trans. W. K. Lowther Clarke (London: SPCK, 1918), 37.

12. Gregory of Nyssa, *Life of St. Macrina* 1, trans. Clark, *Women,* 236.

13. Mary Ann Rossi, "The Passion of Perpetua, Everywoman of Late Antiquity," in *Pagan and Christian Anxiety,* ed. Robert C. Smith and John Lounibus (New York: University Press of America, 1984), 65.

14. Sebastian P. Brock and Susan Ashbrook Harvey, *Holy Women of the Syrian Orient* (Berkeley: University of California Press, 1987), 59.

15. *The Martyrdom of Ss. Perpetua and Felicitas,* in *Acts of the Christian Martyrs,* ed. Herbert Musurillo, (Oxford: Clarendon Press, 1972), 109.

16. *The Acts of Paul and Thecla* 20, trans. Clark, *Women,* 82.

17. This is Robin Lane Fox's term for Christian ascetics in *Pagans and Christians* (New York: Knopf, 1987). Though Fox overuses the term, collapsing a variety of intentions, practices, and life-styles into a generalized picture of yuppie individualism, it is useful for indicating an aspect of asceticism, the yearning to go beyond the expected and ordinary in the religious life.

18. Dennis R. MacDonald, *There Is No Male or Female* (Philadelphia: Fortress, 1987), 99.

19. Male interpreters used accounts of women who "became male" to shame men into similar behavior; if the "weaker sex" can act so heroically, the reasoning went, men should be ashamed not to do likewise. "The prize is greater," Augustine preached, "when the sex is weaker" (*Sermon* 281; see also *Sermons* 280, 282).

20. Philo, *Questiones et solutiones in Genesim* 1.8, quoted in MacDonald, *There Is No Male or Female,* 99.

21. *Gospel of Mary,* in *The Nag Hammadi Library,* ed. James M. Robinson (San Francisco: Harper and Row, 1977), 472.

22. *Gospel of Thomas* 51.19–26, in ibid., 130.

23. *The Gospel of Philip* 71, trans. R. McL. Wilson (London: Mowbray, 1962), 116.

24. Wayne A. Meeks, "The Image of the Androgyne: Some Uses of a Symbol in Earliest Christianity," *History of Religions* 13:3 (February 1974): 194.

25. *Perpetua,* in Musurillo, *Acts of the Christian Martyrs,* 114.

26. *Letter of the Churches of Vienna and Lugdunum;* ANF 8, 780.

27. Brock and Harvey, *Holy Women,* 154–55.

28. Ibid., 163.

29. Ibid., 165.

30. Ibid., 166.

31. Ibid., 110.

32. The late-fourth-century bishop of Milan, Ambrose, described an incident during Thecla's tortures in which Thecla vanquishes a lion by exposing her genitals; see *Concerning Virgins* 3.19; NPN 10, 376.

33. *Acts of Paul and Thecla* 34, in Clark, *Women,* 86.

34. Ibid., 87.

35. Ibid., 88.

36. Accepted as authentic by Peter Dronke and others; see Dronke, *Women Writers of the Middle Ages* (Cambridge: Cambridge University Press, 1984), 1ff.

37. *Perpetua,* in Musurillo, *Acts of the Christian Martyrs,* 109.

38. I am indebted to Barbara Rossing for this observation.

39. Later in the account Perpetua's father seems to acknowledge her rejection of the "other names" that might characterize her—daughter (*filia*), for example; she notes that "he no longer addressed me as his daughter but as a woman" (ibid., 5).

40. *Acta* 9, in Dronke, *Women Writers,* 5.

41. Ibid., 4.

42. Ibid., 10.

43. Ibid., 10.

44. Ibid., 18.

45. Ibid., 20. Sathianathan Clarke attributes the crowd's horror at seeing, in Perpetua's and Felicitas's bodies, evidence of potential and actual childbirth to Roman society's high valuing of women's bodies as reproductive (unpublished paper, presented in seminar, Harvard Divinity School, October 1988).

46. *Acta* 9; Dronke, *Women Writers,* 5. Cf. Euripedes' *Hecuba* 375 for a classical precedent: at the very moment of her execution, Polyxena modestly arranged her skirt. *Euripidis Fabulae* 1, trans. Gilbert Murray (Oxford: Oxford Classical Texts, 1902).

47. Job 1:21; Jerome, *Epistle* 22.7; NPN 6, 25.

48. Jerome, *Epistle* 52.5; NPN 6, 91.

49. *Sayings of the Fathers* 6.16; *Western Asceticism,* 80.

50. Jerome, *Epistle* 28.3; NPN 6, 259.

51. Rossi, "Passion of Perpetua," 68: "There seems to be an inimical polarity between sexuality and equality in women for any androcentric society."

52. My italics; Clement of Alexandria, *Stromateis* 6.12.100; ANF 2, 503; see also Hippolytus, *Refutation* 5.7.15, 5.8.44; ANF 5, 58, 59.

53. See Adrienne Rich, "Compulsory Heterosexuality and Lesbian Existence," *Signs* (Summer 1980): 631–60.

54. Ambrose, *On Virginity* 1.3; NPN 10, 365.

55. Jerome, *Against Jovinianus* 1.47; NPN 6; see Elizabeth Clark's citation of sources describing "the church's traditional ideals regarding married women" in *Ascetic Piety and Women's Faith* (Lewiston: Edward Mellen, 1986), 199 n. 37.

56. Gregory of Nyssa, *On Virginity* 3; NPN 5, 345.

57. Gregory of Nyssa, *On Virginity,* 12; NPN 5, 358.

58. Jerome, *Epistle* 54.4.2; NPN 6, 103.

59. Ibid. 107.11; 194.

60. Ibid. 22.19; 29.

61. Ibid. 22.19; 22.

62. Ambrose, *Concerning Widows* 6.25; NPN 10, 367; trans. Clark, *Ascetic Piety,* 51–52.

63. John Chrysostom, *On Virginity* 56.1; trans. Clark, *Women,* 124–25.

64. *Acts of Thomas,* 1.12; Stevan L. Davies, *The Revolt of the Widows: The Social World of the Apocryphal Acts* (London: Feffer and Sons, 1980), 33.

65. Brock and Harvey, *Holy Women,* 112.

66. A. R. Burn, *"Hic Breve Vivitur," Past and Present* 4 (1953): 12; for bibliography on marriage of prepubescent girls in late antiquity, see Aline Rouselle, *Porneia: On Desire and the Body in Antiquity* (Oxford: Basil Blackwell, 1988), 33 n. 45.

67. Jerome, *Epistle,* 22.6; NPN 6, 23.

68. Ibid.

69. Augustine, *Epistle* 211; trans. Clark, *Women,* 139.

70. Tertullian, *The Apparel of Women* 2.2; NPN 3. For a discussion of Tertullian's views on women's dress, see my essay "Patriarchy as Political Theology," in *Civil Religion and Political Theology,* ed. Leroy S. Rouner (South Bend: University of Notre Dame Press, 1986), 169–86.

71. Davies, *Revolt of the Widows,* passim.

72. Rossi, "Passion of Perpetua," 65.

73. Jerome, *Epistle* 45.3; NPN 6, 59.

74. Ibid. 108.15; 202.

75. Ibid.

76. Brock and Harvey, *Holy Women,* 60.

77. *Vita Antonii* 14.

78. Palladius, *Lausiac History* 5.

79. Augustine, *City of God* 1.16,18, trans. Henry Bettenson (Middlesex, England: Penguin, 1972).

80. For a discussion of the importance of physical virginity to ascetic women in a later period, see Jane Tibbetts Schulenburg, "The Heroics of Virginity: Brides of Christ and Sacrificial Mutilation," in *Women of the Middle Ages and the Renaissance,* ed. Mary Beth Rose (Syracuse: Syracuse University Press, 1986), 29–72.

81. Augustine, *City of God* 1.18.

82. Even if, as Ross Kraemer suggests, "virginity" was frequently construed as present "non-performance" rather than "never-performance" of sexual activity; see *Ecstatics and Ascetics* (Ann Arbor: UMI Research Press, 1976), 207.

83. Musurillo, *Acts of the Christian Martyrs,* 291.

84. Aldhelm, *Patrologia Graeca* 89.128. Schulenberg, "The Heroics of Virginity," 37, states that Aldhelm's tract was "immensely popular up to the Norman conquest."

85. Roger of Wendover, *Flowers of History: Comprising the History of England from the Descent of the Saxons to AD 1235,* trans. J. A. Giles (London: H. G. Bohn, 1885), 225–38; Schulenberg, "The Heroics of Virginity," 48.

86. Geoffrey Galt Harpham, *The Ascetic Imperative in Culture and Criticism* (Chicago: University of Chicago Press, 1987).

87. Ibid., 55–56.

88. Jerome, *Epistle* 22.7; NPN 6, 25; see also a rare attribution of lust to a female ascetic, the Abbess Sarah, in *Sayings of the Fathers* 5.10; *Western Asceticism,* 121.

89. *Sayings of the Fathers* 4.68; *Western Asceticism,* 59.

90. Ibid. 5.22; 65–66.

91. Harpham, *Ascetic Imperative,* 52.

92. Gregory Nazianzus, *De oratione* 6, cited by Herbert Musurillo, S.J., "The Problem of Ascetical Fasting in the Greek Patristic Writers," *Traditio* 12 (1956): 6.

93. Harpham, *Ascetic Imperative,* 235.

## INTRODUCTION TO PART TWO

1. Clothing locates a person socially; dress, as Augustine remarked, "distinguishes the ranks of men." *De doctrina christiana* 2.25.39; trans. D. W. Robertson, Jr., *On Christian Doctrine* (New York: Bobbs-Merrill, 1958), 62.

2. Geoffrey Galt Harpham, *The Ascetic Imperative in Culture and Criticism* (Chicago: University of Chicago Press, 1987), 71. Harpham's perceptive analysis of asceticism as energized by a dynamic of temptation and resistance informs my discussion.

3. Woman localizes or "reduces" temptation as a cook reduces a sauce by boiling it to its essence, eliminating liquid to bring the sauce to its most highly compressed flavor.

4. Harpham, *Ascetic Imperative*, 68.

## 3

### ADAM AND EVE: BEFORE AND AFTER

1. Genesis 3:7.

2. Augustine, *Enarrationes in Psalmos* 132.10; trans. H. Chadwick, *Augustine* (London: Oxford University Press, 1986), 46.

3. Boethius, *Consolation of Philosophy* 3.8 (Indianapolis: Bobbs-Merrill Company, 1962), 55.

4. Tertullian, *The Apparel of Women* 1.1, 1–2; NPN 4, 14–15.

5. Elaine Pagels, *Adam, Eve, and the Serpent* (New York: Random House, 1988).

6. David Warren Sabean, *Power in the Blood: Popular Culture and Village Discourse in Early Modern Germany* (New York: Cambridge University Press, 1984), 95.

7. A rhetorical device frequently signals the use of the figure "woman" in the religious literature of the Christian West: the use of the plural and collective "woman" in passages in which "woman" is the direct parallel to "men." Male authors represented the whole human race collectively as "man," of course, but when they wrote about social arrangements, "woman" was often the grammatical parallel of "men." To my knowledge, the only instance in the literature of early Christianity in which "woman" was used generically is a statement issuing from the 431 Council of Ephesus in which the designation of Mary as "Theotokos" was established. The all-male membership of the Council pronounced, "The Blessed Virgin was woman as we are." NPN 14, 225ff.

8. Although I limit my discussion to religious discourse on "woman" as figure, many others have explored secular imagery in which similar figures are used to characterize woman as untrustworthy or evil. For example, Hanna Fenichel Pitkin examines the highly volatile figure of Fortuna as woman: *Fortune Is a Woman, Gender and Politics in the Thought of Niccolò Machiavelli* (Berkeley: University of California Press, 1984).

9. Tertullian, *On the Veiling of Virgins* 9; NPN 4, 33.

10. Augustine, *The Literal Meaning of Genesis* 9.15; ACW 41.

11. Augustine, *The Literal Meaning of Genesis* 9.11; ACW 41.

12. Alternative interpretations, faithful to the Genesis text, have been proposed: Jane Dempsey Douglas discusses Agrippa of Netesheim's interpretation of the Genesis 1 account of creation as an ascending order in which Eve, created last, represents the apex and crown of creation; she is both intelligent and life-bearing; Henry Cornelius Agrippa, *Declamation on the Nobility and Excellence of the Feminine Sex,* 1509; in Douglas, *Women, Freedom, and Calvin* (Philadelphia: Westminster, 1985), 68.

13. Augustine, *The Good of Marriage* 17.20; FOC 15, 34.

14. 1 Corinthians 11:4–10.

15. Calvin, *Sermon* 1 on 1 Corinthians 11:4–10, trans. Willis P. DeBoer, "Calvin on the Role of Women," in *Exploring the Heritage of John Calvin,* ed. David Holwerda (Grand Rapids: Baker, 1976), 245.

16. Ambrose, *Paradise* 4.24; FOC 42, 301.

17. Ibid., 6.32; 310.

18. Ibid., 6.33; 311.

19. Ibid. 6.34; 312.

20. Italics mine; ibid., 10.48; 327.

21. Ibid.

22. Ibid.

23. Ibid., 11.50; 328–29.

24. Ibid., 12.56; 336.

25. Ibid., 1363; 343. A curious twentieth-century statement that parallels Ambrose's claim that Adam and Eve's act of clothing themselves lies at the heart of the Fall occurs in Paul Ableman, *Anatomy of Nakedness* (London: Orbis, 1982), 86: "The fundamental perversion, to which many, if not all particular perversions are essentially responses, is the concealment of the body that has resulted from the universal adoption of clothes."

26. Ambrose, *Paradise* 13.65 FOC 42, 344.

27. Ibid., 15.73, 351.

28. Genesis 3:13.

29. Ambrose, *Paradise* 14.72; FOC 42, 350.

30. Augustine; *The Literal Meaning of Genesis* II.39; ACW 42, 172. Mieke Bal has pointed out the traditional tendency to correlate physical weakness with moral weakness; see "Sexuality, Sin, and Sorrow: The Emergence of Female Character," in *The Female Body in Western Culture,* ed. Susan R. Suleiman (Cambridge: Harvard University Press, 1986), 317.

31. For references to authors who held this view, see John Hammond Taylor's note to *The Literal Meaning of Genesis* 9.3 in ACW 42, 265 n. 15.

32. Augustine, *City of God* 14.18, treas. Henry Bettinson (Middlesex, England: Penguin, 1972).

33. Ibid., 14.23.

34. Ibid., 14.24.

35. Ibid., 14.23. For the use of "woman as field" in imagery in antiquity, see Page duBois, *Sowing the Body, Psychoanalysis and Ancient Representations of Women* (Chicago: University of Chicago Press, 1988).

36. Augustine, *City of God*, 14.24.

37. In contrast to prelapsarian sexual intercourse "at the bidding of the will," Augustine describes the volatility and "self-willed" character of present sexual impulses. The embarrassment of impotence seems to weigh as heavily as unwanted sexual arousal in Augustine's mind: "Thus strangely does lust refuse to be a servant, not only to the will to beget but even to the lust for lascivious indulgence; and although on the whole it is totally opposed to the mind's control, it is quite often divided against itself. It arouses the mind, but does not follow its own lead by arousing the body." *City of God* 14.16.

38. Augustine, *The Literal Meaniing of Genesis* 9.5; ACW 42, 75.

39. Ibid., 11.30; 161.

40. Compare *City of God* 14.17, here Augustine says of the same event: "There appeared a certain indecent novelty which made nakedness shameful. They were embarrassed at the insubordination of their flesh."

41. Augustine, *The Literal Meaning of Genesis* 11.31, 32; ACW 42, 162–65.

42. Ibid., 11.37; 171. Compare Augustine's discussion of familial and social order in *City of God* 19.13–15.

43. Augustine, *The Literal Meaning of Genesis* 11.37; ACW 42, 171.

44. Augustine makes a similar argument for the perpetuation of slavery in *City of God* 19.15: slavery is also a sign of the fallen condition in which human beings exist; but borne willingly, it can win the slave the future reward of equality in the Kingdom of God, where all human beings will be equal, and "God will be all in all."

45. Italics mine; Augustine, *The Literal Meaning of Genesis* 11.42; ACW 42, 176.

46. 1 Corinthians 11:7.

47. Augustine, *The Literal Meaning of Genesis* 11.42; ACW 42, 176.

48. Ibid.

49. H. W. Janson, *History of Art,* 2d ed. (Englewood Cliffs: Prentice-Hall, 1963), 291. A full analysis of the altarpiece *Adoration of the Lamb* would take me far from this chapter's agenda. Janson argues that the alterpiece is a composite of disparate parts not originally intended to appear together. It was probably begun by Hubert Van Eyck and finished after his death by his brother, Jan. The only panels that can be attributed with confidence to Jan Van Eyck are the Adam and Eve panels of the upper—heavenly—register.

50. Ibid.

51. Ibid., 291.

52. See chapter 6 for further discussion of the Renaissance notion of female beauty. If Janson is correct in saying that Adam and Eve are represented in the original, prelapsarian condition, Eve's rotund belly might imply that Eve's future motherhood was part of the divine plan from before her creation. She may

not, of course, be pregnant, having not yet sinned, in which case the artist has simply painted a female body that corresponds to his society's notion of female beauty, a large-bellied beauty similar to that of the bride in his 1434 painting *Giovanni Arnolfini and His Bride*.

53. Barbara Newman, *Sister of Wisdom: St. Hildegard's Theology of the Feminine* (Berkeley: University of California Press, 1987), 12.

54. Ibid., 93.

55. Hildegard, *De operatione Dei* 2.5.43; trans. in Newman, *Sister of Wisdom*, 93.

56. Newman, *Sister of Wisdom*, 112. Authors such as Gregory the Great sometimes argued that Adam's was the greater sin, responsibility, and guilt. They did so, however, on the grounds that Adam, being more spiritual than Eve, had the greater capacity for sin: "The devil makes the suggestion, the flesh delights in it, and the spirit consents. It was the serpent who suggested the first sin; Eve representing the flesh was delighted by it, and Adam representing the spirit consented to it." *Bede's Ecclesiastical History of the English Church and People*, ed. and trans. Bertram Colgrave and R. A. B. Mynors (London: Oxford University Press, 1969); 100–1. Charles T. Wood comments, "Far from absolving Eve, Gregory merely downplays her responsibility by implicitly denigrating her capacities, for, like all medieval thinkers, he knew that spirit was greater than flesh, and hence that greater sin was imputable to Adam." See "The Doctor's Dilemma: Sin, Salvation, and the Menstrual Cycle in Medieval Thought," *Speculum* 56:4 (October 1981): 712.

57. Peter Dronke, *Women Writers of the Middle Ages: A Critical Study of Texts from Perpetua to Marguerite Porete* (Cambridge: Cambridge University Press, 1984), 149.

58. Ibid., 201.

59. Hildegard, *Causae et curae* 47; trans. Newman, *Sister of Wisdom*, 115.

60. Ibid.

61. Ibid.

62. Illustrations for the *Scivias* were "prepared at Hildegard's own scriptorium, most likely under her supervision." Ibid., 17.

63. Ibid., 100.

64. Italics mine; Hildegard of Bingen's *Scivias* 1.2, trans. Bruce Hozeski (Santa Fe: Bear and Co., 1986), 24.

65. *Scivias* 1.2; Newman, *Sister of Wisdom*, 99.

66. Dronke, *Women Writers*, 176.

67. Ibid.

68. Hildegard, *Fragment* 4.29; trans. Newman, *Sister of Wisdom*, 111.

69. Dronke, *Women Writers*, 176.

70. Trans. Newman, *Sister of Wisdom*, 117. Compare the similar complaint of a contemporary feminist; Luce Irigaray describes twentieth-century heterosexual relations: "Woman's pleasure and the representation that can be made of it and that she can have of it, are—once again—too suppressed, repressed, obscured, or denied for her to be anything but 'frigid.' . . . We need to examine the rela-

tionship between this 'frigidity' and the aggressiveness that devolves upon the male in the sexual function. . . . Perhaps female sexuality does not find its needs met by this violence, this rape, that 'biology' supposedly demands of the male to ensure reproduction." See "The Blind Spot of an Old Dream of Symmetry," *The Speculum of the Other Woman,* trans. Gillian C. Gill (Ithaca: Cornell University Press, 1985), 97.

71. Peter Dronke, *Poetic Individuality in the Middle Ages* (London: Oxford University Press, 1970), 157.

72. Trans. Newman, *Sister of Wisdom,* 111.

73. Trans. Dronke, *Women Writers,* 176.

74. Hildegard, *Causae et curae,* trans. Dronke, *Women Writers,* 176.

75. Genesis 1:26.

76. Luther, *Lectures on Genesis;* LW 1, 56.

77. Ibid., 57.

78. Ibid., 63.

79. Ibid., 62.

80. Ibid., 66.

81. Ibid., 64.

82. Ibid., 63.

83. Ibid., 66.

84. Ibid., 67.

85. Ibid., 115; italics mine.

86. Ibid., 69.

87. Ibid., 219.

88. Ibid., 69.

89. Ibid., 116.

90. Ibid., 70.

91. Several authors have discussed this debate; see, for example, Ian Maclean, *The Renaissance Notion of Woman, A Study in the Fortunes of Scholasticism and Medical Science in European Intellectual Life* (Cambridge: Cambridge University Press, 1983); Joan Kelly, "Early Feminist Theory and the *Querelle des Femmes,* 1400–1789," *Signs* 8:1 (1982): 4–28.

92. Luther, *Lectures;* LW 1, 141; see also Luther's discussion of Genesis 3:7: "What can be a greater depravity than that the nakedness which was formerly a glory is now turned into the greatest disgrace?" Ibid. 165.

93. Ibid., 151–52.

94. Ibid., 167.

95. Ibid., 221.

96. Ibid., 168.

97. Ibid., 151.

98. See Valerie Saiving, "The Human Situation: A Feminine View," *Womanspirit Rising,* ed. Carol P. Christ and Judith Plaskow (San Francisco: Harper and Row, 1979); and Judith Plaskow, *Sex, Sin, and Grace: Women's Experience and the The-*

*ologies of Reinhold Niebuhr and Paul Tillich* (Washington, D.C.: University Press of America, 1980).

99. Luther, *Lectures;* LW 1, 182. Luther himself confessed on another occasion that he had to remind himself frequently that he must not feel and express more gratitude to Katie, his wife, than he did to God, "who has given me so much more."

100. Ibid., 199.

101. Ibid., 200.

102. Ibid., 201.

103. Ibid., 202.

104. Ibid., 202–3. Many Christian authors refer to Eve as the reason for not permitting women to teach: "The woman taught once and for all and upset everything." See Elizabeth Clark, *Women in the Early Church* (Wilmington, DE: Michael Glazier, Inc., 1983), 156ff.

105. Luther, *Lectures;* LW 1, 203. Luther's understanding of the contemporary significance of the Genesis account of the Fall is indicated by his statement that marriage exists so that "those who cannot contain themselves might live content with their own Eve and not touch other women." Ibid., 240–41.

106. Søren Kierkegaard, *The Concept of Anxiety,* trans. Reidar Thomte (Princeton: Princeton University Press, 1980), 64, 66.

107. Ibid., 63–65.

108. Ibid., 41.

109. Ibid., 66.

110. Ibid., 66.

111. Ibid., 47.

112. Newman, *Sister of Wisdom,* 197.

113. Luther, *Lectures;* LW 1, 182.

114. For example, Luther's contemporary, Desiderius Erasmus, in one of the most popular devotional manuals of the sixteenth century, acknowledged that "Eve," in addition to being a seductive woman, is also insidiously seated within men's own nature: "That hellishly slippery serpent, the first destroyer of our peace . . . never ceases to lie in ambush in the heel of woman, whom he once corrupted. Keep in mind that woman is man's sensuous part: she is our Eve, through whom that wiliest of serpents lures our passions into deadly pleasures." *The Enchiridion of Erasmus,* trans. Raymond Himelick (Bloomington: Indiana University Press, 1963), 39.

4

THE FEMALE BODY AS FIGURE

1. Ecclesiasticus 25:24.

2. Dante Alighieri, "The Purgatorio" 29, 22–30, in *The Divine Comedy* trans. John Ciardi (New York: Norton, 1961), 361.

3. Cyril of Jerusalem, *Catechesis* 13.21; FOC 64.

4. See my *Image as Insight: Visual Understanding in Western Christianity and Secular Culture* (Boston: Beacon Press, 1985).

5. Wayne A. Meeks, "The Image of the Androgyne: Some Uses of a Symbol in Earliest Christianity," *History of Religions* 13:3 (February 1974): 182.

6. See my essay "The Virgin with One Bare Breast: Female Nudity and Religious Meaning in Tuscan Early Renaissance Culture," in *The Female Body in Western Culture*, ed. Susan R. Suleiman (Cambridge: Harvard University Press, 1986), 193–208.

7. Helena Michie has discussed the textual strategies by which female characters in Victorian literature are "reduced to a figure rather than a body." Description, the process of metaphorization that creates the figure, replaces the living woman, making her a function in the text, the author's creation. See *The Flesh Made Word: Female Figures and Women's Bodies* (New York: Oxford University Press, 1987), 61 and *passim*.

8. For example, Titian's *Sacred and Profane Love,* in which, as Erwin Panofsky has persuasively argued, the clothed woman represents the profane while the nude—and here "nude" is the correct word, in that the body is posed, its idiosyncrasies removed—represents sacred love. *Sacred and Profane Love,* however, presents a reversal of an established visual cliché—the association of female nakedness with "the flesh," sin, and evil. This chapter presents the evidence for the existence of such a stereotypical visual association; see also Harold Wethey, *The Paintings of Titian,* vol. 3, *The Mythological and Historical Paintings* (London: Phaidon, 1975), 175–79.

9. Gregory the Great: "For all sin is committed in three ways, namely by suggestion, pleasure, and consent. The devil makes the suggestion, the flesh delights in it, and the spirit consents. It was the serpent who suggested the first sin, Eve representing the flesh was delighted by it, and Adam representing the spirit consented to it." *Bede's Ecclesiastical History of the English Church and People,* ed. and trans. Bertram Colgrave and R. A. B. Mynors (London: Oxford University Press, 1969), 100–1.

10. Lionel Rothkrug, "Religious Practices and Collective Perceptions: Hidden Homologies in the Renaissance and Reformation," *Historical Reflections* 7:1 (Spring 1980): 147.

11. Heinrich Kramer and James Sprenger, *The Malleus Maleficarum,* ed. and trans. Montague Summers (New York: Dover, 1971), 41–44; see also Lisa Tichner's important stipulation: "Female lust is insatiable and provocative only in so far as it is arousing to masculine desire, and often only as a prelude to her submission before the phallus." "The Body Politic: Female Sexuality and Women Artists Since 1970," *Art History* 1 (1978): 237.

12. The association of excessive flesh with an inferior development of spirit or intelligence could be traced through centuries from Plato's general suggestion that any person with "more flesh" was "stupid and insensitive" (*Timaeus*

75c−76) to the more specific association of sin (or "the flesh") with female flesh in medieval Christianity.

13. Notice that the story assumes that the Elders are attractive to Susanna, making her refusal a matter of virtue rather than repulsion! From the story's perspective, her own erotic interest—or lack thereof—is not important.

14. Tertullian assumed that Susanna's beauty constituted guilt; he comments that Susanna veiled herself for her trial because she was "ashamed of the disgrace she had brought on herself." *De corona militis* 4; ANF 3.

15. For a bibliography of depictions of Susanna and the Elders before AD 700, see C. R. Morey, *Early Christian Art* (Princeton: Princeton University Press, 1953), and L. Reau, *L'iconographie de l'art crétien,* vol. 2 (Paris, 1957), 393ff. The theme continues to fascinate: Professor Melvin Zabarsky of the University of New Hampshire has recently painted a series of contemporary "Susanna and the Elders" scenes.

16. For a discussion of a woman painter, Artemisia Gentileschi, who painted Susannah and the Elders, see Mary D. Garrard, "Artemesia and Susanna," in *Feminism and Art History* (New York: Harper and Row, 1982), 147−72.

17. Joan Kelly-Gadol, "Did Women Have a Renaissance?" in *Becoming Visible: Women in European History,* ed. Renate Bridenthal and Claudia Koonz (Boston: Houghton Mifflin, 1977), 137−64.

18. Merry Wiesner, "Women's Defense of Their Public Role," *Women in the Middle Ages and the Renaissance,* ed. Mary Beth Rose (Syracuse: Syracuse University Press, 1986), 3.

19. Martha C. Howell, *Women, Production, and Patriarchy in Late Medieval Cities* (Chicago: University of Chicago Press, 1986), 177−78.

20. Natalie Zemon Davis, *Society and Culture in Early Modern France* (Palo Alto: Stanford University Press, 1965), 94.

21. Wiesner, "Women's Defense," 4.

22. Ibid., 8.

23. Ibid.

24. Some scholars attribute to Baldung the illustrations of the first German-language treatise on witchcraft, *Die Emeis* (1517). Against a direct attribution of these illustrations to Baldung, however, see Linda C. Hults, "Baldung and the Witches of Freiburg: The Evidence of Images," *Journal of Interdisciplinary History* 18:2 (Autumn 1987): 265.

25. Hults, "Baldung and the Witches," 263−64.

26. Joseph Koerner, "The Mortification of the Image: Death as Hermeneutic in Hans Baldung Grien," *Representations* 10 (1985): 54.

27. Compare Augustine's statement "Adam did not love Eve because she was beautiful: his love made her beautiful" (Quid enim boni meruit Adam? Et tamen misericors amavit, et sponsus dilexit, non pulchram, sed ut faceret pulchram), *Enarratione in Psalm* 132.10.

28. John Berger's describes "the personification of *Vanitas* as an example of

men's moralizing through the female nude: 'You painted a naked woman because you enjoyed looking at her, you put a mirror in her hand and you called the painting *Vanity,* thus morally condemning the woman whose nakedness you had depicted for your own pleasure.' The real function of the mirror, the symbol of woman's vanity, is to make her 'connive in treating herself as, first and foremost, a sight'." *Ways of Seeing* (London: Penguin, 1972), 45–64. See also Thalia Gouma-Peterson and Patricia Matthews, "The Feminist Critique of Art History," *The Art Bulletin* 69:3 (September 1987): 339.

29. A. Kent Hieatt argues, however, that "the work stands much later in Baldung's career than has been assumed in previous accounts." Hans Baldung Grien's Ottawa *Eve* and its Context," *Art Bulletin* 65:2 (1983): 290.

30. Koerner, "Mortification," 82.

31. Ibid.

32. Ibid., 99 n. 47.

33. Ibid. 83–84.

34. Carol Duncan, "The Aesthetics of Power in Modern Erotic Art," *Heresies* 1 (1977): 46–50.

35. See for example, Linda Nochlin, "Eroticism and Female Imagery in Nineteenth Century Art," in *Woman as Sex Object: Studies in Erotic Art 1730–1970,* ed. Thomas B. Hess and Linda Nochlin (New York: Newsweek, 1972), 9; see also Carol Duncan's redefinition of erotic, "not as a self-evident universal category, but as a culturally-defined concept that is ideological in nature." "Esthetics of Power," 46.

36. Michael Baxandall, *Painting and Experience in Fifteenth Century Italy* (New York: Oxford University Press, 1972), 29ff.

37. Ann Hollander, *Seeing Through Clothes* (New York: Viking, 1980), 98–99.

38. Griselda Pollock, "Women, Art, and Ideology: Questions for Feminist Art Historians," *Women's Art Journal* (Spring/Summer, 1983): 42.

39. Stanislav Andreski has recently argued in "The Syphilitic Shock," *Encounter* 52 (1982): 7–26, that a wave of virulent misogyny coincided with the syphilis epidemic as men blamed prostitutes in particular and women in general for infecting them. "The terror and abhorrence of syphilis," projected on women, was, Andreski says, a fundamental underlying motive for the witch persecutions of the sixteenth century. This hypothesis needs further documentation, but it is a provocative suggestion.

40. Luther, *Lectures on Genesis: LW* 1, 207.

41. *Malleus Maleficarum,* 47.

42. Hults, "Baldung and the Witches of Freiburg"; 273.

43. Katharine M. Rogers has proposed a useful definition of misogyny: it can be identified, she says, where there is apparently "uncalled-for vehemence in the satiric attacks, blurring of the distinction between censurable women and women in general, revelations that women's differences from man invariably make her inferior, and undercurrents of seriousness in the jokes" about women.

See *The Troublesome Helpmate, A History of Misogyny in Litterature* (Seattle: University of Washington Press, 1966), 265.

44. Rothkrug, "Religious Practices and Collective Perceptions," 147.

45. Sandra Clark, "'Hic mulier, Haec vir': The Controversy Over Masculine Women," *Studies in Philology* 82:2 (1985): 169.

46. To assert the illegitimacy of observing and describing figures of women in art and literature, one would have to claim either (1) that they are not present, or (2) that their depiction is "natural," inevitable, representational, inscribed in women's biology, or (3) that representations of women are uninteresting (in the sense that from them the historian can understand nothing—or nothing important—about human societies). If none of these claims seems compelling, historians must continue to explore how gender constructions interact with events and social and sexual arrangements in particular societies.

47. See Colin Eisler, "The Athlete of Virtue: The Iconography of Asceticism," *De Artibus Opuscula: Essays in Honor of Erwin Panofsky* (New York: New York University Press, 1961), 82–97.

48. Ibid., 92ff; cf. Andrée Hayum's reinterpretation of the naked figures as Old Testament figures: "Michelangelo's *Doni Tondo:* Holy Family and Family Myth," *Studies in Iconography* 7–8 (1981–82): 209–51.

49. John Dixon, "The Drama of Donatello's David," *Gazette des Beaux-Arts* 113 (January 1979): 6–12.

50. Eisler, "The Athlete of Virtue," 82f.

51. Leo Steinberg, *The Sexuality of Christ in Renaissance Painting and in Modern Oblivion* (New York: Pantheon, 1984).

52. Ibid., 13.

53. Ibid., 71–72.

54. Ibid., 23.

55. Tertullian, *De carne Christi* 17; ANF 3: "Christ received flesh from the Virgin . . . certain proof that his flesh was human, if he derived its substance from his mother's womb."

56. See my further discussion of Steinberg's thesis in "Nudity, Gender, and Religious Meaning in the Italian Renaissance," *Art as Religious Studies,* ed. Doug Adams and Diane Apostolos-Cappadona (New York: Crossroad, 1987), 101–16.

57. For example, depictions of the apocryphal account of Judith and Holofernes consistently show Judith fully and fashionably clothed until, in the sixteenth century, interpretation of her character shifted from emphasizing her virtue, skill, and power to the threat and danger masked by her seductiveness; when the latter interpretation dominated, she was, for the first time, depicted naked by Hans Baldung Grien. Diane Apostolos-Cappadona demonstrated this in a paper delivered at the American Academy of Religion on December 7, 1987.

5

"CARNAL ABOMINATIONS": THE FEMALE BODY
AS GROTESQUE

1. Plato, *Republic* 452a.

2. Heinrich Kramer and Jacobus Sprenger, *The Malleus Maleficarum*, ed. and trans. Montague Summers (New York: Dover, 1971), 41–48.

3. Michel Foucault, *Discipline and Punish: the Birth of the Prison* (New York: Vintage, 1979), 136.

4. *Mandeville's Travels*, ed. M. C. Seymour (London: Oxford University Press, 1968), 121.

5. Ibid., 17–18.

6. Ibid., 190.

7. Wolfgang Kayser, *The Grotesque in Art and Literature* (Bloomington: Indiana University Press, 1963), 37.

8. M. Pelaez, "Visioni di S. Francesca Romana," *Archivio di Società Romana di storia patria* 14 (Rome, 1891): 364–409; quoted in Piero Camporesi, *The Incorruptible Flesh, Bodily Mutation and Mortification in Religion and Folklore*, trans. Tania Croft-Murray (New York: Cambridge University Press, 1988), 51.

9. Adolf Katzenellenbogen, *Allegories of the Vices and Virtues in Mediaeval Art* (London: The Warburg Institute, 1939; trans. Alan J. P. Crick; republished New York, 1964), 58.

10. Geoffrey Galt Harpham, *On the Grotesque: Strategies of Contradiction in Art and Literature*, (Princeton: Princeton University Press, 1982), 3.

11. Ibid., xv.

12. Ibid., 72.

13. Ibid., 17.

14. Ibid., 191. Analysts of the grotesque have found, within the breadth of these definitions, a great deal of room to critique their predecessors on the basis of a few well-chosen examples. Thus, Mikhail Bakhtin, in a chapter titled, "The Grotesque Image of the Body," reports G. Schneegans's analysis of the components of the grotesque, finding it ultimately a "narrow modern interpretation . . . typical but radically eroneous, . . . the complete neglect of a series of essential aspects of the grotesque." Mikhail Bakhtin, *Rabelais and His World*, trans. Helene Iswolsky (Cambridge: The MIT Press, 1968), 307. Harpham, while crediting Wolfgang Kayser's *The Grotesque in Art and Literature* and Bakhtin's *Rabelais and His World* as "prodigiously well informed, carefully argued, persuasive accounts," draws the starting point of his own argument from the fact that these two authors "manage to contradict each other utterly on the most basic premises." I hesitate to participate in this time-honored academic dynamic, but find it difficult to make my point without demonstrating that former definitions of the grotesque have missed one of its crucial components, namely the essential role of gender in creating the quality of grotesqueness.

15. Harpham, *On the Grotesque*, 14.

16. Ibid., 304.

17. Ibid., 309.

18. Boethius, *The Consolation of Philosophy* 4.3, trans. V. E. Watts (Harmondsworth: Penguin, 1978), 125; quoted by Harpham, *On the Grotesque,* 83.

19. Bakhtin, *Rabelais,* 339.

20. Biddy Martin, "Feminism, Criticism, and Foucault," in *Feminism and Foucault,* ed. Irene Diamond and Lee Quinby (Boston: Northeastern University Press, 1988), 13–14.

21. Peter Stallybrass, "Patriarchal Territories: The Body Enclosed," in *Rewriting the Renaissance,* ed. Margaret W. Ferguson, with Maureen Quilligan and Nancy Vickers (Chicago: University of Chicago Press, 1986), 126.

22. Alain Corbin "Commercial Sexuality in Nineteenth-Century France: A System of Images and Regulations," in *The Making of the Modern Body,* ed. Catherine Gallagher and Thomas Laqueur (Berkeley: University of California Press, 1987), 209–19; see also Luce Irigaray, "Volume-Fluidity," in *Speculum of the Other Woman* (Ithaca: Cornell University Press, 1985), 229, 237.

23. Jerome, *Epistle* 22.25, To Eustochium; NPN 6, 32.

24. Sexuality is a prominent part of both Bakhtin's and Harpham's descriptions of the grotesque, but gender is not.

52. Bakhtin, *Rabelais,* 335. Laughter has a special association with the grotesque: "That is why Baubo, who was able to make the goddess Demeter laugh, is represented as an inverted body: 'a woman's body without head or breast, on whose belly a face is drawn: the lifted dress surrounds this sort of face like a crown of hair.'" Freud, *A Mythological Parallel to a Visual Obsession,* quoted by Hélène Cixous and Catherine Clément, *The Newly Born Woman* (Minneapolis: University of Minnesota Press, 1986), 33.

26. Bakhtin, *Rabelais,* 352.

27. Ibid., 329.

28. Rabelais, *Pantagruel,* in *Great Books of the Western World* 24 (Chicago: Encyclopedia Britannica, Inc., 1952), 72.

29. Jerome, *Epistle* 107.11, NPN 6, 194.

30. Bakhtin, *Rabelais,* 317.

31. Elaine Pagels writes, "Whereas the orthodox often blamed Eve for the fall and pointed to women's submission as appropriate punishment, gnostics often depicted Eve—or the feminine spiritual power she represented—as the source of spiritual awakening." *Adam, Eve, and the Serpent* (New York: Random House, 1988), 66.

32. Jerome, *Epistle* 48.2, To Pammachius; NPN 6, 66.

33. S. Francesca Romana's vision of hell, quoted by Camporesi in *The Incorruptible Flesh,* 51, included the detailed account of punishment for contraception or abortion: "Those women who 'by means of a beverage or some other method try not to conceive or to induce abortion, and those who were mother and have murdered their own babies,' are drowned 'in vats of boiling human blood' and then thrown in an 'icy pool,' their flesh being torn with 'iron hooks,' quartered

by demonic butchers, their hearts opened and their entrails thrown into a 'boiler full of bubbling pitch,' but not before they have been roasted 'inside the belly of a great bronze serpent of fire, where they howl in agony.'"

34. *Malleus Maleficarum,* 56: "Witches who do such things by witchcraft are by law punishable by the extreme penalty."

35. Foucault, *The Use of Pleasure,* trans. Robert Hurley (New York: Pantheon), chapter 3, "Risks and Dangers," 117ff; Aline Rouselle, *Porneia; On Desire and the Body in Antiquity* trans. Felicia Pheasant (Oxford: Basil Blackwell, 1988), chapter 1, "The Bodies of Men," 5ff.

36. Jerome, *Against Jovinian* I.28; NPN 6, 367.

37. For all the reasons indicated by Hildegard in an earlier chapter. Midwives and female physicians also frequently reported women's sexual discontent; Helen Rodnite LeMay, "Some Thirteenth and Fourteenth Century Lectures on Female Sexuality," *International Journal of Women's Studies* 1 (1978): 391–99.

38. Although some medical treatises in antiquity and the Middle Ages urged the necessity or usefulness of female sexual pleasure *for conception,* Aline Rouselle discusses the process by which female sexual pleasure came to be regarded as incidental to conception and thus unimportant. Greek women, as reported in the *Hippocratic Collection,* insisted that they could not conceive without reaching orgasm; however, "Aristotle discovered, or at least he was the first to state, that women would conceive even if they did not reach orgasm." Following Aristotle, Soranus and Galen held that "women conceived without feeling anything." See Rouselle, *Porneia,* 29ff. There is evidence, however, that the issue of the role of female pleasure in relation to conception was not settled by Aristotle's discovery; interestingly, his eleventh-century Arab follower, Avicenna, transmitter to the West of Aristotelian philosophy, "writes in some detail of how a woman may not 'be pleased by' the smallness of her mate's penis 'wherefore she does not emit sperm: and when she does not emit sperm a child is not made.'" See Thomas Laqueur, "Orgasm, Generation, and the Politics of Reproductive Biology," in Gallagher and Laqueur, eds., *The Making of the Modern Body,* 9. Helen LeMay, writing on Anthonius Guainerius's early-fifteenth-century *Tractatus de matricibus* (*Treatise on the Womb*), strongly advocates the view that woman's pleasure contributes to conception and gives detailed instructions on how a man should act to please his partner. In none of this learned debate is women's pleasure desirable in itself, of course, but only as an aid to conception. See LeMay, "Antonius Guainerius and Medieval Gynecology" and "Trotula: Women's Problems and the Professions of Medicine in the Middle Ages," ed. John Benton, *Bulletin of the History of Medicine* 59 (1985): 30–53.

39. For example, sinister and grotesque powers, associated with the women's physical condition or spiritual commitments, were conjectured; menstruating women, postmenopausal women, and witches were frequently accused of possessing a visual ray capable of poisoning the plant, animal, or person on which it falls. LeMay, "Some Thirteenth and Fourteenth Century Lectures on Female Sexuality," 394.

40. Helena Michie, *The Flesh Made Word: Female Figures and Women's Bodies* (New York: Oxford University Press, 1987), 7.

41. For a detailed exploration of threatening women in the works of Machiavelli, see Hanna Fenichel Pitkin, *Fortune Is a Woman: Gender and Politics in the Thought of Niccolò Machiavelli* (Berkeley: University of California, 1987), chapter 5.

42. LeMay, "Anthonius Guainerius," 320ff. John S. Haller and Robin M. Haller, *The Physician and Sexuality in Victorian America* (Urbana: University of Illinois Press, 1974), 8, 9; see also Ian Maclean, *The Renaissance Notion of Woman* (Cambridge: Cambridge University Press, 1980), 40ff. for attitudes toward the uterus.

43. Peter Stallybrass, examining sixteenth-century rhetoric on women's bodies, quotes Barbaro's treatise *On Wifely Duties:* "It is proper that not only arms, but indeed the speech of women never be made public; for the speech of a noble woman can be no less dangerous than the nakedness of her limbs." Stallybrass comments, "The signs of the 'harlot' are her linguistic 'fullness' and her frequenting of public spaces." See "Patriarchal Territories," 127.

44. See Jane Caputi's discussion of twentieth-century interest in murders of women in which the male murderers tortured, killed and dismembered their victims: *The Age of Sex Crime* (Bowling Green: Bowling Green University Popular Press, 1987), especially chapters 1 and 2.

45. Jørgen Andersen, *The Witch on the Wall: Medieval Erotic Sculpture in the British Isles* (Copenhagen: Rosenkilde and Bagger, 1977), 37; compare the account in the third-century *Acts of Paul and Thecla* in which Thecla, condemned to death by wild beasts in the colosseum, repulses a lion by exhibiting her vagina; trans. Elizabeth Clark, *Women in the Early Church,* (Wilmington, Delaware: Michael Glazier, Inc., 1983). See also Saint Ambrose's citation of this incident, *Concerning Virgins* 3.19; NPN 10, 361.

46. Andersen, *The Witch on the Wall,* 48.

47. Ibid., 121.

48. Ibid., 70.

49. Fascination with and horror of the vagina is apparent not only in the Christian West, but appears cross-culturally in images of the *vagina dentata,* the vagina equipped with rows of sharp teeth capable of trapping and biting off the penis of the male who has intercourse with her. Erich Neumann describes the *vagina dentata* as "the destructive side of the Feminine, the destructive and deadly womb that appears . . . in the form of a mouth bristling with teeth." *The Great Mother: An Analysis of the Archetype* (Princeton: Princeton University Press, 1955), 168. In cultures in which the *vagina dentata* plays a large role in mythology, "the hero is the man who overcomes the Terrible Mother, breaks the teeth out of her vagina, and so makes her into a woman." Jill Raitt, "The *Vagina Dentata* and the *Immaculatus Uterus Divini Fontis,*" *Journal of the American Academy of Religion* 48:3 (September 1980): 415–31.

50. For descriptions of the female body from medical texts of the ancient, medieval, and Renaissance periods, see Maclean, *Renaissance Notion;* Rousselle, *Por-*

*neia;* LeMay, "Anthonius Guainerius" and "Some Thirteenth and Fourteenth Century Lectures on Female Sexuality."

51. Maclean, *Renaissance Notion,* 30; Aristotle, *De generatione animalium,* 1.2.

52. Rouselle, *Porneia,* chapter 2; see also Maclean, *Renaissance Notion,* chapter 3.

53. Rouselle, *Porneia,* 26.

54. Ibid., 26–27; Oribasius, *Medical Collection* 24, 32.

55. Quoted in Laqueur, "Orgasm," 5; Galen, *On the Usefulness of the Parts of the Body,* ed. and trans. Margaret May, 2 vols. (Ithaca, New York: Cornell University Press, 1968), 2: 640. This picture of the female body remained virtually uncontested until 1829, when Carl Ludwig Klose argued that "the uterus, woman's most important sex organ, has no analogue in man; hence the comparison with men's organs is worthless." See Londa Schiebinger, "Skeletons in the Closet: The First Illustrations of the Female Skeleton in Eighteenth-Century Anatomy," in Gallagher and Laqueur, *Making of the Modern Body,* 53.

56. Laqueur, "Orgasm" 4.

57. Quoted by Jill Raitt, "*Vagina Dentata,*" 422.

58. Carl Ludwig Klose, quoted in Schiebinger, "Skeletons in the Closet," 53.

59. Page duBois, *Sowing the Body: Psychoanalysis and Ancient Representations of Women* (Chicago: University of Chicago Press, 1988), 184.

60. Thomas Aquinas, *De veritate* 5.9.d.9: "nisi ergo esset aliqua virtus quae interderet femineum sexum, generatio feminae esset omnino a casu, sicut et aliorum monstrorum."

61. Quoted by Kayser, *The Grotesque,* 22.

62. Bakhtin, *Rabelais,* 25–26.

63. Kayser, *The Grotesque,* 181.

64. Thomas Aquinas's conclusion was too theologically nuanced to affect popular thinking on the issue. Thomas found that: "Woman is made in the image of God insofar as image is understood to mean 'an intelligent nature'; but insofar as man, and not woman is, like God, the beginning and end (of woman), woman is not in God's image, but in man's image, being created *ex viro propter virum.*" For Augustine's and Thomas's conclusions on the question, see Maryanne Cline Horowitz, "The Image of God in Man—Is Woman Included?", *Harvard Theological Review* 72:3–4 (July–October, 1979): 175–206.

65. Ellen Messer-Davidow, "The Philosophical Bases of Feminist Literary Criticism," *New Literary History* 19:1 (Autumn 1987): 85.

66. *The Enchiridion of Erasmus,* trans. Raymond Himelick (Bloomington: Indiana University Press, 1963), Introduction, 11–12.

67. Ibid., 58.

68. Ibid., 48.

69. Ibid., 87.

70. Ibid., 177.

71. Ibid., 182.

72. Ibid., 160.

73. Ibid., 178. Erasmus also adds a graphic picture of the soldier wasted by lust (181). One thing, he says, leads to another: "Once pleasure has been tasted it will cloud and beguile your reason in such a way that you will proceed from one nastiness to another until you blindly arrive at a depraved state of consciousness and, hardened in evil, cannot leave off sordid pleasure even when it has already left you in the lurch—something we see happen in many cases, as when, with worn out bodies, raddled looks, rheumy eyes, men still itch without ceasing and are more scandalously obscene in their talk than they were once shameless in practice. What can be more monstrous and deplorable than this condition?"

74. Ibid., 179.

75. Ibid., 83.

76. Broadbent's reminder is relevant here: "To love the attribute is to evade the identity." See *The Body as Medium of Expression,* ed. Jonathan Benthall and Ted Polhemus (London: Allen Lane, 1975), 306. See Martha Nussbaum's discussion of Aristotle's view of love between persons in *The Fragility of Goodness, Luck and Ethics in Greek Tragedy and Philosophy* (Cambridge: Cambridge University Press, 1986), 357 and passim.

77. Erasmus, *Enchiridion,* 182.

78. Ibid., 131; cf. *Timaeus* 91a: "According to the probable account, all those creatures generated as men who proved themselves cowardly and spent their lives in wrongdoing were transformed, at their second incarnation, into women." Trans. R. G. Bury (Cambridge: Harvard University Press, 1955), 249.

79. Stallybrass, "Patriarchal Territories," 127.

80. Ibid., 127.

81. Ibid., 128.

82. Discussed by duBois, *Sowing the Body.*

83. Stallybrass, "Patriarchal Territories," 133.

84. Quoted by Stallybrass, ibid., 135.

85. Compare Boccaccio's statement, placed in the mouth of a young woman, with a twentieth-century parallel. The fourteenth-century author wrote: "Any young girl can tell you that women do not know how to reason in a group when they are without the guidance of some man who knows how to control them. We are fickle, quarrelsome, suspicious, timid, and fearful. . . . Men are truly the leaders of women, and without their guidance, our actions rarely end successfully." *Decameron,* trans. Mark Musa and Peter Bondanella (New York: Mentor, 1982), 15–16. The twentieth century example is from *One Day at a Time in Al-Anon* (New York: Al-Anon Family Group, 1987): A man, despairing over the alcoholism of his wife, joined an Al-Anon group which happened to be all women. Finding it (understandably, the text implies) difficult to "identify with the problems of 'a bunch of gals,'" he was instrumental in getting several other men to join the group. "Finally everyone in the group gratefully realized that the men in the group gave it a stamina and workability it might never have had otherwise."

86. Anne Hollander, *Seeing Through Clothes* (New York: Avon, 1975), 99.

87. Sandra Clark, "'Hic Mulier, Haec Vir:' The Controversy Over Masculine Women," *Studies in Philology* 82:2 (1985): 157–83.
88. Ibid., 170.
89. Quoted by Clark, ibid., 170.
90. Rabelais, *Pantagruel* 96.
91. Maclean, *Renaissance Notion*, 31.
92. See n. 21 for Stallybrass, n. 59 for duBois.
93. Clark, "'*Hic Mulier,*'" 172. On the next, and concluding, chapter we will turn from the history of gendered religious practices and representations in the Christian West to the present post-Christian Western society. To step from the sixteenth century to the present omits other chapters in the representation of female nakedness. They are, however, "chapters" that have been extensively explored by others. Instead of repeating and summarizing studies of the social significance of practices and representations of female nakedness from the seventeenth century forward, I have included in the bibliography references to books that carry the study of gender and representation to the present.

6

NAKEDNESS, GENDER, AND RELIGIOUS MEANING

1. Hélène Cixous, "The Laugh of the Medusa," *Signs* (Summer 1976): 40.
2. Lisa Tichner, "The Body Politic: Female Sexuality and Women Artists Since 1970," *Art History* 1 (1978): 247.
3. Ibid., 220.
4. Elaine Scarry, *The Body in Pain* (New York: Oxford University Press, 1985), 279.
5. Sandra Lee Bartky, "Foucault, Femininity, and the Modernization of Patriarchal Power," *Feminism and Foucault,* 72.
6. Jana Sawicki, "Identity Politics and Sexual Freedom: Feminism and Foucault," in *Feminism and Foucault,* 187; see also my article, "Generosity and Suspicion: Theological Education in a Pluralistic Setting," *Theological Education* 23, Supplement (1987), for an account of the value of difference in an academic setting.
7. Bryan S. Turner, *The Body and Society* (Oxford: Basil Blackwell, 1984), 3.
8. Ibid., 152–53.
9. Ibid., 155.
10. Ibid.
11. Ibid., 156.
12. Ibid., 145.
13. In *The Bonds of Love: Psychoanalysis, Feminism, and the Problem of Domination* (New York: Pantheon, 1988), Jessica Benjamin argues that male domination and female submission cannot be fully understood by examining only the social interaction of men and women, but must be seen as an "interaction of culture and

psychological processes" (81). Both female masochism and male sadism, she claims, originate with "the mother's lack of subjectivity, as perceived by both male and female children" (81). The mother's lack of subjectivity occurs because, in the marital relationship, "one person (the woman) is not allowed to play the subject; one person (the man) arrogates subjectivity only to himself" (82).

Because of the mother's "renunciation of her own will," she cannot respond to the child's self-assertion with both recognition and limit-setting. Even more problematically, she cannot require from him recognition of herself as an individual with her own needs. In Benjamin's striking phrase, mother and child commit "the original sin of denying recognition to the other" (83–84). The result is the reproduction of gender polarity and complementarity, rather than mutuality. Mutual recognition, the decisive moment in which sameness and difference are acknowledged, requires the presence of *two* subjects. Whether we begin with social practices or intersubjective processes, then, the result is similar: women's lack of a developed and confident subjectivity both results from, and perpetuates, gender asymmetry.

Nevertheless, Benjamin's optimism over the possibility that "individuals can integrate the gender division, the two sides of which have previously been considered mutually exclusive and the property of only one sex" (130) seems unwarranted if it is exclusively based on alterations in the dynamics of intersubjectivity. Until the development of women's subjectivity is valued in the public sphere, and reflected and cultivated in social practices and representations, I suspect that real intersubjective changes between men and women will be impossible.

14. See Jane Caputi's analysis of the interconnection of misogynist society, media culture, and serial murders: *The Age of Sex Crime* (Bowling Green: Bowling Green University Popular Press, 1987).

15. Carol Duncan, "The Esthetics of Power in Modern Erotic Art," *Heresies* 1 (1977): 47.

16. Iris Marion Young, "Women Recovering Our Clothes, Perhaps," in *Postmodernism and Continental Philosophy*, ed. Hugh J. Silverman and Donn Welton (Albany: State University of New York Press, 1988), 146.

17. Ibid., 147.

18. Cixous, "The Laugh of the Medusa," 247.

19. Tichner, "The Body Politic," 239.

20. Thalia Gouma-Peterson and Patricia Matthews, "The Feminist Critique of Art History," *The Art Bulletin* 69:3 (September 1987): 326–57, provides extensive bibliography on this issue.

21. Craig Owens, "The Discourse of Others: Feminists and Postmodernism," in *The Anti-Aesthetic, Essays on Postmodern Culture,* ed. Hal Foster (Post Townsend, WA: Bay Press, 1983), 71.

22. Tichner, "The Body Politic," 239.

23. Cixous's advocacy of "writing the body" is founded on an essentialism that

identifies women with body: "More so than men who are coaxed toward social success, toward sublimation, women are body. More body, hence more writing" ("The Laugh of the Medusa," 267).

24. For example, Ruth Iskin formulates the possibility of a "women's art" in the following way: "What does it feel like to be a woman? To be formed around a central core and have a secret place which can be entered and which is also a passageway from which life emerges? What kind of imagery does this state of feeling engender? There is now evidence that many women artists have defined a central orifice whose formal organization is often a metaphor for a woman's body. The center of the painting is the tunnel, the experience of female sexuality." See "Sexual and Self-Imagery in Art—Male and Female," *Womanspace Journal* 3 (June 1973): 11.

25. "Judy Chicago, Talking to Lucy Lippard," in Lucy R. Lippard, ed., *From the Center: Feminist Essays on Women's Art* (New York: E. P. Dutton, 1976), 219.

26. Ibid., 227: "I never meant all women made art like me. I meant that some of us had made art dealing with our sexual experiences as women. I looked at O'Keeffe and Bontecou and Hepworth and I don't care what anybody says, I identified with that work. I knew from my own work what those women were doing. A lot of us used a central format and forms we identified with as if they were our own bodies. . . . I really think that differentiates women's art from men's."

27. Douglas Crimp, "The Photographic Activity of Postmodernism," *October* 15 (Winter 1980): 98.

28. Deborah Haynes, "A Look at What Belongs to What: The Art of Sherrie Levine and Cindy Sherman," unpublished manuscript, October 1988.

29. Peter Schjeldahl and Lisa Phillips, *Cindy Sherman, Essays* (New York: Whitney Museum of Modern Art, 1987), 16.

30. Elaine Showalter, "Feminist Criticism in the Wilderness," in *The New Feminist Criticism,* ed. Elaine Showalter (New York: Pantheon, 1985): 252, 259.

31. Tichner, "Body Politic," 239.

32. Tichner, I assume, uses Carol Duncan's definition of "erotic" as "erotic for men" in advocating the "de-eroticizing" of the female body.

33. Helena Michie, *The Flesh Made Word, Female Figures and Women's Bodies* (New York: Oxford University Press, 1987), 141.

34. See, for example, the late-nineteenth-century portraits of Suzanne Valadon, of which Ruth Iskin writes: "Suzanne Valadon's paintings . . . represent undressed women models, whose figures are robust and heavy; not beautiful in the traditional sense, their age, life, and sufferings are visible. They are powerful images of women as real living members of society." Iskin also proposes that the self-portraits of the twentieth-century artist Marriette Lydis "transcend a male view of a female nude." Iskin, "Sexual and Self-Imagery," 9–10.

35. Young, "Women Recovering Our Clothes," 146.

36. Hans-Georg Gadamer's description of what he calls "the experience of art" (as opposed to "aesthetic experience") describes a visual hermeneutic in which

viewer and art "object" enter something like a conversation in which both are changed because of the other's presence; the work of art is changed in interpretation, and the viewer is changed because of the new experience represented by the work of art. Gadamer, *Truth and Method* (New York: Crossroad, 1984), section 1.

37. Betterton, "How Do Women Look? The Female Nude in the Work of Suzanne Valadon" *Feminist Review* 19 (March 1985), 258.

38. Ibid., 266.

39. Frigge Haug, ed., *Female Sexualization,* trans. Erika Carter (London: Verso, 1987), 39.

### APPENDIX

#### THE POWER OF REPRESENTATION — PRODUCTIVE OR REPRESSIVE?

1. Mary Vetterling-Braggin, ed., *'Femininity,' 'Masculinity,' and 'Androgyny': A Modern Philosophical Discussion* (Totowa, NJ: Rowman and Allenheld, 1982), 59.

2. For a feminist argument against essentialist theories in which authentic sexuality is posited as a basis for women's liberation, see Winifred Woodhull, "Sexuality, Power, and the Question of Rape," in *Feminism and Foucault, Reflections of Resistance,* ed. Irene Diamond and Lee Quinby (Boston: Northeastern University Press, 1988): 167–76; see also Frigga Haug's critique of Foucault's theory of the subject, *Female Sexualization* (London: Verso, 1987), 204.

3. Haug, *Female Sexualization,* 169.

4. Paula J. Caplan, "The Myth of Women's Masochism," in *The Psychology of Women,* ed. Mary Roth Walsh (New Haven: Yale University Press, 1987), 78–98.

5. Haug, 166.

6. Ibid., 88.

7. For a description of female sexualization, in which a girl's desire is turned from her first love object, a woman, to males, see Adrienne Rich, "Compulsory Heterosexuality," *Signs* (Summer 1980): 631–60.

8. Jana Sawicki, "Identity Politics and Sexual Freedom: Foucault and Feminism," *Feminism and Foucault,* 179.

9. Michel Foucault, *Discipline and Punish* (New York: Vintage, 1979), 23–30.

# SELECT BIBLIOGRAPHY

Ableman, Paul. *Anatomy of Nakedness*. London: Orbis, 1982.

Adams, Doug, and Diane Apostolos-Cappadona, eds. *Art as Religious Studies*. New York: Crossroad, 1987.

Amundsen, D. W. "Medieval Canon Law." *Bulletin of the History of Medicine* 52 (1978): 22–44.

Andersen, Jørgen. *The Witch on the Wall: Medieval Erotic Sculpture in the British Isles*. Copenhagen: Rosenkilde and Bagger, 1977.

Andreski, Stanislav. "The Syphilitic Shock." *Encounter* 57 (1982): 7–26.

Arbesmann, Rudolph. "Fasting and Prophecy in Pagan and Christian Antiquity." *Traditio* 7 (1949–51): 1–71.

Aries, P., and A. Bejin. *Western Sexuality: Practice and Precept in Past and Present Times*. London: Oxford University Press, 1985.

Atkinson, Clarissa W. "Precious Balsam in a Fragile Glass: Ideology of Virginity in the Middle Ages." *Journal of Family History* (Summer 1983): 131–43.

Augustine of Hippo. *Sermons on the Liturgical Seasons*. Trans. Sr. Mary S. Muldowney, R.S.M. New York: Fathers of the Church, Inc., 1959.

Aymer, Brandt. *The Young Male Figure*. New York: Crown, 1970.

Bakhtin, Mikhail. *Rabelais and His World*. Trans. Helene Iswolsky. Cambridge: The MIT Press, 1968.

Barker, Francis. *The Tremulous Private Body: Essays on Subjection*. New York: Methuen, 1984.

Barocchi, Paola. *Trattati d'arte del Cinquecento fra manierismo e Controriforma*. 2 vols. Bari: Laterza and Figli, 1960–62.

Barthes, Roland. *The Fashion System*. Trans. Matthew Ward and Richard Howard. New York: Hill and Wang, 1983.

Belting, Hans. *The Image and Its Public in the Middle Ages; Form and Function of Early Passion Illustrations*. Trans. Mark Bartusis with Raymond Meyer. New Rochelle, NY: Aristide D. Caratyas, 1986.

Benedek, Thomas. "The Changing Relationship Between Midwives and Physicians in the Renaissance." *Bulletin of the History of Medicine* 51 (1977): 550–64.

Benhabib, Seyla, and Drucilla Cornell, eds. *Feminism as Critique*. Minneapolis: University of Minnesota Press, 1987.

Benjamin, Jessica. *The Bonds of Love: Psychoanalysis, Feminism, and the Problem of Domination.* New York: Pantheon Books, 1988.

Benko, Stephen. "The Libertine Gnostic Sect of the Phibionites according to Epiphanius." *Vigiliae Christianae* 21 (1967): 103–19.

———. *Pagan Rome and the Early Christians.* Bloomington: Indiana University Press, 1986.

Benthall, Jonathan, and Ted Polhemus, eds. *The Body as a Medium of Expression.* London: Allen Lane, 1975.

Benton, John. "Trotula: Women's Problems and the Professions of Medicine in the Middle Ages." *Bulletin of the History of Medicine* 59 (1985): 30–53.

Berger, John. *Ways of Seeing.* London: Penguin, 1972.

Blonsky, Marshall, ed. *On Signs.* Baltimore: Johns Hopkins University Press, 1985.

Brock, Sebastian P., and Susan Ashbrook Harvey. *Holy Women of the Syrian Orient.* Berkeley: University of California Press, 1987.

Broude, Norma, and Mary Garrard. *Feminism and Art History.* New York: Harper and Row, 1982.

Bugge, John. *Virginitas: An Essay in the History of a Medieval Ideal.* The Hague: M. Nijhoff, 1975.

Bullough, Vern. "Medical and Scientific Views of Women." *Viator* 4 (1973): 485–501.

———. *The Subordinate Sex: A History of Attitudes Towards Women.* Urbana: University of Illinois Press, 1973.

Bynum, Caroline Walker. "The Body of Christ in the Later Middle Ages: A Reply to Leo Steinberg." *Renaissance Quarterly* 39:3 (1987): 399–439.

———. *Holy Feast and Holy Fast: The Religious Significance of Food to Medieval Women.* Berkeley: University of California Press, 1987.

Bynum, Caroline Walker, Stevan Harrell, and Paula Richman, eds. *Gender and Religion: On the Complexity of Symbols.* Boston: Beacon Press, 1986.

Cahn, Susan. *Industry of Devotion: The Transformation of Women's Work in England 1500–1660.* New York: Columbia University Press, 1987.

Camporesi, Piero. *The Incorruptible Flesh, Bodily Mutation and Mortification in Religion and Folklore.* Trans. Tania Croft-Murray. New York: Cambridge University Press, 1988.

Caputi, Jane. *The Age of Sex Crime.* Bowling Green: Bowling Green University Popular Press, 1987.

Carroll, Kenneth L. "Early Quakers and 'Going Naked as a Sign'." *Quaker History* 67 (Autumn 1978): 69–87.

Châtillon, Jean. "Nudum Christum nudus sequere. Note sur les origines et la signification du thème de la nudité spirituelle dans les écrits spirituels de saint Bonaventure." *S. Bonaventura, 1274–1974* 4. Rome: Grottaferrata, 1974, 719–72.

Chicago, Judy. *The Dinner Party: A Symbol of Our Heritage.* New York: Doubleday, 1979.

Cixous, Hélène, "The Laugh of the Medusa." In *New French Feminisms.* Edited by Elaine Marks and Isabelle de Courtivron. Amherst: University of Massachusetts Press, 1980.

Cixous, Hélène, and Catherine Clément. *The Newly Born Woman*. Minneapolis: University of Minnesota Press, 1986.

Clark, Elizabeth A. *Ascetic Piety and Women's Faith*. Lewiston, ME: Edward Mellon, 1986.

———. *Women in the Early Church*. Wilmington: Michael Glazier, Inc., 1983.

Clark, Kenneth. *Feminine Beauty*. New York: Rizzoli, 1980.

———. *The Nude: A Study in Ideal Form*. Garden City, NY: Doubleday, 1956.

Clark, Sandra. "'Hic mulier, Haec Vir:' The Controversy Over Masculine Women." *Studies in Philology* 82:2 (1985): 157–83.

Constable, Giles. "'Nudus Nudum Christum Sequi' and Parallel Formulas in the Twelfth Century." In *Continuity and Discontinuity in Church History: Essays Presented to George Hunston Williams*. Edited by F. Forrester Church and Timothy George. Leiden: Brill, 1979: 83–91.

Cropper, Elizabeth. "On Beautiful Women: Parmigianino, Petrarchismo, and the Vernacular Style." *Art Bulletin* 58:3 (1976): 374–94.

———. "The Beauty of Women: Problems in the Rhetoric of Renaissance Portraiture." In *Rewriting the Renaissance: The Discourses of Sexual Difference in Early Modern Europe*. Edited by Margaret W. Ferguson, Maureen Quilligan, and Nancy J. Vickers. Chicago: University of Chicago Press, 1986.

Culianu, Ioan P. *Eros and Magic in the Renaissance*. Trans. Margaret Cook. Chicago: University of Chicago Press, 1987.

Davies, Stevan L. *The Revolt of the Widows: The Social World of the Apocryphal Acts*. London: Feffer and Sons, 1980.

De Laurentis, Teresa. *Alice Doesn't: Feminism, Semiotics, Cinema*. Bloomington: Indiana University Press, 1984.

Derrett, J. Duncan. "Religious Hair." In *Studies in the New Testament I: Glimpses of the Legal and Social Presuppositions of the Authors*. Leiden: Brill, 1977.

Derrida, Jacques. "Sending: On Representation." *Social Research* 49:2 (Summer 1982): 295–326.

Diamond, Irene, and Lee Quinby, eds. *Feminism and Foucault*. Boston: Northeastern University Press, 1988.

Dixon, John. "The Drama of Donatello's David." *Gazette des Beaux-Arts* 113 (January 1979): 6–12.

Dondeyne, A. "La discipline des scrutins dans l'église latine avant Charlemagne." *Revue d'histoire écclesiastique* 28:2 (January 1932): 5–33.

Dronke, Peter. *Women Writers of the Middle Ages. A Critical Study of Texts from Perpetua to Marguerite Porete*. New York: Cambridge University Press, 1984.

duBois, Page. *Sowing the Body, Psychoanalysis and Ancient Representations of Women*. Chicago: University of Chicago Press, 1988.

Dufrenne, Suzy. "Psautiers Byzantins." *L'Oeil* 167 (November 1968): 2–9, 86.

Duncan, Carol. "The Esthetics of Power in Modern Erotic Art." *Heresies* 1 (1977): 46–50.

Eisenstein, Hester, and Alice Jardine. *The Future of Difference*. New Brunswick: Rutgers University Press, 1987.

Eisler, Colin. "The Athlete of Virtue. The Iconography of Asceticism." In *De Artibus Opuscula. Essays in Honor of Erwin Panofsky*. Edited by Millard Meiss. New York: New York University Press, 1961.

Erasmus. *The Enchiridion of Erasmus*. Trans. Raymond Himelick. Bloomington: Indiana University Press, 1963.

Evans, Ernst. *Tertullian's Treatise on Baptism*. London: SPCK, 1964.

Ferguson, M., M. Quilligan, N. Vickers, eds. *Rewriting the Renaissance*. Chicago: University of Chicago Press, 1986.

Ferrante, Joan. *Woman as Image in Medieval Literature from the Twelfth Century to Dante*. Durham: Labyrinth Press, 1985.

Flandrin, Jean Louis. "Sex in Married Life in the Early Middle Ages." In *Western Sexuality*. Edited by Philippe Ariès and André Béjin. London: Blackwell, 1985.

Forbes, T. R. *The Midwife and the Witch*. New Haven: Yale University Press, 1966.

Foster, Hal, ed. *The Anti-Aesthetic, Essays on Postmodern Culture*. Port Townsend, WA: Bay Press, 1983.

Foucault, Michel. *The Care of the Self*. Trans. Robert Hurley. New York: Pantheon, 1986.

———. *Discipline and Punish: The Birth of the Prison*. Trans. Alan Sheridan. New York: Vintage, 1979.

———. *History of Sexuality*. Volume 1. Trans. Robert Hurley. New York: Random House, 1980.

———. *The Use of Pleasure*. Trans. Robert Hurley. New York: Pantheon, 1985.

Frey, Linda, Marsha Frey, and Joanne Schneider, eds. *Women in Western European History*. Westport, CT: Greenwood Press, 1982.

Fuller, Peter. *Seeing Berger: A Revaluation*. London: Writers and Readers, 1980.

Furnivall, F. J., ed. *Hali meidenhad: An Alliterative Homily of the Thirteenth Century*. London: Oxford University Press, 1922.

Gager, John G. "Body Symbols and Social Reality: Resurrection, Incarnation and Asceticism in Early Christianity." *Religion* 12 (1982): 345–63.

Gallagher, Catherine, and Laqueur, Thomas. *The Making of the Modern Body: Sexuality and Society in the Nineteenth Century*. Berkeley: University of California Press, 1987.

Gallop, Jane. *The Daughter's Seduction: Feminism and Psychoanalysis*. Ithaca: Cornell University Press, 1982.

Garnier, Francois. *Le langue de l'image au moyen âge*. Paris: Léopard d'or, 1982.

Garrard, Mary D. "Artemesia and Susanna." In *Feminism and Art History*. Edited by Norma Broude and Mary D. Garrard. New York: Harper and Row, 1982.

———. *Artemesia Gentileschi, The Image of the Female in Italian Baroque Art*. Princeton: Princeton University Press, 1989.

Gold, Penny Schine. *The Lady and the Unicorn: Image, Attitude, and Expression in Twelfth-Century France*. Chicago: University of Chicago Press, 1985.

Gougaud, Louis. *Dévotions et pratiques ascétiques du moyen âge*. Paris: Abbaye de Maredsous, 1925.

Gouma-Peterson, Thalia, and Patricia Matthews. "The Feminist Critique of Art History." *The Art Bulletin* 69:3 (September 1987): 326–57.

Grant, Robert M. *Gnosticism: A Sourcebook of Heretical Writings from the Early Christian Period*. New York: Harper and Row, 1961.

Greer, Germaine. *The Obstacle Race: The Fortunes of Women Painters and Their Work*. New York: Farrar, Straus, Giroux, 1979.

Gregoire, Reginald. "L'adage ascétique 'Nudus nudum Christum sequi'." *Studi storici in onore de Ottorino Bertolini* 1 (Pisa, 1972): 395–409.

———. "Nudité." *Dictionnaire de spiritualité*. Volume 11. Paris: Beauchesne, 1982. Cols. 508–13.

Gubar, Susan. "'The Blank Page' and Issues of Female Creativity." *Critical Inquiry*. 8:2 (Winter 1982): 243–63.

Habermas, Jurgen. "Modernity—An Incomplete Project." In *The Anti-Aesthetic, Essays on Postmodern Culture*. Edited by Hal Foster. Port Townsend, WA: Bay Press, 1983.

Hallett, Judith P. *Fathers and Daughters in Roman Society*. Princeton: Princeton University Press, 1984.

Harl, Marguerite. "La prise de conscience de la 'nudite' d'Adam; Une interpretation de Genese 3, 7 chez les Peres Grecs." *Texte und Utersuchungen zur Geschichte der Altechristichen Literatur* 92 (1966): 486–95.

Harpham, Geoffrey Galt. *The Ascetic Imperative in Culture and Criticism*. Chicago: University of Chicago Press, 1987.

———. *On the Grotesque: Strategies of Contradiction in Art and Literature*. Princeton: Princeton University Press, 1982.

Harré, Rom. *Personal Being: A Theory for Individual Psychology*. Cambridge: Harvard University Press, 1984.

Harvey, Susan Ashbrook. "Women in Early Syrian Christianity." In *Images of Women in Antiquity*." Edited by A. Cameron and A. Kuhrt. Detroit: Wayne State University Press, 1984.

Haug, Frigga, ed. *Female Sexualization*. Trans. Erika Carter. London: Verso, 1987.

Hentsch, A. *De la littérature didactique du moyen âge s'addressant spécialement aux femmes*. Cahors, 1903; reprint Geneva, 1975.

Herrin, Judith. "Women and the Faith in Icons in Early Christianity." In *Culture, Ideology, and Politics*. Edited by Raphael Samuel. Boston: Routledge and Kegan Paul, 198.

Hess, Thomas B., and Elizabeth C. Baker, eds. *Art and Sexual Politics*. New York: Macmillan, 1971.

Hess, Thomas B., and Linda Nochlin, eds. *Woman as Sex Object: Studies in Erotic Art 1730–1970*. New York: Newsweek, 1972.

Hieatt, A. Kent. "Hans Baldung Grien's Ottawa *Eve* and Its Context." *Art Bulletin* 65:2 (1983): 290–304.

Himmelman, Nikolaus, "Ideale Nacktheit." *Zeitschrift fur Kunstgeschichte* 48 (1985): 1–28.

Hoak, Dale. "The Great European Witchhunts: A Historical Perspective." *American Journal of Sociology* 88 (1983): 171–74.

———. "Witch-Hunting and Women in the Art of the Renaissance." *History Today* (February 1981): 22–26.

Hollander, Anne. *Seeing Through Clothes*. New York: Avon, 1975.

Holt, Elizabeth Gilmore. *A Documentary History of Art* 2 vols. Princeton: Princeton University Press, 1981.

Horowitz, Maryanne Cline. "Aristotle and Women." *Journal of the History of Biology* 9 (1976): 183–213.

———. "The Image of God in Man: Is Woman Included?" *Harvard Theological Review* 72:9–4 (July–October 1979): 175–206.

Howell, Martha C. *Women, Production, and Patriarchy in Late Medieval Cities*. Chicago: University of Chicago Press, 1986.

Hults, Linda C. "Baldung and the Witches of Freiburg: The Evidence of Images." *Journal of Interdisciplinary History* 18 (1987): 249–76.

———. "Hans Baldung Grien's 'Weather Witches' in Frankfurt." *Pantheon* 40 (1982): 124–30.

Huyssen, Andreas. *After the Great Divide: Modernism, Mass Culture, Postmodernism*. Bloomington: Indiana University Press, 1986.

Irigaray, Luce. *This Sex Which is not One*. Trans. Catherine Porter. Ithaca: Cornell University Press, 1985.

———. *Speculum of the Other Woman*. Trans. Gillian C. Gill. Ithaca: Cornell University Press, 1985.

Jacobs, Michael. *Nude Painting*. Oxford: Phaidon, 1979.

Jacobus da Voragine. *The Golden Legend*. Trans. Granger Ryan and Helmut Ripperger. London: Longmans, Green and Company, 1941.

Jameson, Frederic. "Postmodernism, or the Cultural Logic of Late Capitalism." *New Left Review* 146 (July–August 1984): 53–92.

Jardine, Alice, and Paul Smith, eds. *Men in Feminism*. New York: Methuen, 1987.

Jencks, Charles. *Post-Modernism: The New Classicism in Art and Architecture*. New York: Rizzoli, 1987.

———. *What is Postmodernism?* New York: St. Martin's Press, 1986.

Kahr, Madilyn. "Danae: Virtuous, Voluptuous, Venal Woman." *Art Bulletin* 60 (March 1978): 43–55.

Kaplan, Cora. *Sea Changes: Culture and Feminism*. London: Verso, 1986.

Kappeler, Susanne. *The Pornography of Representation*. Minneapolis: University of Minnesota Press, 1986.

Karl, Frederick R. *Modern and Modernism*. New York: Atheneum, 1985.

Katzenellenbogen, Adolf. *Allegories of the Vices and Virtues in Mediaeval Art*. Trans. Alan J. P. Crick. London: The Warburg Institute, 1939; republished New York: Norton, 1964.

Kayser, Wolfgang. *The Grotesque in Art and Literature*. Bloomington: Indiana University Press, 1963.

Kelly, Joan. "Early Feminist Theory and the *Querelle des Femmes* 1400–1789." *Signs* 8:1 (1982): 4–28.

Kelly-Gadol, Joan. "Did Women Have a Renaissance?" In *Becoming Visible: Women in European History*. Edited by Renate Bridenthal and Claudia Koonz. Boston: Houghton Mifflin, 1977.

Kibre, Pearl. "The Faculty of Medicine and Unlicensed Medical Practitioners in the Late Middle Ages." *Bulletin of the History of Medicine* 27 (1953): 1–20.

King, Margot. *The Desert Mothers: A Survey of the Feminine Anchorite Tradition in Western Europe*. London: Oxford University Press, 1985.

Klapisch-Zuber, Christiane. *Women, Family, and Ritual in Renaissance Italy*. Trans. Lydia G. Cochrane. Chicago: University of Chicago Press, 1987.

Koch, Robert A. *Hans Baldung Grien: Eve, The Serpent and Death*. Ottawa: National Gallery of Canada, 1974.

Koerner, J. "The Mortification of the Image: Death as Hermeneutic in Hans Baldung Grien." *Representations* 10 (1985): 52–101.

Kraemer, Ross. *Ecstatics and Ascetics*. Ann Arbor: UMI Research Press, 1976.

Kramer, Heinrich, and James Sprenger. *Malleus Maleficarum*. Ed. and trans. Montague Summers. New York: Dover, 1971.

Kuhn, Annette. *The Power of the Image: Essays on Representation and Sexuality*. London: Routledge and Kegan Paul, 1985.

Labowitz, Leslie, and Suzanne Lacy. "Mass Media, Popular Culture, and Fine Art." In *Social Works*. Los Angeles: Los Angeles Institute of Contemporary Art, 1979; reprinted in Richard Hertz, *Theories of Contemporary Art*. Englewood Cliffs: Prentice-Hall, Inc., 1985.

Lakoff, George. *Women, Fire, and Dangerous Things: What Categories Reveal About the Mind*. Chicago: University of Chicago Press, 1987.

Leach, M. C. "Rubens 'Susanna and the Elders' in Munich and Some Early Copies." *Print Review* 5 (1976): 120–27.

Leach, Patricia. "Images of Political Triumph: Donatello's Iconography of Heroes." Ph.D. dissertation, Princeton University, 1984.

Leclercq, H. "Adam et Ève"; "Nu dans l'art chrétien"; "Nudité baptismale"; "Nudité des condamnes." *Dictionnaire d'archeologie chretienne* 12:2. Paris: Librarie Letouzey et Ane, 1936.

Leclercq, Jean. *La femme et les femmes dans l'oeuvre de saint Bernard*. Paris: Téqui, 1982.

LeGoff, Jacques. "Un témoin de l'antiféminisme du moyen âge." *Revue Benedictine* 80 (1970): 304–9.

LeMay, Helen R. "Anthonius Guainerius and Medieval Gynecology." In "Trotula: Women's Problems and the Professions of Medicine in the Middle Ages." John Benton, ed. *Bulletin of the History of Medicine* 59 (1985): 217–336.

———. "Some Thirteenth and Fourteenth Century Lectures on Female Sexuality." *International Journal of Women's Studies* 1 (1978): 391–99.

Linker, Kate. *Difference: On Representation and Sexuality*. New York: New Museum of Contemporary Art, 1985.

———. "Representation and Sexuality." In *Art After Modernism: Rethinking Representation*. Edited by Brian Wallis. New York: New Museum on Contemporary Art, 1984.

Lippard, Lucy R. ed. *From the Center: Feminist Essays on Women's Art*. New York: E. P. Dutton, 1976.

Lucas, Angela M. *Women in the Middle Ages, Religion, Marriage, and Letters*. Sussex: Harvester, 1984.

Lucie-Smith, Edward. *The Body: Images of the Nude*. London: Thames and Hudson, 1981.

———, ed. *The Male Nude: A Modern View: An Exhibition Organized by François de Louville*. Oxford: Phaidon, 1985.

MacDonald, Dennis R. *There is No Male or Female*. Philadelphia: Fortress, 1987.

Maclean, Ian. *The Renaissance Notion of Woman*. Cambridge: Cambridge University Press, 1980.

MacNamara, Jo Ann. *A New Song: Celibate Women in the First Three Christian Centuries*. New York: Haworth Press, 1983.

———. "Sexual Equality and the Cult of Virginity in Early Christian Thought." *Feminist Studies* 3:3/4 (Spring/Summer 1976): 145–58.

MacNamara, Jo Ann, and Barbara J. Harris, eds. *Women and the Structure of Society: Selected Research from the Fifth Berkshire Conference on the History of Women*. Durham: Duke University Press, 1984.

Makowski, Elizabeth M. "The Conjugal Debt and Medieval Canon Law." *Journal of Medieval History* 3 (1977): 99–114.

*The Malleus Maleficarum of Heinrich Kramer and James Sprenger*. Trans. Montague Summers. New York: Dover, 1971.

Maquet, Jacques. *The Aesthetic Experience: An Anthropologist Looks at the Visual Arts*. New Haven: Yale University Press, 1987.

Marks, Elaine, and De Courtivron, Isabelle, eds. *New French Feminisms*. Amherst: University of Massachusetts Press, 1980.

Marnhac, Anne de. *Femmes au Bain: Les Métamorphoses de la Beauté*. Paris: Berger-Levrault, 1986.

Matthews Grieco, Sara F. "Mito ed Immagine della Donna nelle Incisioni del Cinquecento Francese: Il Discorso Morale sulla Sessualit." In *Profili di Donna mita immagine realta fra medioevo ed eta contemporanea*. Edited by Benedetto Vetere and Paolo Renzi. Rome: Galatina [Lecce], 1986.

McGrath, Elizabeth. "Rubens's 'Susanna and the Elders' and Moralizing Interpretations on Prints." In *Wort und Bild in der niederlandischen Kunst und Literatur des 16. und 17. Jahrhunderts*. Edited by Herman Vekeman and Justus Muller Hofstede. Erfstadt: Lukassen, 1984.

Meeks, Wayne A. "The Image of the Androgyne: Some Uses of a Symbol in Earliest Christianity." *History of Religions* 13:3 (February 1974): 165–208.

McNeill, John T., and Helena M. Gamer. *Medieval Handbooks of Penance*. New York: Columbia University Press, 1938.

Meer, Frederic van der. *Augustine the Bishop*. Trans. B. Battershaw and G. R. Lamb. London: Sheed and Ward, 1961.

Messana, V. "La nudité d'Adam et d'Eve chez Diadoque." In *Studia Patristica* 17. Edited by Elizabeth Livingstone. Elmsford, NY: Pergamon, 1982.

Messer-Davidow, Ellen. "The Philosophical Bases of Feminist Literary Criticisms." *New Literary History* 19:1 (Autumn 1987): 63–104.

Michie, Helena. *The Flesh Made Word: Female Figures and Women's Bodies*. New York: Oxford University Press, 1987.

Miles, Margaret R. *Augustine on the Body*. Missoula, MT: Scholars Press, 1979.

———. *Fullness of Life: Historical Foundations for a New Asceticism*. Philadelphia: Westminster, 1981.

———. *Image as Insight: Visual Understanding in Western Christianity and Secular Culture*. Boston: Beacon, 1985.

———. "The Virgin's One Bare Breast: Female Nudity and Religious Meaning in Tuscan Early Renaissance Culture." In *The Female Body in Western Culture*. Edited by Susan Rubin Suleiman. Cambridge: Harvard University Press, 1986.

Milhaven, Giles. "Thomas Aquinas on Sexual Pleasure." *Journal of Religious Education* 5:2 (1977): 157–81.

Millon, Henry A., ed. *Studies in Italian Art and Architecture, Fifteenth through Eighteenth Centuries*. Rome: American Academy in Rome, 1980.

Mulvey, Laura. "Visual Pleasure and Narrative Cinema." In *Art After Modernism: Rethinking Representation*. Edited by Brian Wallis. New York: New Museum of Contemporary Art, 1984.

Murray, Robert. "The Exhortation to Candidates for Ascetical Vows in the Ancient Syrian Church." *New Testament Studies* 21 (October 1974): 59–80.

Musurillo, Herbert, S.J. *Acts of the Christian Martyrs*. Oxford: Clarendon Press, 1972.

———. *Acts of the Pagan Martyrs: Acta Alexandrinorum*. Oxford: Clarendon Press, 1954.

———. "The Problem of Ascetical Fasting in the Greek Patristic Writers." *Traditio* 12 (1956): 1–64.

Newman, Barbara. *Sister of Wisdom: St. Hildegard's Theology of the Feminine*. Berkeley: University of California Press, 1987.

Nochlin, Linda, "Eroticism and Female Imagery." In *Woman as Sex Object*. Edited by Thomas B. Hess and Linda Nochlin. New York: Newsweek, 1972.

———. "Toward a Juster Vision. How Feminism Can Change Our Ways of Looking at Art History." In *Feminist Collage*. Edited by Judy Loeb. New York: Teachers College Press, 1979.

———. "Why Have There Been No Great Women Artists?" In *Art and Sexual Politics*. Edited by Thomas B. Hess and Elizabeth Baker. New York: Macmillan, 1971.

Otis, Leah Lydia. *Prostitution in Medieval Society*. Chicago: University of Chicago Press, 1985.

Owens, Craig. "The Discourse of Others: Feminists and Postmodernism." In *The Anti-Aesthetic, Essays on Postmodern Culture*. Edited by Hal Foster. Port Townsend, WA: Bay Press, 1983.

――――. "Posing." In *Difference: On Representation and Sexuality*. Edited by Kate Linker. New York: New Museum of Contemporary Art, 1985.

――――. "Representation, Appropriation, and Power." *Art in America* 70:5 (May 1982): 9–21.

Pagels, Elaine. *Adam, Eve, and the Serpent*. New York: Random House, 1988.

Palladius. *The Lausiac History*. Trans. W. K. Lowther Clarke. London: SPCK, 1918.

Panofsky, Erwin. "Erasmus and the Visual Arts." *Journal of the Warburg and Courtauld Institutes* 32 (1969): 200–27.

Parker, Rozsika, and Griselda Pollock. *Old Mistresses: Women, Art, and Ideology*. New York: Pantheon Books, 1981.

Payer, P. J. *Sex and the Penitentials*. Toronto: University of Toronto Press, 1984.

Pevsner, Nikolaus. *Academies of Art, Past and Present*. Cambridge: Cambridge University Press, 1940.

Pinto, Lucille. "The Folk Practice of Gynecology and Obstetrics in the Middle Ages." *Bulletin of the History of Medicine* 47 (1973): 513–23.

Pitkin, Hanna Fenichel. *Fortune is a Woman: Gender and Politics in the Thought of Niccolò Machiavelli*. Berkeley, University of California Press, 1984.

Polhemus, Ted, and Lynn Proctor. *Fashion and Anti-Fashion: The Anthropology of Clothing and Adornment*. London: Thomas and Hudson, 1978.

Pollock, Griselda. "Women, Art, and Ideology: Questions for Feminist Art Historians." *Woman's Art Journal* 4 (Spring/Summer 1983): 39–47.

Puniet, P. de. "Baptême: Rit Africain." *Dictionnaire d'archeologie chrétienne*. Paris: Librarie Letouzey et Ane, 1936. Cols. 309ff.

Raitt, Jill. "The *Vagina Dentata* and the *Immaculatus Uterus Divini Fontis*." *Journal of the American Academy of Religion* 48:3 (September 1980): 415–31.

Réau, Louis. *L'iconographie de l'art chrétien*. Volume 2. Paris, 1957.

Regnier-Bohler, Danielle. "Le corps mis a nu: Perception et valeur symbolique de la nudite dans les écrits du Moyen Age." *Europe* 654 (October, 1983): 51–52.

Rich, Adrienne. "Compulsory Heterosexuality and Lesbian Existence." *Signs* 5 (Summer 1980): 631–60.

Robb, Theodore K., and Jonathan Brown. "The Evidence of Art: Images and Meaning in History." *Interdisciplinary History* 17 (1986): 1–6.

Robinson, Hilary. *Visibly Female: Feminism and Art*. New York: Universe Books, 1988.

Rogers, Katherine M. *The Troublesome Helpmate: A History of Misogyny in Literature*. Seattle: University of Washington Press, 1966.

Rose, Jacqueline. *Sexuality in the Field of Vision*. London: Verso, 1986.

Rose, M. B. *Women in the Middle Ages and the Renaissance*. Syracuse: Syracuse University Press, 1986.

Rossi, J. B. "Insigne vetro sul quale è effigiato il battesimo d'una fanciulla." *Bulletin di archeologia christiana*. Ser. 3:1 (1876): 7–14.

Rossi, Mary Ann, "The Passion of Perpetua, Everywoman of Late Antiquity."

In *Pagan and Christian Anxiety*. Edited by Robert C. Smith and John Lounibos. New York: University Press of America, 1984.

Rotberg, Robert I., and Theodore K. Rabb. *Art and History: Images and Their Meaning*. New York: Cambridge University Press, 1988.

Rouselle, Aline. *Porneia: On Desire and the Body in Antiquity*. Oxford: Basil Blackwell, 1988.

Sabean, David Warren. *Power in the Blood: Popular Culture and Village Discourse in Early Modern Germany*. New York: Cambridge University Press, 1984.

Salu, M. B., ed. and trans. *The Ancrene Riwle*. London: Burns and Oates, 1955.

Sasson, Jack. "Genesis 2:25 and Its Implications." *Biblica* 66:3 (1985): 418–21.

Scarry, Elaine. *The Body in Pain: The Making and Unmaking of the World*. New York: Oxford University Press, 1985.

Schulenburg, Jane Tibbetts. "The Heroics of Virginity: Brides of Christ and Sacrificial Mutilation." In *Women of the Middle Ages and the Renaissance*. Edited by M. B. Rose. Syracuse: Syracuse University Press, 1986.

———. "Sexism and the Celestial Gynaeceum—From 500 to 1200." *Journal of Medieval History* 4 (1978): 117–33.

Schuler, Jane. "The *Malleus Maleficarum* and Baldung's *Witches' Sabbath*." *Source* 6:3 (Spring 1987): 20–26.

Schultz, Bernard. *Art and Anatomy in Renaissance Italy*. Ann Arbor: UMI Research Press, 1985.

Scott, Joan W. "Gender: A Useful Category of Historical Analysis." *American Historical Review* 91 (December 1986): 1053–75.

Seymour, M. C., ed. *Mandeville's Travels*. Oxford: Clarendon Press, 1968.

Shaw, J. R. "Scientific Empiricism in the Middle Ages: Albertus Magnus on Sexual Anatomy and Physiology." *Clio Medica* 10:1 (1975): 53–64.

Shewring, W. H. *Perpetua, Saint and Martyr*. London: Sheed and Ward, 1931.

Shweder, Richard A., and LeVine, Robert A. *Culture Theory: Essays on Mind, Self, and Emotion*. Cambridge: Cambridge University Press, 1984.

Showalter, Elaine, "Feminist Criticism in the Wilderness," in *The New Feminist Criticism*. Edited by Elaine Showalter. New York: Pantheon, 1985.

Silverman, Hugh J., and Donn Welton, eds. *Postmodernism and Continental Philosophy*. Albany: State University of New York Press, 1988.

Smith, Jonathan Z. "Garments of Shame." *History of Religions* 5 (1966): 217–38.

Smith, Robert C., and John Lounibos. *Pagan and Christian Anxiety*. New York: University Press of America, 1984.

Spelman, Elizabeth V. "Woman as Body: Ancient and Contemporary Views." *Feminist Studies* 8:1 (Spring 1982): 109–31.

Steele, Valerie. *Fashion and Eroticism: Ideals of Feminine Beauty from the Victorian Era to the Jazz Age*. New York: Oxford University Press, 1985.

Steinberg, Leo. *The Sexuality of Christ in Renaissance Painting and in Modern Oblivion*. New York: Pantheon, 1983.

Stinger, Charles. *Renaissance in Rome*. Bloomington: Indiana University Press, 1985.

Suleiman, Susan Rubin, ed. *The Female Body in Western Culture*. Cambridge: Harvard University Press, 1986.

Talbot, Charles, "Baldung and the Female Nude." In *Hans Baldung Grien: Prints and Drawings*. Edited by James Marrow and Alan Shestack. New Haven: Yale University Press, 1981.

Thompson, John L. "Creata ad Imaginem Dei, Licet Secundo Gradu: Woman as the Image of God according to John Calvin." *Harvard Theological Review* 81:2 (April 1988): 125–44.

Tichner, Lisa. "The Body Politic: Female Sexuality and Women Artists Since 1970." *Art History* 1 (1978): 236–47.

Toulmin, Stephen. "The Construal of Reality: Criticism in Modern and Post-modern Science." *Critical Inquiry* 9 (September 1982): 93–111.

Trask, Haunani-Kay. *Eros and Power: The Promise of Feminist Theory*. Philadelphia: University of Pennsylvania Press, 1986.

Turner, Bryan S. *The Body in Society*. Oxford: Basil Blackwell, 1984.

Van Unnik, W. C. "Les cheveux défaits des femmes baptisées." *Vigilae Christianae* 1 (1947): 77–100.

Verdier, Philippe. "Women in the Marginalia of Gothic Manuscripts and Related Works." In *The Role of Woman in the Middle Ages*. Edited by Rosmarie T. Morewedge. Albany: State University of New York Press, 1975.

Voobus, Arthur. *A History of Asceticism in the Syrian Orient*. Louvain: Secrétariat du Corpus, SCO, 1958–60.

Walker, D. P. *Unclean Spirits, Possession and Exorcism in France and England in the Late Sixteenth and Early Seventeenth Centuries*. London: Scholars Press, 1981.

Walsh, Mary Roth, ed. *The Psychology of Women*. New Haven: Yale University Press, 1987.

Walters, Margaret. *The Nude Male: A New Perspective*. New York: Paddington Press, 1979.

Watson, Paul F. *The Garden of Love in Tuscan Art of the Early Renaissance*. Philadelphia: Art Alliance Press, 1979.

Wethey, Harold. *The Paintings of Titian*. Vol. 3: *The Mythological and Historical Paintings*. London: Phaidon, 1975.

Wildridge, T. Tindall. *The Grotesque in Church Art*. London: William Andrews, 1899; republished Detroit: Gale Research, 1969.

Wilson, Katarina M., ed. *Women Writers of the Renaissance and Reformation*. Athens: University of Georgia Press, 1987.

Wolff, Janet. *Hermeneutic Philosophy and the Sociology of Art*. Boston: Routledge and Paul, 1975.

Wood, Charles T. "The Doctor's Dilemma: Sin, Salvation, and the Menstrual Cycle." *Speculum* 56:4 (October 1981): 710–27.

# INDEX

Abel, 98
Abortion, 22, 154, 221n
*Acta,* 56, 57, 59–63, 70
*Acts of Paul and Thecla,* 58
Acts of Thomas, 68
Adam, and Eve, story of, 43, 45,
    50, 85–116; in Augustine, 87–88,
    93–99, 105, 114–16, 117; Bal-
    dung's depictions of, 127–38;
    figures of, on the walls of Chris-
    tian catacombs, 26, 27; and the
    naming of Eve, 107; relevance
    of, to present gender relations,
    119–21
—and Eve's creation, 56, 87, 88,
    91, 121; and Aristotle's doctrine
    of women as deformed, 162; and
    gender hierarchy, 115–16; Hilde-
    gard on, 101, 103; and virginity,
    nature of, 154. *See also* Eve;
    Fall, the
Adultery, 51
Aesthetics, 6, 113
Agapê, Saint, 74
Agnes, Saint, 156
Aldhelm, 74
Alexander Severus (emperor), 28
Alexandria, 72
Amazonia, 145–46
Ambrose, Saint, 68, 88, 89–93, 99,
    105, 114, 117
Andersen, Jørgen, 156, 159

Angelico, Fra, 142
Annunciation, 144
Anthony, Saint, 72
Antioch, 71
Anxiety, 112, 154, 165
Apostle's Creed, 38
*Apostolic Constitutions,* 28, 42–43, 48
Aquinas, Thomas, 161, 224n
Aristotle, 5, 108, 159, 161, 162
Art, 12, 18, 26, 81, 219n, 228n–
    29n; women's 179–84, 228n
Asceticism, 13, 32, 53–77, 81, 152,
    189; athletic, 142, 143; in Augus-
    tine, 40; Christ's specific instruc-
    tions on, 21; and the fetishization
    of the female body, 63, 69, 76;
    in Tertullian, 35; and women's
    beauty, 82–83. *See also* Fasting
Athanasius, 42
Athleticism, 17, 29, 40, 57–58, 72,
    142–43
Augustine, 6, 17, 29, 32, 37, 154;
    on Adam and Eve, 87–88, 93–
    99, 105, 114–16, 117; on bap-
    tism, 32–33, 36, 39–41; the
    body and the soul in, 30, 94;
    *Confessions,* 31; conversion of,
    31–32; Easter sermons of, 38;
    fasting in, 42; marriage in, 88–
    89; patriarchal order in, 23;
    prayer in, 42; on the sexual as-
    sault of women, 72–73; on